War Memory and
Popular Culture

War Memory and Popular Culture

*Essays on Modes of
Remembrance and
Commemoration*

Edited by
MICHAEL KEREN *and*
HOLGER H. HERWIG

McFarland & Company, Inc., Publishers
Jefferson, North Carolina, and London

LIBRARY OF CONGRESS CATALOGUING-IN-PUBLICATION DATA

War memory and popular culture : essays on modes of
  remembrance and commemoration / edited by Michael Keren
  and Holger H. Herwig.
      p.   cm.
  Includes bibliographical references and index.

  ISBN 978-0-7864-4141-9
  softcover : 50# alkaline paper

  1. War and society.   2. War memorials—Social aspects.
3. Memorialization—Social aspects.   4. Psychic trauma—
Social aspects.   5. Collective memory—Social aspects.
6. War in art.   7. War in mass media.   I. Keren, Michael.
II. Herwig, Holger H.
HM554.W373   2009
303.6'6—dc22   2008044943

British Library cataloguing data are available

On the cover: Vietnam Veterans Memorial ©2008 Photos.com

Manufactured in the United States of America

*McFarland & Company, Inc., Publishers
  Box 611, Jefferson, North Carolina 28640
  www.mcfarlandpub.com*

Table of Contents

Introduction
Michael Keren   1

Part I: The Popularization of War Memory: Remembering or Forgetting?

Commemorating Jewish Martyrdom
Michael Keren   9

The Ninetieth Anniversary of the Battle of the Somme
Dan Todman   23

Popular Memory in Northern Ireland
Rebecca Lynn Graff-McRae   41

Manufacturing Memory at Gallipoli
Bruce C. Scates   57

Commemoration and Consumption in Normandy, 1945–1994
Sam Edwards   76

Nuclear War and Popular Culture
Arthur G. Neal   92

Part II: The Media of War Memory: Erosion of Hegemony?

The Cult of Heroic Death in Nazi Architecture
Holger H. Herwig   105

The Superhero Comic Book as War Memorial
Bart Beaty   120

The BBC's "People's War" Website
Lucy Noakes   135

Inscribing Narratives of Occupation in Israeli Popular Memory
　　Tamar Katriel　　　　　　　　　　　　　　　　　　　　150

The *Operation Victory* Video Game
　　Janis L. Goldie　　　　　　　　　　　　　　　　　　　166

The Rwandan Genocide in Film
　　Kirsten McAllister　　　　　　　　　　　　　　　　　185

About the Contributors　　　　　　　　　　　　　　　　201
Index　　　　　　　　　　　　　　　　　　　　　　　　203

Introduction

Michael Keren

War veterans are often frustrated as a result of their realization that the war memories they are haunted by, or indulging in, are not transferable. When the war they fought is considered glorious and justified, state leaders may build memorials and organize ceremonies honoring veterans and themselves. When, on the other hand, the war is controversial, veterans may have to fight hard battles to get memorials erected and ceremonies set. Yet, even when these battles are successful, frustration grows every year while the ranks of those who hold memories of the war shrink, and while a new generation of youngsters comes on stage, often disinterested in its elders' war stories.

Nothing makes war veterans happier than groups of school children showing interest in the artifacts exhibited or lectures given in a war museum. The veterans' urge to share their heritage with future generations is enormous, stemming from a variety of reasons: the obligation to fallen comrades, the need to make sense of a traumatic experience, the willingness to revive the excitements of one's youth, and the sense of mission to pass on virtues believed to have been gained in war such as heroism, sacrifice, bravery, comradeship, abolition of class barriers, devotion to a higher cause, and ingenuity.

Traditionally, these virtues were considered building blocks of the nation state, which has therefore encouraged select veterans' groups to turn their war experiences into "social memory," defined as "an artificial recollection of some experiences by some groups, institutions, or individuals in society organized according to recognizable scripts and having a moral dimension."[1] The experiences recollected along a moral script by military forces allowed the nation state to endow itself with the virtues exhibited in the veterans' legacies. This process has been analyzed by George Mosse who showed how virtues attributed to fallen soldiers in

1

World War I have served European intellectuals in the construction of interwar nationalism.[2] Omer Bartov has shown how small military elite units took up the traditional role of the hero-king in providing the nation state with an example of heroism: "The Homeric hero, the medieval knight, the SS officer, the French paratrooper, all represent a view of human existence, reflecting and molding a social and political reality by practicing their image of war on the battlefield, and striving to adapt the reality of their civilian environment to their martial ethos."[3]

In recent decades, however, with the decline of the nation state as a main molder of virtues, the turning away of intellectuals from historical narrative, the objection to war commemoration by feminist groups objecting to the masculine heritage involved, a general antiwar sentiment, and the dominance of popular culture in the public sphere, veterans find it harder and harder to initiate acts of commemoration.[4] Their moral scripts cannot compete with the rhythm of rock music, the noise of video arcades and the speedy communication on MTV. This is familiar from other attempts to reach out to the young in parental sermons, antismoking ads, and history lessons in schools, but no scene seems more pathetic than that of a war veteran telling war stories to an inattentive youth, or that of a memorial day devoted to shopping:

> Ask an average American when or what Armistice Day is and you're likely to draw a blank state; ask about Veterans Day and you're not likely to do much better. One of those awkward anniversaries that insist upon being tied to a specific date, unsuitable for shuffling off to a nearby Monday to satisfy car dealers and department stores, November 11 has become an orphan holiday.[5]

Veterans not only feel orphaned but often perceive their heritage to be distorted, as indicated by the many controversies over heritage. In the United States, a famous controversy concerned the National Air and Space Museum's plan in 1994 to exhibit the Enola Gay, the B-29 that dropped the atomic bomb on Hiroshima. This led to a huge public scandal steered mainly by the Air Force Association, which ultimately resulted in the abolishment of the exhibition by the Smithsonian Institution.[6] In Canada, a famous controversy concerned the 1992 CBC documentary series *The Valour and the Horror*, produced by Brian and Terry McKenna, which depicted several World War II battles, formerly seen as symbols of Canadian bravery, as catastrophic blunders. The outrage by veterans led to a high profile public investigation by a Senate subcommittee that ended in strong denunciation of the series, to the dismay of artistic communities and the press.[7] Another controversy concerned the decision by the Canadian War Museum in Ottawa to allocate funds for a Holocaust gallery.

Although Canadian soldiers took part in fighting the Nazis and liberating the concentration camps, many of them felt that the Holocaust had little to do with Canada's military history.[8]

The frustration by veterans over the neglect or distortion of their message frequently leads them to put their faith in the agents of popular culture themselves. Feeling that time is running out, they fight a last battle over memory by raising funds to recruit popular songwriters, bestselling authors, renowned painters, professional organizers of mass events, creative museum designers, and other agents expected to effectively disseminate the message in a public sphere considered mostly hostile. This has become a widespread tactic in "the politics of recognition,"[9] the long term effect of which is still hard to assess in spite of a massive scholarly literature on war commemoration.[10]

The scholarly literature has made important contributions in setting the arena for the study of the relations between veterans' memories and their representation in popular culture. Jay Winter and Emmanuel Sivan have emphasized the distinction between private and public modes of remembering, reminding us that collective remembrance "in ceremony, in ritual, in stone, in film, in verse, in art"[11] is not simply the sum of memories by ordinary soldiers. The authors accept neither the position that private memories are ineffable and individual nor that they are socially determined, and argue that "the effort to create artifacts or ceremonies in the aftermath of war has been so widespread that it is time to consider them not as reflections of current political authority, or a general consensus—although some clearly are one or the other, but rather as a set of profound and evanescent expressions of the force of civil society itself."[12]

While agreeing that the study of memory should focus not on individual memories but on the interaction between different agencies of remembering and forgetting in civil society, T. G. Ashplant, Graham Dawson and Michael Roper note that the nation state is still a major player in this interaction. The politics of memory is thus seen by them as "a process of negotiation between interested parties (including the armed forces, veterans' organizations and the Churches) brokered by the government."[13] The authors fall short of including makers of popular culture, who develop artistic and commercial interests of their own, as important players in the negotiation process, although they note that "artistic groups in civil society, drawing on individual and shared memories which they help connect up into sectional memories, may help to generate a dissenting or oppositional narrative which can challenge dominant official memory."[14]

Artistic groups have always played a role in the process of war commemoration. Even in instances in which a strong nation state dictated how a war would be remembered, the monuments, statues, museums, paintings, posters, films, and other representations were subjected to artistic creativity. In the early twenty-first century, however, the role of creators of popular culture has become more salient in the process of commemoration as a result of what Alison Landsberg has called "the commodification of mass culture."[15] Commodification, she writes, which is at the heart of mass cultural representations, makes images and narratives widely available to people who did not experience them themselves. Landsberg refers to these narratives and images as "prosthetic memories," that is, "privately felt public memories that develop after an encounter with a mass cultural representation of the past, when new images and ideas come into contact with a person's own archive of experience."[16] The power of this term, she writes, derives in part from its challenge to the idea that a particular set of memories belongs exclusively to a particular group. "With the aid of mass cultural technologies, it becomes possible for a person to acquire memories that are not his or her 'natural' or biological inheritance and thus to feel a sense of kinship with people who might otherwise seem very different."[17] And while prosthetic memory appears more radical in some cases than in others, Landsberg calls on scholars and intellectuals to take seriously the popularity of new cultural surfaces, such as experimental museums, and recognize the power of new media "to affect people and shape their politics."[18]

This book responds to the challenge to take seriously the means of popular culture and the new media used to represent war and considers their role in the negotiation process over memory in which war veterans, their families, civil society groups, governments, political parties and, not the least, the makers of popular culture take part. The book originated in a 2006 workshop sponsored by the University of Calgary, Veterans Affairs Canada and SSHRC Canada devoted to the transition from traditional commemoration activities such as memorial services and parades to activities responding to the needs, demands and tastes of contemporary mass cultures with use of new media like the Internet and video games. The workshop brought together historians, social scientists, communication scholars, and experts on popular culture from Australia, Canada, Great Britain, Israel and the United States in an attempt to explore the nature of the popularization of war memory and the role of new media in that process.

The essays are divided into two parts in accordance with these two themes. The first part takes on the question of whether the popularization of war memory, that is, the use of modes of remembrance oriented to mass cultures, implies the remembering or forgetting of war. The second part considers the transition to new media of war commemoration in an attempt to explore whether that transition implies erosion in the hegemony of the state over social memory.

My essay, "Commemorating Jewish Martyrdom," which opens the first part, discusses a case in which Jewish Poet Saul Tchernichowski, in his extremely popular poem "Baruch of Magenza," has given in the early twentieth century a face and a voice to hundreds of Jews killed in the Rhineland massacres during the First Crusade. The essay shows how the popularization of the event through the personification of the victims not only commemorated it but turned it into a major pillar of modern Jewish nationalism.

Dan Todman's "The Ninetieth Anniversary of the Battle of the Somme" places the 2006 anniversary of the 1916 battle in the context of the recent "memory boom," illustrating how in spite of the fact that this was the first anniversary in which war veterans were no longer present, a strong sense of remembrance was achieved through detailed memories of the battle by bereaved relatives, nurtured by the contemporary interest in family histories, as well as others whose memory was based on secondary cultural sources. The essay emphasizes the importance of traditions of commemoration which turned reenactments of the battle into an acceptable way to remember. "The Somme in 2006," Todman writes, "was full of people remembering."

Rebecca Lynn Graff-McRae's "Popular Memory in Northern Ireland" addresses the discourse over memory in postwar Northern Ireland, where cab tours of former Trouble spots promote messages of reconciliation, murals are repainted to promote a similar message and a maximum security prison is being transformed into a commercial and community center as a symbol of shared space, while the ghosts of the past continue to haunt these projects which figure differently in the memory of Unionists and Republicans. "[T]he complex and conflicting memories of the Troubles," the author writes, "continually demand, like restless ghosts, to be addressed, reconfigured and reproduced, despite — or because of — the powerful paradox of conflict memory."

Bruce C. Scates's "Manufacturing Memory at Gallipoli" discusses the amazing phenomenon of battlefield tourism in Gallipoli, especially since the early 1990s when Gallipoli became a site of pilgrimage for thousands of Australian backpackers. Studying the testimony of young Australian visitors to the peninsula on which their ancestors fought and died in World War I, the author objects to the dismissal of the emotions expressed by them in guest books as "invented," pointing rather to the hunger for ritual and meaning, and the search for transcendence, satisfied by the memory manufactured in Gallipoli.

Sam Edwards in "Commemoration and Consumption in Normandy, 1945–1994" asks whether the production and consumption of souvenirs, as well as the development and expansion of commercial tourism in Normandy, violates the sense of solemn mourning and implies forgetting rather than remembering the war experience. Studying the "commercialization of memory" initiated by local Norman communities in cooperation with American veterans, the author concludes that commerce and commemoration are not necessarily opposites and that a new form of commemoration has emerged.

Arthur G. Neal's essay "Nuclear War and Popular Culture" examines the continuity of the symbolism of Hiroshima in the fears and anxieties underlying collective memories in the United States. Describing the tensions during the cold war and the difficulty to answer the questions posed by a nuclear world, the author shows how Americans turned to such forms of popular culture as movies, novels, and music, mixing humor with tragedy for reflections on their underlying anxieties. These means of popular culture, he argues, "were grass roots attempts to deal with incomplete information and the uncertainty inherent in modern social life."

Part II opens with Holger H. Herwig's essay "The Cult of Heroic Death in Nazi Architecture," which highlights one of the strongest instances of state hegemony in the construction of memory. The author surveys gigantic architectural projects designed by Adolf Hitler and architect Wilhelm Kreis to memorialize the Nazi experience and demonstrates the fascination with death found, for instance, in the design of memorials to the dead of the future or in the incredible plan to construct "castles of the dead" along the invasion route of Operation Barbarossa, that would evoke memories of Teutonic Knights.

Bart Beaty in "The Superhero Comic Book as War Memorial" shows the difficulty to express grief over real world trauma through the media of popular culture. Analyzing the depiction of America's 9/11 trauma in "Captain America's New Deal" comic book, the differences between civic or national memorials and a popular medium open to disparate readings are nicely illustrated. "In short, while both traditional war memorials and their newer counterparts seek consensus through the narrating of discursive entry points and the minimization of ambiguity," writes the author, "popular culture works awkwardly as a memorializing enterprise insofar as its narrative demands to authorize potentially contradictory, and therefore inflammatory, discursive regimes."

Lucy Noakes in "The BBC's 'People's War' Website" introduces the

Internet as a key site for the collection and transmission of individual wartime memories and their transformation into new, shared sites of remembrance "from below." Focusing on the BBC's "People's War" Website, she identifies a "hierarchy of memory," meaning that some stories are more visible than others, with gender being the main factor that shapes the stories entered on the Website. "It appears that, although the war is largely remembered within Britain as a 'people's war,' which touched every aspect of national life, and in which every member of the nation played a part," writes the author, "war itself is still perceived as an essentially masculine affair, sitting comfortably within naturalized discourses of masculinity."

Tamar Katriel in "Inscribing Narratives of Occupation in Israeli Popular Memory" surveys a variety of media by which a group of Israeli soldiers protesting their role in the Palestinian occupied territories brought their firsthand testimonies to the general public: exhibitions, videotaped interviews, a Website, popular online newspapers, and the like. The author attributes the continued resonance of the group's counter-hegemonic message to the effective fusion of digital communication and more traditional protest practices, and demonstrates how this allowed the group to force society to take into consideration aspects of the ongoing war with the Palestinians that would otherwise be doomed to oblivion.

Janis L. Goldie in "The *Operation Victory* Video Game" analyzes a strategy game based on Canada's role in World War II as a text of commemoration constructing a particular version of Canadian national identity that consists of reluctance to go to war but resilience when forced into it.

Finally, Kirsten McAllister in "The Rwandan Genocide in Film" analyzes *Hotel Rwanda* and *Sometimes in April*, two films offering audiences insight into the failed role of peacekeeping in Rwanda and discusses the ways these films mediate the burden of guilt by the international community over the genocide of 1994. The author argues that "while *Hotel Rwanda* restores faith in Western nation states and attempts to offer closure, *Sometimes in April* shows audiences that there is no closure for those affected by genocide and that only in a commitment to the long and complex process of reconciliation is there a possibility for resolution."

While the various questions discussed here are, of course, not fully answered, as scholarly questions never are, the interdisciplinary and intercultural research effort contained in this book should open the door to further research on the complex relations between war memory and popular culture. It should inspire those in many societies today who are concerned with the need to remember our past to do so in liberation from the hegemony of both the nation state and the forces of popular culture.

NOTES

1. John Nerone, "Professional History and Social Memory," *Communication* 11 (1989): 92.

2. George L. Mosse, *Fallen Soldiers: Reshaping the Memory of the World Wars* (New York, 1990).

3. Omer Bartov, "Man and the Mass: Reality and the Heroic Image in War," *History @ Memory* 1 (Fall/Winter 1989): 116.

4. See Susan A. Crane, "Memory, Distortion, and History in the Museum," *History and Theory* 36 (1997): 44–63; Jacqueline Scott and Lilian Zac, "Collective Memories in Britain and the United States," *The Public Opinion Quarterly* 57 (1993): 315–331.

5. Stephen Budiansky, "Have We Forgotten to Remember?," *U.S. News & World Report* 119, 13 November 1995, p. 20.

6. Martin Harwit, *An Exhibit Denied: Lobbying the History of Enola Gay* (New York, 1996).

7. David Taras, "The Struggle over *The Valour and the Horror*: Media Power and the Portrayal of War," *Canadian Journal of Political Science* 28 (December 1995): 725–48; David J. Bercuson and Sidney F. Wise. *The Valour and the Horror Revisited* (Montreal, 1994).

8. Barbara Amiel, "Controversy over a Delicate Matter," *Maclean's* 110, 29 December 1997, p. 13.

9. Barry Schwartz and Todd Bayma, "Commemoration and the Politics of Recognition," *The American Behavioral Scientists* 42 (March 1999), p. 946.

10. See Maurice Halbwachs, *On Collective Memory*, ed. and trans. Lewis A. Coser (Chicago, 1992); Pierre Nora ed. *Les Lieux de mémoire* (7 vols., Paris, 1984–1992); Jay M. Winter, *Sites of Memory, Sites of Mourning: The Great War in European Cultural History* (Cambridge, 1995).

11. Jay Winter and Emmanuel Sivan, eds., *War and Remembrance in the Twentieth Century* (Cambridge, 2000), p. 9.

12. *Ibid.*, p. 10.

13. T. G. Ashplant, Graham Dawson and Michael Roper, eds., *The Politics of War Memory and Commemoration* (London, 2000), p. 26.

14. *Ibid.*, p. 32.

15. Alison Landsberg, *Prosthetic Memory: The Transformation of American Remembrance in the Age of Mass Culture* (New York, 2004), p. 20.

16. *Ibid.*, p. 19.

17. *Ibid.*, p. 22.

18. *Ibid.*, p. 21.

Commemorating
Jewish Martyrdom

Michael Keren

Any commemoration of a past event consists to some degree of popularization, that is, making it comprehensive and attractive to many. Nothing makes an event more popular than its personification, its presentation in relation to one individual with whom it is easy to identify. This was understood by ancient Jewish sages who, being concerned with the commemoration of the Exodus, demanded that "in every generation it is one's duty to regard himself as though he personally had gone out of Egypt."[1] "Baruch of Magenza," a poem written by Shaul Tchernichowsky in the late nineteenth century, provides an effective illustration of an act of commemoration in which the voiceless victims of war — here, Jewish victims of the massacres in the Rhineland during the First Crusade — are personalized. The poem tells the story of one victim in the first tense singular, thus turning him into a household icon serving Jewish nationalism in the twentieth century. In this essay, I analyze the process in which the massacre in the Rhineland has been developed by Tchernichowsky into a personalized tale, and the political implications of that process.

The Event

Following the conquest of Jerusalem by the Seljuk Turks in 1071, Pope Urban II in 1095 convened the Council of Clermont in which he called for a crusade to rescue the Holy Land from the Moslem invaders. In 1096 the first of a series of crusades was launched in which armies of knights accompanied by peasants, children and unorganized bands marched toward Constantinople and Jerusalem. In 1099 the crusaders captured Jerusalem and established a Latin kingdom in the Holy Land. On the way, they slaughtered populations regarded as heretical such as Cathars, Muslims and Jews. The main massacres of Jews occurred in the Rhineland cities of Speyer, Worms, Mainz, and Cologne in May 1096. These massacres were recorded in Christian and Jewish chronicles including those by Albert of Aachen, a eulogist of Christian military service who recorded the history of the crusades from 1095 to 1121; Ekkehard of Aura, a Benedictine monk who detailed the history of Germany from 1080 to 1125[2]; and Solomon Bar Samson, a Rhineland Jew who wrote in 1140 on the massacre in Mainz.[3]

Albert of Aachen provides a grim picture of the beginning of the event when an army of the faithful had been gathered in France, England, Flanders, and Lorraine. "I know not whether by judgment of the Lord, or by some error of mind," he writes of the crusaders, "they rose in a spirit of cruelty against the Jewish people scattered throughout these cities and slaughtered them without mercy, especially in the Kingdom of Lorraine, asserting it to be the beginning of their expedition and their duty against the enemies of the Christian faith." He tells of the destruction of houses and synagogues of Jews in Cologne and of the arrival of a great multitude of pilgrims at Mainz, where Count Emico, a powerful nobleman, was awaiting them.

Ekkehard of Aura describes Count Emico as "a man of very ill repute on account of his tyrannical mode of life. Called by divine revelation, like another Saul, as he maintained, to the practice of religion of this kind, he usurped to himself the command of almost twelve thousand cross bearers." The Jews of Mainz, aware of the fate of their brethren in Cologne, fled to the local bishop's house where he offered them safety in return for a large sum of money. However, when Emico and the rest of his band attacked the hall with arrows and lances, the Bishop and his men fled and the Jews were left to their fate. Albert of Aachen then provides details of the attack:

> Breaking the bolts and doors, they killed the Jews, about seven hundred in number, who in vain resisted the force and attack of so many thousands. They killed the women, also, and with their swords pierced tender children, and that they were sparing no age, likewise fell upon one another, brothers, children, wives, and sisters, and thus they perished at each other's hands. Horrible to say, mothers cut the throats of nursing children with knives and stabbed others, preferring them to perish thus by their own hands rather than to be killed by the weapons of the uncircumcised. From this cruel slaughter of the Jews a few escaped; and a few because of fear, rather than because of love of the Christian faith, were baptized.

The description of the massacre in Solomon Bar Samson's chronicle shows that forced baptism was worse than death, which could be justified as God's will:

When the children of the covenant saw that the heavenly decree of death has been issued and that the enemy had conquered them and had entered the courtyard, then all of them — old and young, virgins and children, servants and maids—cried out together to their Father in heaven and, weeping for themselves and for their lives, accepted as just the sentence of God.... As soon as the enemy came into the courtyard they found some of the very pious there with our brilliant master, Isaac Ben Moses. He stretched out his neck, and his head they cut off first. The others, wrapped by their fringed prayingshawls, sat by themselves in the courtyard, eager to do the will of their Creator. They did not care to flee into the chamber to save themselves for this temporal life, but out of love they received upon themselves the sentence of God.

Self slaughter was mainly a way of parents to prevent the forced baptism of their children:

The women there girded their loins with strength and slew their sons and their daughters and then themselves. Many men, too, plucked up courage and killed their wives, their sons, their infants. The tender and delicate mother slaughtered the babe she had played with, all of them, men and women arose and slaughtered one another. The maidens and the young brides and grooms looked out of the Windows and in a loud voice cried: "Look and see, O our God, what we do for the sanctification of Thy great name in order not to exchange you for a hanged and crucified one...."

Sanctification of the Name

The difficulty to explain the murder of Jews, Moslems and unfaithful Christians during the First Crusade is apparent in all three chronicles. Albert of Aachen, as we have seen, is not sure whether the murders could be committed by judgment of the Lord; Ekkehard of Aura, commenting on Amico's atrocities against Hungarians, claims they were committed "for God, though not according to the knowledge of God"; and Solomon Bar Samson asks in a way reminiscent of the biblical sermons of Job: "Why did the heavens not grow dark and the stars not withdraw their brightness? Why did not the moon and the sun grow dark in their heavens when on one day, on the third of Sivan, on a Tuesday, eleven hundred souls were killed and slaughtered, among them many infants and sucklings who had not transgressed nor sinned, many poor, innocent souls?"

In spite of this call to heaven, the chronicler never doubts the belief, prevalent among Jews in the Middle Ages, that their persecution had divine meaning: "For thy sake it was that these numberless souls were killed." This belief stems from an important pillar of Jewish theology: the status of God in the world depends on the people who entered into a covenant with him, as noted in *Leviticus* 22/32: "I will be hallowed among the children of Israel." Therefore, death is to be chosen over the abandonment of the covenant, which is a direct offense against God. A Jew who is forced to baptize and submits to death in order to avoid it is seen as sanctifying the name of God and those who have done so were commemorated as martyrs. As Susan Einbinder, in a study of martyrdom in medieval France, writes, "The poems of martyrdom commemorated Jewish victims as figures of exceptional piety and courage who put virtue to the ultimate test and 'sanctified the Name' in death." She also notes, however, that in so doing, most murdered Jews were forgotten, for the poems of martyrdom "memorialized as heroes the men and women who achieved the poetic ideal while assigning to oblivion those who did not."[4]

Since Jews have traditionally perceived history as unfolding in accordance with a divine will, the notion of "sanctification of the name" served for centuries as an explanation of the persecutions inflicted on them. This notion was not free of theological difficulties because biblical law sanctifies life and Talmudic interpretation prohibits suicide. As Jeremy Cohen puts it, "*submitting to death* to avoid transgression was one thing; *inflicting death*, upon oneself or upon someone else, was very much another."[5] Yet despite these difficulties, individuals like Isaac Ben Moses mentioned above were singled out for their willingness to die for a divine cause, which reflected on the death of all other anonymous Jewish men, women and children.

This became unwarranted to Jewish intellectuals in the nineteenth century, and not for theological reasons. Influenced by the eighteenth-century European Enlightenment, many of them replaced religion with science and rationality. The solution to the problem of persecution was seen by them as related to the replacement of religious customs by universal modes of thinking and behavior. The Jewish enlightenment movement, originating in Germany in the late eighteenth century, spreading to other European countries, and culminating in the gathering of Jewish intellectuals in Odessa at the end of the nineteenth century, opted for political emancipation of Jews in their respective countries, which was seen as dependent on their abandonment of notions associated with Ghetto life, such as the "sanctification of the name."[6]

The hopes for emancipation were shattered in 1881 when, following the assassination of Tsar Alexander II, anti–Jewish pogroms in Russia did not distinguish between "enlightened" and "unenlightened" incumbents of the Jewish race. But the Odessa intellectuals experiencing the pogroms have not framed them as "sanctification of the name," which was no longer part of their symbol system. As Alan Mintz notes, "The world that had once been thick with symbols and texts, sacred times and covenanted obligations, providential signs and redemptive promises was, suddenly, not there."[7] A new symbolism, framed in the new language of enlightenment, was needed to give meaning to the pogroms, and nobody was more suitable to provide it than Shaul Tchernichowsky.

Origins of the Poem

Shaul Tchernichowsky was born in 1875 in the village of Mikhailovka in the Crimea where he lived a rural life and, in contrast to his fellow Jews who were mostly educated in parochial religious institutions, attended a Russian school. He was versed in both Hebrew and Russian literature and fluent in many languages—Hebrew, Russian, English, French, German, Greek, and Latin—which made him a prolific translator. In 1890 he studied in Odessa and in 1899 went to study medicine as well as mathematics and German literature in Heidelberg and Lausanne. On his return to Russia, he could not get a permanent position, worked for a while as a military doctor and after World War I settled in Germany. In 1931 he immigrated to Palestine where he was employed as a school doctor until his death in 1943. Throughout his life, he composed hundreds of poems and other literary works.

Tchernichowsky was exposed to the Jewish chronicles of the Mainz massacre when they were published in Berlin in 1892.[8] Two of the chronicles—by Eliezer Bar Nathan and by Solomon Bar Samson—tell of a community warden, Isaac the Pious, who was forced to baptize and whose wife was killed in the pogrom. Three days later, however, he regretted his conversion, killed his daughters and his mother, and set his house and the synagogue on fire. "Baruch of Magenza" ("Magenza" is the Latin name for Mainz) revokes this tale. Tchernichowsky began to work on the poem in Odessa in 1896, exactly 800 years after the massacre, and completed it in Heidelberg in 1902. The time he spent in Heidelberg was described by his biographer, Joseph Klausner, as the best of his life. The combination of spectacular beauty, ruins from the Middle Ages and a modern, vibrant intellectual culture marked by a strong Jewish-German symbiosis attracted him greatly.[9] In that period, Tchernichowsky composed a series of poems expressing his admiration for ancient Hellenistic ideals of beauty, in the European tradition of body worship. In "Before the Statue of Apollo," for instance, a Jew is described as facing the statue of the Greek god of the sun. He recalls the enmity between Judaism and Hellenism but kneels to the statue representing "the noble and the true."[10] He cherishes the values associated with Apollo as against the culture he belongs to, which has its origins in the same free spirit of Hellenism but has bounded its God of gods in phylacteries (a Jewish religious artifact worn in prayer).

This unusual attraction to the pagan spirit of Hellenism has been explained by Athena Leoussi and David Aberbach as an outgrowth of the Jewish enlightenment. As they put it, "Theological adaptations of Hellenism could further Jewish emancipation and assimilation into European society as the traditional anti–Hellenism and anti–Judaism of the Church were laid open to attack."[11] In specific reference to "Before the Statue of Apollo," they write of the poet: "He rejects the alleged over-intellectualization of Judaism, its excessive moral rigour and lack of joy and sensuality, as sources of inhibition and corruption. Violent revenge is preferred to Hebraic suffering and martyrdom."[12] It is this shift from inhibition to revenge that signifies "Baruch of Magenza," and it is this shift which transforms the faceless and voiceless victims of the Mainz massacre into characters with a unique face and loud voice.

As a poem of revenge, "Baruch of Magenza" has often been associated with another poem, "In the City of Slaughter," written a few years later by Haim Nachman Bialik, the master poet of modern Jewish nationalism. That poem, considered "the most influential public poem in the annals of modern Hebrew literature,"[13] was written by Bialik after a visit to the city of Kishinev shortly after the massacre of 45 Jews there in 1903.[14] But two major differences between the poems must be noted. First, "In the City of Slaughter" expresses extreme resentment toward the Kishinev pogrom's victims; Bialik bashes the victims without mercy, especially for their passivity in the face of anti–Semitic attacks. "For since they have met pain with resignation/ And have made peace with shame, / What shall avail thy consolation? / They are too wretched to evoke thy scorn. / They are too lost thy pity to evoke."[15]

Second, in contrast to "Baruch of Magenza," Bialik's victims remain faceless. As Dan Miron states, while the eye witnesses with whom Bialik had met in Kishinev in 1903 were vivid, glowing, vibrant individuals telling their stories in a multitude of styles and having unique personalities that were often impressive, the poet ignored the uniqueness of both the perpetrators and the victims. Miron believes that Bialik made an explicit choice to exclude the victims' humanity from his poem and to turn them into "non entities,"[16] which helped their depiction as passive (and led to the establishment of Jewish self-defense units in the Russian Empire and in Palestine). In this regard, Bialik can be seen as having deserted the victims while Tchernichowsky has not. In Ephraim Broido's words, "He was ... a rebel, not a deserter. He sought to save God from his bloodless champions, not to damn him."[17]

The Victims' Voice

The rebellious nature of "Baruch of Magenza" has been noted in Alan Mintz's book *Hurban* (destruction), on responses to catastrophe in Hebrew literature. Mintz considers the poem part of an interrogation of the normative response of the Jewish intelligentsia to the pogroms of 1881, especially the tendency to read the situation as a recurrence of the persecution of the Middle Ages and thus attribute courage, loyalty and self-sacrifice to the victims. This normative response, he claims, is shattered by the figure of Baruch who represents a deviation from the norm: "Like the classic dramatic monologue on the model of Browning and Tennyson, the poem is based on a dynamic of judgment and sympathy: the judgment that the reader makes of the speaker for his violation of moral norms and the sympathy that the speaker manages to win for himself by virtue of his voice, his presence, and the disclosure of his motives."[18]

This analysis overlooks two important points. First, the consideration of the narrator as a man whose behavior deviates from a norm is too limited, as Baruch is not one individual among many but a personification of an anonymous mass. Second, the fact that Baruch holds a monologue is not obvious and may be seen as the most important component of the poet's rebellion. Let me provide a reading of the poem that emphasizes both points: the use of the first tense singular as a way to give an anonymous mass a voice and the rebellious nature of this literary device.[19]

"Here are the graves! Yours too among them!" The opening line points at the anonymity of the victims. Baruch, who comes to the Mainz cemetery three days after the massacre, cannot find his wife's place of rest for "all the bloody sacrifices" were cast in a mass grave that he can only assume to have found. He comes to the cemetery to tell his wife a story that cannot be told. Like many victims of horrible crimes he feels he died on the day of the horror, when he was forced to convert to Christianity and then killed his two daughters: "And I *am* dead! For now another / man am I, abhorred." The new man he has turned into is capable of telling the story which resembles no story that had been told before in Jewish history, if only because the narrator considers himself, in sharp contrast to former traditions, as having been abandoned by God.

Baruch's story has many references to voices. It begins with the loud voices of pogrom: "The clanging brass's message rang, / the courtyard astounding / 'Down with the Jews!'- from tower to tower / the dread alarm astounding." The victims' cries are blended in the general commotion: "groans of the dying, children weeping, / women's pleading voices; / broken vessels, cloths in tatters, / blood in the mud like water, / shouts that fill the soul with quaking: / 'Beat them! To the slaughter!'" Within the commotion, the stunned victim is silent. Facing a thronging mob flashing a knife at him, brutish, savage faces waiting for him to say the blessing of baptism, Baruch is speechless: "in a muffled voice I cried an answer...." The only voices heard now are those of the cathedral: "organ's tones, and light, / seas of voices rising, soaring, everywhere prevailing / seas of song!"

Once Baruch abandons his religion, he is faced with dumbness: "Then stone idols, dumb and cold, / on my walls were raised." His new gods are made of stone and do not speak to him. The ironic description of dumb idols declaring nevertheless: "we are thy gods" makes one wonder whether "Before the Statue of Apollo" may not have been ironic too, especially in light of Baruch's indulgence in memories of his Bar-Mizvah when he put on phylacteries. However that may be, the memories of the narrator's boyhood do not include (and indeed do not require) a voice; this was a time in which he lived in full harmony with God, who is worshipped in silence: "what thrills of awe and exultation / tremble through the boy!" As the Bar-Mizvah boy participates in the traditional seven rounds with the Torah, he counts in silence: "one and two ... / five ... and seven turns."

And then comes the horrible tale that cannot be told, for who can tell of the murder of one's children? Indeed, Baruch speaks with no voice: "I'll whisper to you in the darkness, / in the night dissembling, / lest you eyes see while I'm speaking, / lips that move with trembling." He tells his wife of killing their two daughters for reasons that are quite different from those appearing in the Jewish chronicles of the Middle Ages. According to Solomon Bar Samson's chronicle, Isaac the Pious asked his children if they want him to sacrifice them to God and they answered: "Do with us what you wish."[20] In Tchernichowsky's poem, however, the daughters do not want to die and their death is not sanctifying God. Their father kills them because he refuses to see them fall into enemy hands and give birth to new generations of murderers of Jews. He cannot bear the thought of his own daughter's children coming "to shout in glee as they watch the game; / the roasting of Jews on tongues of flame."

The chronicling of the killing and later of Baruch's burning down the town is accompanied by a long depiction, in the tradition of Russian pastoral literature, of the family's former life in the village. It is marked, like the Bar-Mizvah paragraphs, by references to a silent harmony, which stands in sharp contrast to the noises of the pogrom as well as to the meaningless silence at the church.

> Remember yet: at eventide, / silently dreaming, side by side, / around us network of blue and the hush, / the lindens steeped in a secret flush ... And

darkness grew, a spreading pall, / and slowly there faded away the call / of
the ringing bell's artless prayer / ... Then when silence was complete, / dust
clouds billowed down the street, ... Before the mounting of the moon / the
village grew still, was sleeping soon ... Peace eternal in the silence of night, /
its shadow-charms, uncertain light, its secrets, voices of mystery, / that
echo near and far-off flee; the wheel of a wagon, heaped with grain, /
shricks as it passes a narrow lane; / the voice of a dog, a voice of fear, / now
heard, now fading on the ear ... Silently night has come and flown. / The
milky Way has wandered down ... Then suddenly, down from heaven
falling, / rain jubilant shouts as of sweet-sounding voices: / a waking lark
in the village rejoices.

The family home was "a nest full of song and full of light" and the
tiny garden a place where "The breeze stealing, soft and tender, / made
softly eloquent the leaves, / like one who tells secrets or relieves / heart's
infinite burden, song without end, / in the graceful ear of a loving friend.
/ The apple tree, standing dumb; / and all the day, the quiet hum / about
it, swarming bold ... the birds that twittered, every one, / from early morn
till day was done."

This amazing compilation of silent sounds in the poem is not incidental; it points at the poet's concern with the harmony he has experienced as a young Jew in the Crimea between humanity, nature and God,
and the interruption of that harmony by the loud noises of pogroms committed to the ringing of church bells. Tchernichowsky, a man in his twen-
ties, expresses fear of a new silence of death and destruction. He describes
the silence of those who went through forced conversion and were facing
"stone idols, dumb and cold" which left them equally dumb. It seems the
poet was less concerned with the conversion itself than with the victims'
voicelessness. Baruch, finding himself after the conversion in a monk's
high tower, is expecting his God to council him and point a way amidst
the destruction inflicted on his people, but God is also silent: "Alone I
stood before my God, / my rock and my Lawgiver, / high above the noisy
world /and foolish evil's taint, / waiting for my command, I listened–."

The narrator is waiting for a word of God that is not spoken. God
has abandoned his people and the poet, an incumbent of the Jewish
national movement of the late nineteenth century, does not allow him to
accept it in passivity. Tchernichowsky depicts the victims of the Mainz
massacre in a new light, as individuals having a voice, who do not just
remain stunned and helpless when God is not speaking, who do not accept
their harsh fate as sanctifying the name of a God, and who refuse to consider the murder of two girls as sanctification. In "Baruch of Magenza"
the voiceless victims of the Mainz pogrom are given a voice for the first
time in 800 years. Not only are they rescued from oblivion by their

personification in the form of an individual with a name, but that individual takes his fate in his own hands, sets fire to the town, and speaks about his actions clearly and loudly. The following stanza, composed as a strident declaration, has become the most famous in the poem:

> "I am the man, the father I,
> Who slew his daughters, saw them die,
> And did not turn his knife away,
> Till he was steeped in blood as they!"

Political Implications

The fame and impact of the above stanza in Jewish national thought of the twentieth century must be understood against the strong influence of Friedrich Nietzsche's ideas on Russian literature at the turn of the century. Writing on the popularization, verging on vulgarization, of Nietzsche's idea of the *Übermensch* in Russia, Edith Clowes shows how young Russian intellectuals at the time had found in it a solution to social, moral and spiritual ills. They associated the concept with renewed attention to individual will, subjective perception, self-reliance, physical, and sexual liberation and artistic creativity. As she puts it, "In the 1890s and 1900s a faith in the creative self replaced the predominant self-denying ethic of social service."[21]

Nietzsche's influence was particularly strong among Hebrew writers of the Russian Empire. As Menachem Brinker writes, "Nietzsche appealed to them because of his trenchant criticism of exaggerated spirituality, asceticism, and all forms of faith in the supernatural. It was these that Hebrew secularists identified as the historical limitations of traditional Judaism."[22] Tchernichowsky in particular viewed monotheistic faith as a repression of the vibrant Dionysian drives of the ancient Hebrews, and cherished the worship of pagan deities rejected in Judaism. He was a major contributor to the romantic literature of the turn of the century expressing a love of nature and conceiving nature as a source of the formation of a new, healthy, masculine Jewish prototype, connected to the soil and conducting a liberated, productive life. This, as Brinker explains, was strongly connected to Nietzsche's ideas. "The new Hebrew man envisioned by Jewish critics and writers, and later by political Zionists, was Nietzschean to the extent that courage, physical well-being, and virility were valued and all forms of otherworldliness rejected."[23]

Nietzsche, who abhorred traditional priestly Judaism as much as he abhorred Christianity but admired the modern European Jew breaking the chains of religion and emerging into a new and free existence, provided

a philosophical base for Hebrew writers who abandoned religious traditions and were searching for a new way. To Nietzsche, the Jews were
"beyond any doubt the strongest, toughest and purest race now living in
Europe; they know how to prevail even under the worst conditions (even
better than under favorable conditions), by means of virtues that today
one would like to mark as vices, thanks above all to a resolute faith that
need not be ashamed of modern ideas."[24] Opposing both nationalist solu-
tions and imitative assimilation, he assigned them a major role within a
new Europe: "*creative assimilation*, in which the Jews are secularized, excel
in all European matters and serve as catalysts in a new revolution of values—this time a curative, Dionysian revolution...."[25]

Tchernichowsky was seen as a torchbearer of that revolution not only
because of his Hellenistic sentiments but because he relentlessly promoted
the model of the "new Jew" who, in the manner of the *Übermensch*, overcomes cultural repression, creates himself, and attains "maturity, authenticity and power."[26] Literary critic Hilel Barzel has found Nietzschean
elements in many of Tchernichowsky's poems: a rebellious attitude; an
emphasis on masculinity; an objection to Judeo-Christian moral codes; a
fascination with destruction; a belief in art as the greatest achievement of
the human spirit; and a preference for the mythical over the rational,
among others.[27]

On the face of it, "Baruch of Magenza" can indeed be seen as part of
a Dionysian revolution inspired by Nietzsche in its bold endorsement of
death, insanity and orgiastic revenge, and its rejection of all laws and
norms prevailing in Jewish life, from "Thou shalt not kill" to "Do not
rejoice at the fall of your enemy." Toward the end of the poem, Baruch
(whose name in Hebrew ironically means "blessed he") curses the pred-
ators in terms unprecedented in Hebrew letters and indulges in their death
in a manner reminiscent of the cult of death in Richard Wagner's operas:
"Every night we'd rise / from graves where we have sunk, / to drink the
blood of these butchers / until our souls were drunk." Baruch speaks like
a drunk when he describes the fire he set: "and in the furnace of those
rooms- / rivers of fire part, / crackling, roaring in the streams, / and in
sparks upstart." His behavior is that of a madman: "In the noise and confusion I / ran through the street / to see my enemies' broken spirits, / witness their defeat.... I laughed, I laughed, in the city streets / at the weeping
dames, / when a fellow fled from his burning house, / his coat in flames!"
His entire outlook is now molded by the fire to the extent of envisioning
a palace of fire, hinted to be fire from hell, in which he and his dead family would reside in glory. "And like a gleaming, glorious vision / created
by magic names, / on the great black cliff there rose a palace / of glowing

flames.... Here it is cold, but there, on high, / in that other flame, our daughters wait, / with holiday singing in the sky."

However, neither the poet nor his fictional hero has been associated with a cult of death, insanity and orgiastic revenge. Such elements can sometimes be found in later poetry, especially after the Holocaust, but they have not become part of the jargon of Jewish nationalism in the first half of the twentieth century for reasons related in large part to Tchernichowsky himself. It is not incidental that when he describes the rise of the dead, he refrains from the first tense singular. This turns the scene into a foreign mythology put forward, in my opinion, with a great deal of irony. For we are constantly reminded that Baruch, even when indulging in the fantasies of fire, remains an individual whispering to his dead wife in a dark corner of the cemetery. He asks, "Why, my dove, have you come to rest / here, in the darkness of the pit?" The masses killed in the Mainz pogrom are embodied in the figure of Baruch, but are never turned back into a mass. To the contrary, the individual emerging in "Baruch of Magenza," however defiant of the European Enlightenment that launched a pogrom against him, remains the "I" of the Enlightenment, not the "we" of twentieth century ultra-nationalism. Apollo rather than Dionysus continues to be Tchernichowsky's ideal; the faceless and voiceless victims are given a face and a voice, not torches to carry in a new march of the masses.

Tchernichowsky, who read Nietzsche in the original, was more familiar with his writings than many of his contemporaries who were mainly introduced to vulgar versions of these writings. As such, he was probably less impressed by Nietzsche than they were, as Brinker claims in a recent article.[28] The German philosopher sought victory of the human spirit over nature, while the Jewish poet sought a return to nature. The Jewish people, banned from owning land and from agricultural work, engaged for generations in what Tchernichowsky considered an overly reflective existence, but the "new Jew" to emerge was not, to him, an authentic, nihilistic *Übermensch* but an incumbent of a social, political, national group, of the kind Nietzsche detested. Tchernichowsky's poetic romanticism never shattered his concern with a national home for the persecuted Jews of Europe built on such foundations of European culture as socialism and liberalism.[29]

"Baruch of Magenza" may thus be seen as a bold attempt to commemorate Jewish history in a new light, that is, to construct a tale that turns the anonymous victims of the Crusades 800 years ago into individuals capable of taking their fate into their own hands. The highly successful popularization of the tale in a *fin de siècle* poem has become a major building bloc of an ideology giving Jews an identity as people who, while asserting their national will, are rooted in nature, history, and the international environment.

NOTES

1. This sentence appears in the Passover tale of the Exodus ("Haggadah").

2. "Albert of Aix and Ekkehard of Aura: Emico and the Slaughter of the Rhineland Jews." Internet Medieval Sourcebook, Paul Halsall, ed., (http://www.fordham.edu/halsall/source/1096jews.html).

3. "Soloman bar Samson: The Crusaders in Mainz, May 27, 1096." Internet Medieval Sourcebook. (http://www.fordham.edu/halsall/source/1096jews-mainz.html).

4. Susan L. Einbinder, *Beautiful Death: Jewish Poetry of Martyrdom in Medieval France* (Princeton, 2002), p. 1.

5. Jeremy Cohen, *Sanctifying the name of God* (Philadelphia, 2004), p. 13.

6. See Amos Elon, *The Pity of It All: A Portrait of the German-Jewish Epoch, 1743–1933* (New York, 2002).

7. Alan Mintz, *"Banished from their Father's Table": Loss of Faith and Hebrew Autobiography* (Bloomington, IN, 1989), p. 4.

8. See Me'ir Bussak, "Limkorot Baruch Mi'magnza." *Moznayim* 17 (November 1963): 442. (In Hebrew).

9. Howard Zvi Adelman, "Germany as Museum of Jewish History and Laboratory for Jewish-Christian Relations," *Textures and Meaning.* Online publication of the Department of Judaic and Near Eastern Studies, University of Massachusetts Amherst, 2004 (http://www.umass.edu/judaic/anniversaryvolume/articles/04-A2-Adelman.pdf).

10. "Before the Statue of Apollo." In Menachem Ribalow, *The Flowering of Modern Hebrew Literature*, edited and translated by Judah Nadich (New York, 1959), pp. 113–14.

11. Athena S. Leroussi and David Aberbach, "Hellenism and Jewish Nationalism: Ambivalence and its Ancient Roots," *Ethnic and Racial Studies* 25 (September 2002): 763.

12. "Hellenism and Jewish Nationalism," p. 770.

13. Dan Miron, "Mi'be'ir Ha'hariga va'hal'ah..." *Alpayim* 28 (2005): 152. (In Hebrew).

14. Iris Milner, "In the City of Slaughter: the Hidden Voice of the Pogrom Victims (Critical Essay)," *Prooftexts: Journal of Jewish Literary History* 25 (Winter–Spring 2005): 60–73.

15. H.N. Bialik, "The City of Slaughter," in *Complete Poetic Works of Hayyim Nahman Bialik*, vol. 1, ed. Israel Efros (New York, 1948), pp. 129–43.

16. "Mi'be'ir Ha'hariga va'hal'ah, p. 163.

17. Ephriam Broido, *Shaul Tchernichowsky*, published by the Education Department of the Zionist Federation of Great Britain and Ireland, undated, p. 8.

18. Alan Mintz, *Hurban: Responses to Catastrophe in Hebrew Literature* (New York, 1984), p. 124.

19. All quotations are from "Baruch of Magenza," in *The Flowering of Modern Hebrew Literature*, pp. 114–34.

20. Quoted in *Sanctifying the Name of God*, p. 93.

21. Edith W. Clowes, "Literary Reception as Vulgarization: Nietzsche's Idea of the Superman in Neo-Realist Fiction," in *Nietzsche in Russia*, ed. Bernice Glatzer Rosenthal (Princeton, 1986), p. 318.

22. Menacherm Brinker, "Nietzsche's Influence on Hebrew Writers of the Russian Empire," in *Nietzsche and Soviet Culture: Ally and Adversary*, ed. Bernice Glatzer Rosenthal (Cambridge, 1994), p. 396.

23. "Nietzsche's Influence...," p. 408.

24. Friedrich Nietzsche, *Beyond Good and Evil* (Chicago, 1955), pp. 377–78.

25. Yirmiyahu Yovel, "Nietzsche and the Jews: The structure of an ambivalence," in *Nietzsche and Jewish Culture*, ed. Jacob J. Golomb (Florence, KY, 1997), p. 129.

26. Jacob J. Golomb, "Nietzsche and the Marginal Jews," in *Nietzsche and Jewish Culture*, p. 175.

27. Hilel Barzel, "Nietzcschean Motives in Tchernichowski's Poetry," in *Nietzsche, Zionism and Hebrew Culture*, ed. Jacob Golomb (Jerusalem, 2002), pp. 181–216. (In Hebrew).

28. Menachem Brinker, "Nietzsche and the Hebrew Writers: An attempt at a Comprehensive Look," in *Nietzsche, Zionism and Hebrew Culture*.

29. See Robert Alter, *After the Tradition: Essays on Modern Jewish Writing* (New York, 1969).

The Ninetieth Anniversary of the Battle of the Somme[*]

Dan Todman

This essay examines British efforts to commemorate the 90th Anniversary of the 1916 Battle of the Somme. It seeks to illuminate current tensions in the history of memory and remembrance, and to explore the "popularization of war memory" at a moment when participants in the original event were on the point of extinction. It argues that at such points, historians need to pay particular attention to *who* is remembering *what*, to traditions in remembrance and the means by which these are communicated and transmitted, rather than how later generations might inherit ancestral experience.

The Somme in 2006 is an excellent example of what has been called the "memory boom": a widespread fascination with thought and activity about the past, whether personally experienced, from the last decades of the twentieth century into the twenty-first. This "boom" is seen as novel in its scale and intensity. This broad definition can include almost any reference, textual, symbolic, integral, or glancing, to the past. Examples might include the popularity of archaeological and genealogical television programs, the success of memoirs of abuse, the growth in historical reenactment, and rising museum attendances.[1] Many of these are connected to war, and particularly the two world wars. In films, computer programs, battlefield tours, plays, and books, the wars are subject, setting and point of main attraction. The "memory boom" in popular culture has been replicated within the academy. In the 1990s "memory" became one of the key buzzwords of the arts and social sciences. As a result, we now

[*]I am grateful to a number of practitioners for their assistance in providing information for this paper, but it should be stressed that the views and opinions expressed here are mine and do not reflect those held by these individuals or the institutions for which they work.

have access to an enormous body of work, of varying quality, that examines "memory" in one form or another.[2] Here, too, there is a focus on the "memory" of violence. It can seem that historians of war are now more likely to write about how conflicts were remembered than how they were decided.

Yet "memory" is by no means a settled field, and those who study it continue to argue about fundamental aspects of their work. Given its breadth, it would be unrealistic to catalog the subject's every twist and turn, but four themes in particular need to be discussed.

First, we have naming of parts. It is not necessarily to our advantage that "memory" has now broadened to include almost any facet of what used to be termed "culture." Both popular and academic writers have treated "memory" and its variants as unproblematic, or as representing a theoretical improvement over other terms.[3] Yet "memory" is so easily applied that its use can be misleading. Jay Winter has suggested in relation to discussions of cinema and "memory" that the greatest problem of the field is that people "refer to collective memory or national memory without reflecting on what these terms actually mean."[4]

The use of "memory" has methodological and theoretical implications that are too seldom interrogated. While "cultural memory" is more elegant than "commonly shared beliefs about the past as represented in texts," its use leads us to reify that "memory" without considering how it actually works. More damagingly, we run the risk of applying concepts developed in terms of individual psychoanalysis and memory to whole societies with an unspoken assumption that they operate in the same way. As Kerwin Lee Klein has noted, terms such as "repression"—commonly used in discussions of culture and "memory"— are not conceived in a vacuum. "Strangely, although the new memory studies frequently invoke the ways in which memory is socially constructed, Freudian vocabularies are far more common than Halbwachsian or even Lacanian ones."[5]

Those who define their terms more carefully have to confront two key distinctions: the individual and the collective processes that affect "memory," and the experienced and unexperienced past. Together, these form a second, but related, field of debate. As the work that takes account of neurology and psychiatry as well as history and cultural analysis suggests, memories are individual in basis.[6] Memory traces are laid down in the brain at the moment of personal experience. This is not to say that memories are in some ways a perfect, accurate, unalterable recording. Before, during and afterwards, individual interpretations of events are shaped by a range of factors, including prior assumptions, personal life schema and subsequent knowledge and experience. The nature of the event itself affects how it is remembered. The violence that is definitive of war changes how memories are created. When the adrenalin is pumping and the pulse is high, memory traces are denser, but are formed at a different location within the brain. The resulting memories may be extremely vivid and intense, but they can also be harder to access and more difficult to render into a coherent narrative. The historian Marc Bloch, writing years later of his first day of combat as a soldier in World War I, described his memories of what he was sure, as it happened, was an important experience, like a set of individual frames from a film reel. Bloch knew for certain that many of the frames were missing, that others were distorted, and that those that remained had been put into the wrong order. But try as he might, he could not reassemble the original film.[7]

Although held individually, memories are shaped socially. Social influences contribute to the personal schema that distort memories as they are laid down and set the context in which those memories are rehearsed. Rehearsal—a social act in which memories are described to others—is fundamental to the process of memory. The more frequently a story is told, the more likely it is to be remembered, but the more it will be subject to interference from the prevalent assumptions shared by the group in which it takes place. In response to the reactions of their audience, the person remembering adapts their story, often unconsciously, to gain approval and minimize discomfort. The result is that memories change over time. Where shared beliefs are particularly influential, individuals may even be led to make up stories about their pasts, stories that they may come to believe with as much force as if they drew on actual events.[8]

Bearing this in mind, it might be tempting to dismiss the role of individuals, to take a Halbswachsian approach, and to concentrate on socially shared beliefs. This is in practice what many "memory" studies undertake by examining the physical manifestations of those beliefs in the form of texts. Yet writing out the individual comes with its own problems. Most obviously, it leaves unclear how the people who make up societies form their ideas about the past. Does it make any sense to talk about what a society "remembers," when there is no physical location for those memories except the brains of individuals, each looking back to a version of the past that is socially shaped but personally experienced? Over-emphasizing the influence of society also risks obscuring the persistence of individual memories that may contradict the prevalent shared beliefs. As Alistair Thomson's work shows, individual memories that go against the social mores of the time may not be rehearsed, but that does not necessarily mean they disappear. On the contrary, they can remain, to reemerge at a moment when they will be met with more approval.[9]

The notion of "collective memory" is complicated even when societies undergo the sort of events that encourage discussion and agreement over memories as they are formed, such as assassinations and the outbreak and ending of wars.[10] It becomes even more so if we consider what happens subsequently, when those who were not present or even alive at the time form their ideas about the past. While they may communicate with those who were present, within the boundaries of discourse shaped by society as a whole, they hold no memory traces, heavily or otherwise distorted, of the event itself. "I can tell you about the complex, plastic, unstable ideas I have developed about my own experience, but I cannot pass them on to you like a gift or an heirloom."[11] Does it make any sense to talk about these latecomers "remembering" a past that is not theirs? Or do we need different words to describe a process that must take place in a different way?

In connection with his work on modern war, Winter has suggested a useful distinction between memory and remembrance. Memory is limited to the individual with personal experience of the past they are remembering; remembrance is a social phenomenon in which individual ideas about the past are created, shaped or passed on. Remembrance can therefore include acts of memory, either by the individuals who experienced the wars Winter studies firsthand, or by those who knew them only after the event had passed. But it can also include those moments when we develop or share our sense of a past to which we have no experiential connection. This Winter terms "historical remembrance." It may draw on, but is different from, the work of professional historians. The history that they write — shaped by personal experiences and the societies in which they live — is also in part an act of remembrance. Despite these influences, history is separated from memory and from historical remembrance by its basis in evidence, in discussion and revision.[12] Winter's definitions will be used from this point on, with the additional distinctions that "commemoration" refers to that remembrance activity explicitly designed to mark the loss of life, and that whereas memory refers to the individual act of reference to an experienced event in the past, "memory" refers to discussion of the subject in the present.

The "Memory Boom"

The study of the aftermath of World War I has been a particularly fruitful field for studies of how remembrance worked in practice. These have examined how the combination of sacred and profane as very different versions of the war were accommodated within a public discourse acceptable to all interest groups, the strong influence of popular behavior in shaping moments of national remembrance, and the role of local political, structural and economic factors in forming memorials and remembrance activities around specific sites, both real and imagined. Such practices often derived strength from their references to established traditions, rather than seeking new means of expression and remembrance.[13]

In an overview of this work, Winter has suggested that many of the commemorative forms with which we are now left — including memorials, rituals and shared ideas about the war — are the remnants of a scaffolding of belief erected by the bereaved as they sought to come to terms with the horrendous losses of the war.[14] This idea of a framework, originally erected to meet a dire emotional need that can remain even after those who put it up have gone, relates to the third point of discussion around the "memory boom": endurance. For, even if we accept Winter's distinction between individual memory and collective remembrance, it is apparent that those who have not experienced events such as war firsthand can feel an intensely strong emotional relationship to them. They hold to their beliefs about these events with a fierceness that suggests personal experience and that can confuse definitions of memory based on experiential connection.[15] How do those who were not there form such a strong sense of their version of the past, and what are the implications for remembrance? Here much work — both inside and outside the academy — has concentrated on the ways in which trauma was imagined and recorded within families, seemingly a key vector for remembrance. Marianne Hirsch in *Family Frames* considered family photographs (often of the dead or absent), a nineteenth-century innovation in relationships and concepts of the past, and came up with the notion of "postmemory." This describes the phenomenon in which individuals could grow up "dominated by narratives that preceded their birth." Aside from the stories they were told, children and grandchildren would carry with them their own memories of the lasting pain inflicted on their relatives by events that took place before their birth.[16]

Other trends in contemporary media and museum practice may currently be encouraging individuals to develop a strong sense of emotional involvement with the imagined past. In her 2004 book of the same name, Alison Landsberg developed the notion of "prosthetic memory" to describe the situation in which individuals, thanks to developing technology, mass culture and popular fascination with historical remembrance, develop their knowledge and understanding of the past experientially. The deeply-felt emotions that result are not the memories of unlived events, but they do represent a moment of connection that should be welcomed and even exploited by academics and institutions. Landsberg suggested that those who seek to experience the past develop "prosthetic memories" that bring them closer to the original events. Her work suffers from the syntactic difficulties outlined above — there is too little discussion of what "memory" actually means and too often "history" is used as a synonym for "the imagined past." Landsberg's positive interpretations of "prosthetic memories" lead her to treat them all as equally historically valid, and any reaction against them as the retrograde backlash of academics overly concerned with their professional status. Nevertheless, Landsberg is surely right to argue that technological and cultural developments need to be borne in mind in considering the changing construction of "memory" over time.[17]

The fourth and final area of debate around the "memory boom" is the origin of that boom itself. A number of different explanations exist, many of them drawing on the ideas of Pierre Nora, whose *lieux de memoire* project was based on the assumption that there is something distinct and unprecedented about contemporaries' sense of history, memory and the past.[18] From various different directions and over different timescales, the boom is interpreted as a reaction to the distinct wounds of modernity, to the severing of more localized links to the past, and to the failures of traditional narratives in the face of decolonization and democratization. It was further encouraged and shaped by the economic and social

Articles mentioning Somme from selection of UK national papers, 1 June–1 Sept 1994–2006

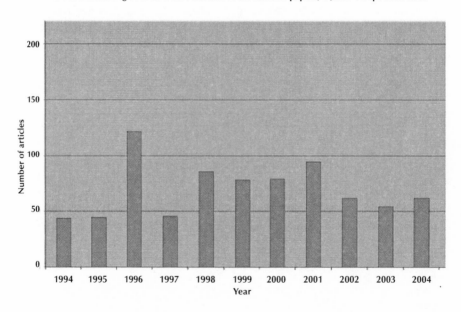

moment in which it has taken place. As a generation of baby boomers find themselves not only historically displaced but with relatively plentiful disposable income and leisure time, they have been able to use the past as a site of literal and imaginary tourism. Provocatively, Klein has suggested two further explanations. The first is located in identity politics at the turn of the twentieth and twenty-first centuries. The notion of "collective memory" became important here as a means to bind groups that would otherwise drift apart. Klein quotes with approval Allan Megill's proposition that as identity grows more problematic, so memory becomes more important.[19] But as Klein points out, a problem in any study of this phenomenon is that statements about identity are so much a part of "memory" discourse that to disentangle them is close to impossible. He also suggests that in academic terms, we should see the boom in studies of "memory" as a reaction to the challenges posed by post-structuralism. Analyzing "memory" allowed academics to acknowledge deconstruction without necessarily rejecting the essentialism that was so important to their sense of self– worth.[20] While this area of intellectual history is beyond the scope of this paper, we should acknowledge that our sensitivity to "war memory" may have as much to do with our professional awareness of the difficulties of composing coherent narratives of war as with an irreversible cultural shift.

Here, then, are four problematic areas: how to define "memory"; how it works for individuals and groups; the relationship between history, memory, family, and trauma in the production of ideas about the unlived past; and possible explanations for the "memory boom." How are these illuminated by a consideration of the remembrance activities undertaken by Britons during the 90th Anniversary of the Somme?

The Somme 2006

The 2006 anniversary is a particularly useful one for considerations of what memory and "memory" mean, in both popular and academic terms. Ceremonies in Britain and in France and the media reporting of them made frequent references to the need to "remember" the battle and those who had died during it. But the number of those who could actually do so was now extremely limited. The commemorations in 2006 were the first major anniversary at which no veteran of the 1916 battle was present. As this is written, surviving British World War I veterans can be numbered on one hand; by the time it is read, it is probable that they will have died out completely. This is a moment that has been prematurely expected since 1976, with veterans persistently outlasting commentator's prognostications that this would be the last anniversary they would attend. The only man who in July 2006 might have qualified as a veteran of the Somme, Harry Patch, was too frail to cross the Channel, or to comment extensively on the commemorations. In terms of public representation, therefore, no one was remembering the battle based on personal experience. What acts of memory were they performing instead?

Some participants had known those who had fought in the battle firsthand. The World War I veteran who did attend the ceremonies on the Somme in 2006 made this clear when he spoke to reporters. Britain's oldest man, Henry Allingham, served with the Royal Naval Air Service and recovered planes from the Somme battlefield in 1918, but he was not there in 1916. He was present, earlier in that year, at the naval Battle of Jutland, but this is a significant moment that the British have not chosen to commemorate. Allingham explicitly stated that he was present not as a participant but as a mourner: "I'm not here for myself. I'm here for the boys who did so much more than me, who never came home. If I hadn't come to the Somme today then I wouldn't have been showing them the respect they deserve, and so I had no choice. I had to be here."[21]

If relatively few Britons by 2006 had known those who died in the battle, many more had known those who had fought and survived as parents and grandparents. Despite the horrific losses of 1 July 1916 and the aura of death that is still associated with World War I, most of those who served in the British armed forces returned home at the war's end. Some had passed on the knowledge of their participation to their offspring who, if they could not remember the battle, could remember others rehearsing their memories of it. Since all but one of those veterans who survived the battle had subsequently died, they could be included in the rhetoric of personal remembrance and tribute. The BBC news website, for example, followed one historical re-enactor, Neil McGurk, a Cambridge engineer who retraced the steps of his grandfather and great-uncles to the Somme. He described it thus:

> [A] ... chance in a lifetime. I think these sort of things are worthwhile doing because the number of veterans are becoming fewer and fewer...
> For me it's less about the politics [of war], more about the sacrifice of those people who were swept up in it. It makes me realise how lucky I was to have been born. My grandfather survived, and so I am here.[22]

In other cases it was apparent that participants in the 2006 commemoration were remembering the pain of family members who had been bereaved by the battle. The grief and loss caused by untimely death had endured for those left behind and been seen firsthand by later generations. Prince Charles, in his 1 July speech at Thiepval, was careful to point out that he found it especially poignant because his wife had lost three great uncles, and he one, in World War I.[23] Family history was a theme of many news reports and BBC News Online devoted a message board to asking relatives to send in their family stories. In two weeks, some 929 messages were left: a remarkable level of public response by the standards of the site.[24] Particularly in its opening stages, before it received extensive publicity and attracted more opinionated surfers, the messages on this site were a poignant reminder of the longevity of grief and the persistence of tragic narratives as a reference point within families.

> My uncle, Angus Calder Macaulay, Lt Corp [*sic*; Lance Corporal?] in the Royal Warwickshire Regiment, was killed on the Somme 23.7.16. He was just 23 years old, and a talented artist, planning to train in France. His family never came to terms with his death, and it was seldom talked about by my father, his younger brother, who found it too painful. I found his "memorial" this year, a moving experience.[25]

Again, however, it is necessary to take care in defining exactly what was taking place. In most cases this did not seem to be "traumatic memory" in the sense of a lasting and damaging recollection of personal experience, the rehearsal of which was beyond individual control. There were, however, many individual memories of trauma: Britons in 2006 could still recall the pain inflicted on others by traumatic experience. The majority of those remembering were two generations removed from those who had fought, with 55 percent of those who contributed to the BBC site mentioning grandfathers or great-uncles. They were close enough not just to have been told about the war and its impact by those who had lived through it, but to have felt the emotional force of their experiences. The level of detail associated with some of these narratives indicated their importance within families—a good example of Hirsch's "postmemory."

We should, however, be careful before we assume that remembrance activity in 2006 was based solely on memories of bereaved relatives, still scarred by their wartime losses long after the event, or on connections to returning veterans, now added by time to the roll call of the dead. Not everyone could easily claim a familial link. While there was an obvious need in wartime for a socially unifying rhetoric that emphasized universal participation, in practice nearly half the male population did not serve in the armed forces, even if the contribution of civilian workers was as important in time of "total war" as those of soldiers. Many families (including my own) could not therefore point to ancestors who had been soldiers. Even on a site supposedly dedicated to family "memory," 132 out of 929 messages on the BBC board had no mention of a family member. For others, the imperfect processes of family remembrance meant that many connections had been lost, forgotten, or only very partially transmitted, so that many messages concentrated on rediscovery, rather than preservation. By 2006, after repeated appearances in novels, documentaries and news reporting, the rhetoric of family history as a means of participation in the commemoration of World War I had become so strong that those who could not draw a link would either seek one out or be left jealous and bereft. As one contributor to the BBC site put it, "I am not sure who if anyone my family lost during that war/battle, but I nonetheless feel our loss as keenly as anyone."[26]

Whether they could personally remember World War I or its veterans, most of those who took part in remembrance activity in 2006 had strong ideas about what the war had been like and what it had meant. But these were not derived unadulterated from the personal experience by their forebears and handed down from one generation to another. Instead, Britons in 2006 derived their sense of World War I from a broad range of cultural sources, constructed during and after the war and re-imagined and reworked in later years. When they pictured the Somme, they drew on a mass of secondary material, including works of popular history, school lessons and television programs. For example, one later contributor to the BBC message board expressed his antagonism towards British generals in terms that directly recalled existing secondary texts— Alan Clark's 1960 account of *The Donkeys* and the 1989 BBC television comedy series *Blackadder Goes Forth*:

> "Lions led by donkies," what a waste of human life when the senior officers treated their men like the lead soldiers they used to throw around on pretend battlefields. Throwing infantry armed with rifles against machine guns was a monumental disaster, the leaders should have been court-marhsalled [*sic*].[27]

It might be suggested that this represented at some level the presentation of an antiestablishment "counter-narrative" of the war as experienced by its lowest ranking soldiers. This would, indeed, have run counter to the official discourse of wartime propaganda. It was, however, absolutely in line with how the war was subsequently distilled and re-imagined in British popular culture. The strength of such beliefs— derived from individual memories of secondary texts, rather than heirloomed memories handed on from veterans—formed a major barrier to a more historical understanding of the war; that is to say, one based on the critical assessment of evidence and the development of argument. As the new books published in 2006 indicated, historians still do not agree about the Somme.[28] But their researches have revealed the complexity of experience at the time — even on the disastrous first day — and questioned some of the most popular myths of the Somme, including the image of soldiers advancing at 7.30 A.M. in long lines "as if on parade at Aldershot."[29] Despite their representation in popular formats, including the drama documentary broadcast by the BBC to mark the 90th Anniversary, these new interpretations did not gain widespread popular acceptance. Critical reaction to the documentary, indeed, suggested bafflement when audiences were presented with a version of the battle that did not fit their preexisting assumptions. If anything, it is the work of professional historians, read by that small selection of the public that is obsessed with the Great War, which forms the "alternative" narrative of the war.

The diverse roots and uses of this "war in the head," to borrow Samuel Hynes' phrase,[30] highlight one of the problems with Landsberg's concept of "prosthetic memory." Among the remembrance activities associated with the Somme in general and the 90th Anniversary in particular were a number of forms that offered the opportunity for "experiential learning," including interactive museum exhibits, battlefield tours, the presence of re-enactors, and even a chance for physical exertion on the Somme marathon (run by some in period uniform).[31] But few if any of those who took these opportunities were *tabulae rasae*, previously ignorant of World War I. On the contrary, those who visited museums or reenactments were often eager consumers of the range of historical products associated with the war. The strength of this market is indicated by the way in which publishers timed book releases to meet the anniversary, and the range of special paid-entry events put on for it. Participants might well use their chance to "experience" World War I to develop their own sense that they understood it better. In practice, however, the tendency was often to reinforce what they already thought they knew about the war, rather than to bring them closer to the experiential world of combatants. For many veterans, for example, the war, for all its horrors and trials, contained moments that they could portray to themselves in positive terms. Either at the time or in retrospect, the war could be turned into a redeemable experience. Yet efforts to make this point by academic and museum historians, documentary makers and commentators, fell flat before the overwhelmingly negative reputation of World War I and the cemeteries that form the focal point for commemoration: it cannot be anything other than a tragedy. Cultural baggage has a crucial influence in shaping "experiential learning" and the "prosthetic memories" that result. To pursue Landsberg's metaphor, the problem with these "prostheses" is that legless men and women may sometimes choose to strap bionic arms onto their stumps.

As noted above, much analysis of remembrance and World War I in Britain has focused on the interwar period. How did the patterns established in the war's aftermath adapt to the passage of time and the disappearance of veterans, and how did remembrance work in the absence of firsthand war memory? Analysis of the 90th Anniversary suggests the continued importance of activity "from below"; the establishment of traditions in remembrance, memories of which inform behavior and attitudes in the present and the interaction of commemorations with contemporary news culture.

Even though some of the ceremonies were officially supported and attended by politicians and members of the royal family, just as in previous decades the form of remembrance was shaped by popular rather than state action. One significant site of commemorative activity, for example, was the Lochnagar Crater—created by an enormous explosion set off beneath the German lines on 1 July 1916 and privately purchased by Richard Dunning in 1978 to preserve it for posterity. The re-enactors from various organizations, whose marches across the battlefield were such a distinctive feature of 2006, did soon their own initiative, although some received logistical aid from the British Army.[32] Individual choices therefore helped to decide where and how the Somme was commemorated.

Remembrance in 2006 was also shaped by the memory of previous commemorations. After ninety years of ceremonial and media activity, and particularly since the revival of popular interest in the 1960s, certain traditions have become established around the major anniversaries of the war.[33] It was anticipated, for example, that the BBC would mark 1 July 2006 with a documentary (as it had done in 1976, 1986 and 1996, although not always with fresh material). Perhaps the clearest example of the force of these commemorative traditions was the need to represent veterans in the reporting of commemoration. So strong was this trope that it could overcome the minor inconvenience of no veterans actually being available. So Henry Allingham, for all his protestations that he too was a mourner, was present because he fulfilled the symbolic role of veteran. While most newspaper reports made it clear that he had not fought on the Somme in 1916, his place in the visual reporting of the ceremonies was identical with that filled in previous years by those who had. The BBC television news that night did, in fact, describe him as a veteran of the battle. If an actual veteran could not be found, then one who was near enough would do—a trend taken to absurdity by the BBC when it recorded the thoughts of a veteran of World War II at the ceremony about "what it must have been like" for his forebears. His image was captioned, tellingly, "War Veteran."[34] It is to be expected that this trend for "old soldiers, general issue" will heighten as both world wars grow further away.

The absence of actual combatants from the Somme may help to

explain the prominent place given to re-enactors. A number of different British reenactment or living history groups were on the Somme in July 2006, along with some counterparts from France and Germany. Two British groups staged marches across the battlefield. Re-enactors took place in many commemorative events, including that at the Lochnagar Crater. In America and Europe, military reenactment has been a minority hobby since the 1960s. British hobbyists have reenacted World War I since the late 1970s on a small scale, and since the 1990s on an increasingly large one. They not only attempt to commemorate and "experience" aspects of wartime life in private, but take place in public events organized by the historical leisure and preservation sector. World War I re-enactors place more emphasis than most on the broader experience of history and less on the recreation of combat: unlike those who reenact the English Civil or Napoleonic Wars, battles are not restaged.[35]

This was not a totally new departure. Less formal reenacting has always taken place, not least by veterans themselves, some of whom came together in the years after 1918 to recreate wartime camaraderie and belonging.[36] Whether such redemption and explanation could be undertaken by those who were not veterans had, however, previously been a subject of dispute. The 2001 BBC series *The Trench*, which put forty modern volunteers through Great War training before sending them out to live in dugouts in the French countryside for three weeks, was widely criticized as an attempt to impose the standards of reality television on the remembrance of war. In contrast, in 2006 it was extremely hard to find any negative comment on the presence of re-enactors on the Somme. Their presence was publicly accepted as respectful rather than distasteful. Arguably, it was more acceptable because their public performances—the march across the battlefield and the participation in commemorative ceremonies—concentrated either on the buildup to the battle or to its remembrance, rather than on the moment of assault and death. They also functioned, however, to replace the actual veterans who could no longer be present. Protected by the aura of remembrance and the requirement to replace vanished veterans, in 2006 reenactment was seen as tribute, not travesty.[37]

Although it drew heavily on established traditions, commemoration in 2006 was widely reported because it also fitted the content needs of the contemporary news media. The constant but slow changes of drawn-out remembrance provided a steady drip of developments that could be displayed on 24-hour news channels. On the screen, to war and tragedy could be added tearful relatives, the royal family and journeys of personal discovery. Crucially, for a news media culture in which eye-witnessing and individual emotional reaction were established modes of representation, there were numerous opportunities to ask people how they felt. This was a significant reason for the place given to re-enactors in news reports. They provided an easily accessible human interest story through which to present the complex events of ninety years before. For one re-enactor, the principal memory of his participation was the constant presence of a microphone, accompanied by the question: "How do you feel?"[38] This structural attraction helps to explain why the Somme was more prominent in British newspapers in the summer of 2006 than it had been in the same period over the previous decade.

Conclusions

How does the anniversary of the Somme help us to understand the popularity of the "memory boom" in general? This survey indicates the large number of different factors that need to be taken into account when trying to explain particular eruptions within the "boom." The sheer range of actors involved and the difficulty of unpacking each individual's relationship to a past that has been conveyed to them in so many different ways must encourage us to caution. It might be useful to divide explanations for the popularity of remembrance into inspirational and permissive factors. Remembrance, at this remove, is much more a choice rather than the overriding necessity that it was to those bereaved by the war. Among the factors that encouraged Britons to make that choice in 2006 were the cultural fashion for family history, the need to resolve their memories of the trauma suffered by others close to them, and a desire to confirm their identity. It has become a cliché that a British identity founded on military and imperial endeavor and religious xenophobia has become increasingly problematic in the modern era, and that English national identity in particular lacks socially acceptable outlets.[39] There certainly was room within the Somme commemorations to assert national identity:

> Having two Grandparents in this conflict, I reflect on the present state of this country and wonder what it was all about. I myself served in the armed forces. But I did not serve to be ruled by bods in Germany and France Common Market, European LAW TOTAL RUBBISH Common sense has disappeared from society [sic].[40]

It might seem, therefore, that Megill's proposition is valid, and that "memory" becomes more attractive as identity grows more problematic. But in practice, the sort of extreme Europhobic nationalism expressed here was rare. Instead, a sense that an important event in national history should be marked was widespread, particularly because it was about to slip over the horizon of lived memory. The re-enactor Neil McGurk wrote:

> I hope that anyone who's seen some of us daft enough to do something like this will take an interest, do what I've done and see what they can find out [about their family history] and realise this is part of British history. Because nearly everybody has a connection with the Great War. The next generation has never known anyone who went through it. I think I'm one of the last few who really got to know anyone who went through it.[41]

As this statement indicates, national identity *per se* was perhaps less important than the location of complex individual identities within broader narratives of family, generation, community, and nation. Commemorating the Somme was less about what it meant to be British and more about finding a moment when participants' forebears had stuck their head over the parapet and appeared, briefly, in British history.

Perhaps surprisingly, there was remarkably little attempt to apply historical remembrance to the contemporary sphere. The continued presence of the war in British popular culture has in part been based on the ways in which it can be recast to meet the needs of the moment. Representations of the war changed to fit the disillusionment of the 1920s; the need for national mobilization and hope for the future in the 1940s; and the fear of nuclear Armageddon in the 1960s. Even though British forces were at war in 2006, such conflicts received little direct mention in response to the anniversary. Neither did England's involvement in a crucial World Cup game with Portugal — worthy of mention, given the country's tradition of combining sport and war in national narratives.

In combination with these inspirational factors, we also need to bear in mind the permissive factors that made remembrance easy and attractive in the twenty-first century. The creation and preservation of individual artifacts such as photographs and medals has left a legacy of potential routes back into the past within families. The bureaucratic effort necessary to mobilize the country for war matched this with detailed records of enlistment and deaths, some of which are now available online. The presence and ease of access of this information, combined with increased leisure and disposable income for the baby-boomer generation, has made family history an attractive choice as a hobby.[42] The worldwide web provides a location at which those who are interested in remembrance can find out more information and make contact with others who share their interest and seek guidance.[43] Future research might well concentrate on finding out whether the web has rejuvenated the fictive kinships which Winter identifies as so important to postwar remembrance.

We should bear in mind that the "memory boom" has developed its own momentum. The Somme was also prominent in the media in 2006 because a number of institutional actors had worked very hard to put it there. As a result of changes in funding and professional culture, museums in Britain now take a much more proactive approach to the media than they once did. They are more conscious than previously of a need to "sell" their institutions and to promote public awareness of their activities. In 1996, for example, the historians at the Imperial War Museum in London logged two major interviews with newspapers in connection with the 80th Anniversary of the Somme. Ten years later, they logged ten interviews and six briefings for radio, television and print media, as well as leading a two-day tour of the battlefields for five journalists. These figures may not be an accurate guide to the exact quantity of media interaction, but the fact that museum staff is now required to record these contacts in such detail is itself indicative of a change in approach.[44] The National Army Museum, which was making an effort to increase its profile generally, under the influence of a new director seized the moment to promote not only its own exhibition but its educational activities more generally. Museum staff joined re-enactors marching across the battlefield in the days before 1 July and provided a reliable resource for interviews.[45] One effect of the "memory boom," therefore, has been to develop a professional body dedicated to exploiting and perpetuating it.

In a well-known discussion in the *American Historical Review* ten years ago, Alon Confino demanded that historians become both more precise, theoretically and methodologically, in their studies of "memory," but also more "anarchic": turning their attention to the enormous range of different factors that can influence memory and remembrance, and placing events in their cultural context.[46] This paper bears out the sense in Confino's demands and indicates the importance of individual memories in historical remembrance. The Somme in 2006 was full of people remembering, after all, but none of them were remembering the battle itself. Instead, they thought back to what they had been told about the battle and the war by those who had been there, or those who had known them, recalled what they had seen on screen or on the page, or cast their minds back to previous commemorations. It would be misleading to say that many of these people had any memory of the Somme in 1916. This distinction matters: they had formed their "war in the head" in a cultural context in which the reductive processes of mythologizing had already been at work. From the 1960s onward, the commonly shared beliefs in Britain about World War I have stabilized around its representation as a futile, ill-fought slaughter. Rather than the complexities of wartime experience being subjected to the simplifying effect of collective remembrance, later generations began with that reduced version. At the same time, it would be unhelpful to dismiss the emotional force of these memories and the sense of familial connection that often accompanied them, merely because they were not based on personal experience of the event being commemorated. The sense that 1916 could and should be remembered was hugely important to participants for a variety of reasons, including locating the self and the nation in historic terms. It remains to be seen whether World War I will retain this ability to entrance subsequent generations, or whether, as it too slips over the edge of lived memory, World War II will fulfill a similar function for Britons in the future.

NOTES

1. J. Winter, "The Generation of Memory: Reflections on the 'Memory Boom' in Contemporary Historical Studies," *Bulletin of the German Historical Institute Washington* (2000).

2. P. Fritsche, "Review: The Case of Modern History," *Journal of Modern History* 73 (March 2001): 87–117; K. L. Klein, "On the Emergence of Memory in Historical Discourse," *Representations* 69 (Winter 2000): 127–50.

3. For example, *ibid.*, pp. 136, 144. See also J. Bodnar, *Remaking America: Public Memory, Commemoration, and Patriotism in the Twentieth Century* (Princeton, 1992); and J. Young, *The Texture of Memory: Holocaust Memorials and Meaning* (New Haven, CT, 1993).

4. J. Winter, *Remembering War: The Great War Between Memory and History in the Twentieth Century* (New Haven, CT, 2006), p. 185.

5. Klein, "On the Emergence of Memory," p. 135.

6. See J. Winter and E. Sivan, eds., *War and Remembrance in the Twentieth Century* (Cambridge, 1999); J. Young, *The Texture of Memory: Holocaust Memorials and Meaning* (New Haven, CT, 1993), p. xi, notes how little cultural historical work engages with the scientific study of how memory works in the brain.

7. M. Bloch, *Memoirs of War* (Ithaca, NY, 1980), p. 85.

8. D. Todman, *The Great War, Myth and Memory* (London, 2005), pp. 204–10.

9. A. Thomson, *Anzac Memories: Living with the Legend* (Oxford, 1994).

10. Winter, *Remembering War*, pp. 5–6.

11. Todman, *The Great* War, p. 382.

12. Winter, *Remembering War*, pp. 5–6, 278.

13. For example, George Mosse, *Fallen Soldiers: Reshaping the Memory of the World Wars* (Oxford, 1990); and A. Gregory, *The Silence of Memory: Armistice Day, 1919–1946* (Oxford, 1994).

14. J. Winter, *Sites of Memory, Sites of Mourning: The Great War in European Cultural History* (Cambridge, 1995), pp. 30, 53, 225; "Forms of Kinship and Remembrance in the Aftermath of the Great War," in Winter and Sivan, eds., *War and Remembrance*, p. 60.

15. Winter, *Remembering War*, p. 278.

16. M. Hirsch, *Family Frames: Photography, Narrative, and Postmemory* (Cambridge, MA, 1997), p. 48.

17. A. Landsberg, *Prosthetic Memory: The Transformation of American Remembrance in the Age of Mass Culture* (New York, 2004), pp. 18–43 and passim.

18. P. Nora, "General Introduction: Between Memory and History," in P. Nora, ed., *Realms of Memory: Rethinking the French Past* (New York, 1996), vol. 1, p. 2; Klein, "On the Emergence of Memory," p. 142.

19. A. Megill, "History, Memory and Identity," *History and the Human Sciences* 11 (August 1998): 37–38.

20. Klein, "On the Emergence of Memory, p. 142.

21. "In praise of Henry Allingham," *Guardian*, http://www.guardian.co.uk/com mentisfree/story/0,1807633,00.html, accessed 23 October 2006; "Henry Allingham," *Daily Telegraph*, http://www.telegraph.co.uk/opinion/main.jhtml?xml=/opinion/2006/06/01/ d10103.xml

22. N. McGurk, "An emotional day at the Somme," http://news.bbc.uk/1/hi/uk/ 5128494.stm, accessed 10 October 2006.

23. D. Smith, "Royals Pay Tribute to Fallen of the Somme," *Observer*, 2 July 2006, p. 12.

24. "BBC News Have Your Say: The Battle of the Somme," http://newsforums.bbc. co.uk/nol/thread.jspa?sortBy=1&threadID=2226&start=1&t, p. 1, accessed 31 October 2006.

25. *Ibid.*, p. 46.

26. *Ibid.*, p., 60.

27. *Ibid.*, p. 45.

28. M. Gilbert, *The Battle of the Somme: The Heroism and the Horror of War* (London, 2006); R. Prior and T. Wilson, *The Somme* (London, 2006); G. Sheffield, *The Somme: A New History* (London, 2004); P. Hart, *The Somme* (London, 2006).

29. Prior and Wilson, *The Somme*, pp. 112–18.

30. S. Hynes, *The Soldiers' Tale* (London, 1995), p. 54.

31. "Guide to Somme Events," http://www.essentialsomme.com/events.htm, accessed 22 October 2006; Department of the Somme Calendar 2006, http://www.somme-battlefields.co.uk/en/-making/calendar.aspx, p. 5; accessed 22 October 2006.

32. My thanks to Andrew Robertshaw and Julian Farrance of the National Army Museum for supplying me with this information.

33. S. Crane, "Memory and Distortion in the Museum," *History and Theory* 36 (December 1997), pp. 47, 51.

34. "Battle of the Somme Commemorated," http://search.bbc.co.uk/cgibin/search/ results.pl?q=somme+battle+commemorated&x=0&y=0&scope=all&edition=d&tab=av& recipe=all, accessed 30 October 2006.

35. A. Smith, "National Identity, Re-enactment and Conflict: A usable Past?," in H. Brocklehurst and R. Phillips, eds., *History, Nationhood and the Question of Britain* (London, 2003), pp. 303–04.

36. "Fiftieth Anniversary of the Battle of the Somme," Arras and District Branch, British Legion, Harrod Papers, Imperial War Museum Department of Documents, 99/52/1; see also J. Vance, *A Death so Noble: Memory, Meaning and the First World War* (Vancouver, 1997).

37. Todman, *The Great War*.

38. Personal information.

39. R. Weight, *Patriots: National Identity in Britain, 1930–2000* (London, 2003).

40. "BBC News Have Your Say," p. 480.

41. See McGurk, "An emotional day at the Somme."

42. Winter, "The Generation of Memory."

43. For example, see the efforts by other users to assist those searching for relatives' graves on the BBC site. Thirty posts in total offered aid to other users: "BBC News Have Your Say."

44. My thanks to Terry Charman of the Imperial War Museum for supplying me with these figures. Charman to Todman (email), 11 October 2006.

45. Again, my thanks to Andrew Robertshaw and Julian Farrance for discussing this topic with me.

46. A. Confino, "Collective Memory and Cultural History: Problems of Method," *American Historical Review* 102 (December 1997): 1402.

Popular Memory in Northern Ireland[1]

Rebecca Lynn Graff-McRae

In the aftermath of traumatic political conflict, the lingering memories of violence intersect with the desire to shape a new and different society. Memorialization of conflict therefore comes into direct contact with questions of cultural identity: that is, how the society is to be perceived, both internally and externally. In *Everything is Illuminated* (a work inextricably tied to conflicts of memory) Jonathan Safran Foer comments on this tension between war memory, cultural identity, and tourism, through his narrator Alex:

> Father toils for a travel agency, denominated Heritage Touring. It is for Jewish people, [...] who have cravings to leave that ennobled country America and visit humble towns in Poland and Ukraine. [...] before the voyage I had the opinion that [these] people were having shit between their brains. This is because all I knew of [these] people is that they paid Father very much currency in order to make vacations *from* America *to* Ukraine.[2]

The significance of Alex's wry observation can be found not in its obvious ignorance, but rather in its appropriateness to post-conflict societies. If we were to causally substitute "Northern Ireland" for "Ukraine" in the above quote, the result would be remarkably similar to the comments I received upon arriving for the first time in Belfast.

As in the novel, the difficulty lays not just in a society struggling to re-imagine itself after prolonged internal conflict, but more deeply in the necessity of addressing the past; that is, "How can others come here seeking answers to their pasts, when we cannot even begin to ask questions of our own?" While tourists often come in search of a simple clarification of "their" past — ancestry, culture, nostalgia, etc. — in Northern Ireland, the issue at stake is thornier: parties cannot agree on "whose" past should be addressed, or how, or even if it should be acknowledged at all.

This dissention is a necessary consequence of political and social conflict:

> After traumatic events, there is a struggle over memory. Some forms of remembering can be seen as ways of forgetting: ways of recovering from trauma by putting its lessons to one side, refusing to acknowledge that anything has changed, restoring the pretence.[3]

The struggle over popular memory of the conflict thus becomes an integral component and continuation of the conflict itself. However, as Jenny Edkins points out, this is not a straight-forward dichotomy of remembering (as "keeping the faith") versus forgetting (as "selective amnesia"). Rather that memory and forgetting are interdependent, mutually constitutive dynamics.

In the essay, I seek to frame this struggle of memory and forgetting in reference to Jacques Derrida's work on spectrality and encryption. These concepts allow us to perceive commemoration as a tension between repetition, rupture, and reiteration — one that is at the heart of lingering political division in Northern Ireland. Moreover, it is a tension that hinges on a particular formulation of the relationship between popular memory, conflict and tourist culture. When Simon Calder, the travel editor for the United Kingdom (UK) broadsheet newspaper *The Independent*, wrote that, "When conflict passes into tourist attraction, the world is a better place,"[4] Northern Ireland navel-gazers hailed it as pointing to a remarkable development: when sites of conflict can be associated with postcards rather than petrol bombs, they no longer have the power of violence. Such a development signals that the conflict has passed into the past. However, from another, more critical perspective, this pronouncement can and must be challenged. Read through spectrality and encryption it suggests, equally, that ways of memorializing the conflicts of the past are in fact processes of reproducing those conflicts in the safer confines of the present. Derrida identifies in the specter "a politics of memory, of inheritance, and of generations."[5] What does it mean when the bitterest of enmities is deemed to be contained in the past? Can the troublesome ghosts of memory be suppressed, or does the conflict merely shift to other arenas? Through several recent examples, I argue that one of these arenas is the issue of popular memory itself: how the Troubles can and should be memorialized, remembered, or forgotten, has become a battlefield both within, and between Unionist and Republican political bases.

Re-visiting, Re-imaging and Re-telling the Troubles: Tourism and Conflict Memory

My first example takes us back to my first days in Belfast in 2000, in the aftermath of the historic Good Friday Agreement. At that time, despite the peace agreement and the simultaneous ceasefires of the major paramilitary organizations, many sections of the city, such as the Falls and the Shankill, were still "no-go areas." While friends and family at home persisted in trying to send me a flak jacket ("Just in case"), I noticed that many of my American counterparts were eager to visit these areas, to see the sites of thirty years of turmoil firsthand. My Northern Irish friends derisively labeled these adventurers as "Troubles Tourists," or, more sardonically, "eejits." There were unwritten rules to navigating Belfast — put so memorably by the poet Ciaran Carson, "The city is a map of the city."[6]

Fast-forwarding a little to 2006, on returning from a short stay in Edinburgh, my fiancé and I were assailed with offers for "black cab tours"— that is, "authentic" Belfast-born cabbies would drive us through the most contested streets of the city, pointing out sites of significance to the conflict, regaling us with a by-now mythologized version of its history.[7] What had changed in Northern Ireland to make way for "political tourism," and how can we trace the implications of this shift? One website, for Belfast Political Tours, encapsulates this sea change through an introduction to its tours of the Falls and Shankill Roads:

> Two roads. One story. A unique opportunity in time.
>   Who else could tell you the real story of these **two infamous roads** [the Falls and the Shankill] but real people. **Real combatants....** Now they have come together, **in peace**, to bring you this unique opportunity to see ... their story as it really happened and to discover the real and friendly people of these two areas. People who are renowned the world over for their **friendliness and hospitality.**[8]

Less than ten years before, these roads had been effectively off-limits; in access and in conversation they evoked nervousness and caution. They allowed no intersection. Now, "in peace," the roads are claimed to offer a common ground, where "[the] story as it really happened" can be told.

This particular advertisement epitomizes a discourse in which sites of conflict are (re)appropriated as spaces of reconciliation. The journey through Belfast's most notorious neighborhoods, while evoking a lingering degree of the fear and isolation experienced by residents and visitors in the past, is effectively rewritten as a metaphoric path from terror to harmony — or at least, to a level of relative normality. In an article for BBC News (26 February 2007), the link between tourism and the peace process is drawn as a unique arena by which to re-tell and remember the history of the Troubles: "There is a new kind of tourist in Northern Ireland. They are the ones eager to turn their back on the usual tourist trail and head into the heart of Belfast's former trouble spots."[9] Jan Nugent of the Northern Ireland Tourist Board encapsulates this shift, saying, "I wasn't too keen when the Black Cab tours started up — I thought it could almost be seen as terror tourism. [...] But now it's seen as the edgy thing to do — people can go home and say, 'I toured the trouble spots.' It's given communities a real drive to spruce up their murals and their local area as well."[10] The promise of transformation or transcendence of violence, division, and deprivation therefore links the promotion of tourism — the very possibility of a permissible space for political tourism — to the engineering of social change.

By playing on the contentious past in order to emphasize the advantages of the present, this discourse seeks to call on the spectral memory of the Troubles and to channel it towards its own ends. It attempts to suggest that there is only one purpose for Troubles memory: to illustrate that the ghosts of the past are no longer troublesome. Rather, they are intended to provide the lesson that it is only from the present that the past can be viewed with an unjaundiced eye. The present offers "a unique opportunity in time," in which history and memory can be brought out, examined, and then sealed carefully away.

What this discourse fails to acknowledge, however, is that the specter can be contained only partially — that is, temporarily, incompletely and with bias. Neither the memory of the past nor its meaning is content to remain conveniently static until they are useful. The political, social, and cultural resonance of the past shifts and changes, just like the neighborhoods of the Falls and the Shankill. As communities formerly situated at sites of conflict (termed "interface areas") are assimilated into the "tourist trail," the drive to "spruce up" their murals and repaint their kerbstones seems at odds with itself. To repaint the past encompasses two contradictory rationales: to retrace the original image, "new and improved," that is, the same picture only cleaner, more aesthetically pleasing; or to paint over, to draw a new image, one that itself possesses a shared or neutral history.

The "Re-imaging Communities" initiative, launched in July 2007, aspires to the latter: the program encourages the creation of shared, inclusive space through the visual transformation of public space.[11] Among the projects to receive funding are the "makeovers" of several murals in Northern Ireland's interface areas. The Greater Village Regeneration Trust, a nonprofit organization formed by local residents, links the transformation of murals to urban revitalization of "The Village," a primarily Protestant, working-class area of South Belfast:

> Murals have a strong tradition in Northern Ireland and in particular in the Village where they are seen by some as part of the heritage of the area. Murals expressing territorialism however are not generally conducive to investment and regeneration.
>
> The community must now explore new, more constructive ways of expressing its cultural identity.[12]

Under the "Re-imaging Communities" scheme, the Greater Village Trust will be embarking on new visual projects entitled "Now and Then," "Hope" and "Reflect," indicating a desire for the community to place conflict, deprivation, and paramilitarism firmly in the past. The transformation of visual space — through the removal or repainting of murals — corresponds to cultural and political change.

Other significant examples seem to signify an explicit attempt to forge (and reinforce) a sense of "neutral" or "inclusive" culture in Northern Ireland. The repainting of a Loyalist Red Hand Commandos mural in Ballymacarrett Road now displays a collage of images to celebrate the centenary of Belfast author C.S. Lewis (Convention Court, Ballymacarrett Road[13]). In similar fashion, the mural of late footballer George Best (Portadown, East Belfast) covers an image of the notorious Billy Wright, a member of the Loyalist Volunteer Force who was shot dead while serving time in the Maze prison. Cyril Moorhead of Portadown Local Action for Community Engagement says that the new mural shows that "paramilitarism is a thing of the past."[14] These examples, along with the proliferation of murals featuring the *Titanic* (most prominently, on the Lower Newtownards Road) claim to renovate the social and political landscape via the visual; thus, a shared image of culture — literature, sport, or engineering — literally takes the place of divisive, territorial markers.

While the program has been widely lauded, there has been concern over the apparent erasure of many visible reminders of the Troubles — what amounts to cosmetic surgery for murals to emphasize shared, inclusive, non-threatening imagery and symbolism. The metaphoric, (en)cryptic significance affixed to the concept of "re-painting" history is telling. In an article of that title, the UK newspaper *Guardian* poses the question thus: "Belfast is trying to put its troubled past behind it, while keeping its heritage intact. So should the paramilitary murals adorning its housing estates be preserved — or destroyed?"[15] The question is framed as though this were an either/or decision; however, the paradox of remembering and forgetting the past refuses to allow one to take precedence over the other. In the article, a local community worker oscillates between the choices, unwilling to embrace the contentious past, yet unable to erase it. "Tour guides have called and said, 'Don't take them down.' They want to take the backpackers around the streets in summer on tour buses. Even I sometimes wonder whether we are simply painting over divisions. Is it a denial of our past history?"[16] The repetition, reproduction and reiteration of the past vie with each other for political space.

Neil Jarman contextualizes the shifting of meaning expressed through murals by defining them as explicitly political sites: murals "inherit" their message context from within the site, while the very presence of the mural simultaneously changes the site physically, visually, symbolically, and politically. Murals in this way provide a critical example of encryption: first, in the sense of code — the changing visual and symbolic message of the murals acts as a cipher, an enigma machine which encodes the history of the Troubles to be read in a particular way. The physical and conceptual existence of the murals themselves, the changing function they fulfill, ascribes a particular space for Troubles memory, thereby encoding permissible/impermissible interpretations of their history. Second, memory is contained within that space, in the sense of burial. Thus, encryption "embodies" the paradox of the dead past:

> [t]he dividing line [which] passes between a mechanical reproduction of the specter and an appropriation that is so alive, so interiorizing, so assimilating of the inheritance and of the "spirits of the past" that is none other than the life of forgetting, life as forgetting itself.[17]

These two emerging tendencies in presenting Northern Ireland's history as a tourist attraction characterize a pull between memory as repeating, reproducing and revisiting the past in conjunction with, and in opposition to, a process of transcending or erasing the past. On the surface, this tension is tied to conflicting Republican and Unionist political interests and ideologies. But essentially, it represents the very question of how to reconcile the ghosts of the past: exorcize and exhume, or inter and enshrine?

Amidst the cacophony of debate surrounding murals we find what Derrida, in *Specters of Marx*, perceives as a "deafening consensus" of the "fearful voice," in calls to (re)bury the past — those attempts to ensure

> that what is, it says, indeed dead, remain dead indeed. [...] As in the work of mourning, after a trauma, the conjuration has to make sure that the dead will not come back: quick do whatever is needed to keep the cadaver localized, in a safe place, decomposing right where it was inhumed.[18]

For Derrida, however, the return of the ghost of the past, the figure of the ghost itself, is neither hegemonic nor subversive; rather, it produces a rupture even as it lays claim to continuity. The "deafening consensus," in its insistence on exorcism, therefore "arouses a suspicion. It awakens us where it would like to put us to sleep."[19] This is suggestive of Edkins' concept of "the troubling" of dominant narratives; that is, what troubles the Troubles? In the next section, I address the troublesome question of ghosts in reference to the proposed transformation of the Maze prison site.

The Maze/Long Kesh: Transforming Memory or Enshrining Conflict?

The Maze prison has many guises. Primarily referred to by Republicans as Long Kesh for the World War II airfield on which it is situated, or "the H-Blocks" for the distinctive shape of the prisoner wings, the site has a long and complex history. The former maximum-security facility, located near Lisburn just south of the city of Belfast, sits at the intersection of several conflicting or competing sites of memory. There history collides with politics and popular culture; Unionist confronts Republican; violence meets transformation; and armalite meets ballot box; and, most controversially, sports stadium shares ground with conflict museum. The proposed transformation of the Maze is therefore directly and precariously linked to the reiteration of the conflict, the retelling of history, and the setting of a future direction of Northern Ireland. As such, it presents opportunities both for shared space and divisive memorials.

Following the ratification of the Good Friday (Belfast) Agreement of 1998, which initiated an early release program for prisoners connected to the Troubles, the prison was finally closed in September 2000. In her article "The Legacy of the Hunger Strikes," written amidst the 25th anniversary commemorations of the 1981 Hunger Strikes, journalist Melanie McFayden describes the empty Maze prison, the site of the strikes, in ghostly detail:

> In a lay-by on a country road a few miles outside of Belfast are some high, pad-locked gates. Beyond the gates, the deserted compounds of Long Kesh jail stretch bleakly into the distance. These days, you can push your way through brambles and disconnected barbed wire and climb into its eerie, grey expanses. The jail is empty [...], its maximum-security fence breachable, its searchlights dismantled. But its fearsome reputation lives on.[20]

The image painted presents the Maze as spectral, encrypted: what cannot, but must, be contained in the past. At this point, the Maze is a liminal space — neither past, present nor future. It can only become future-oriented with the implementation of the Masterplan.

The first recommendations for regeneration of the site were made by a cross-party Maze Consultation Panel. The final proposal was recently released as the Maze/Long Kesh Masterplan and Implementation Strategy. The Masterplan for the Maze identifies its prime objective: "To accelerate and provide a physical expression of the on-going transformation from conflict to peace which builds on the heritage of the site and creates a neutral and welcoming venue which is accessible to all."[21] The panel suggests a multi-purpose sports stadium, an International Center for Conflict Transformation, leisure and equestrian facilities, and commercial space. It highlights key issues, opportunities and potential obstacles, primarily regarding economic viability, transportation, and the like. It reiterates that the

> [r]egeneration of the Maze/Long Kesh site offers the potential to bring significant long term social and economic benefits to the whole community. The overall objective is to provide a physical expression of the ongoing transformation from conflict to peace and to provide an inclusive and shared resource for the whole community.[22]

The proposal continually emphasizes the historical and social significance of the site, but fails to address the highly controversial impact of the plan. While it recognizes "Equality and Inclusiveness" as issues to acknowledge, this is relegated to a quarter page under "Key Issues."[23] The aim to "provide a physical expression of the ongoing transformation from conflict to peace" indicates both a recognition of the site's transitional symbolism and a desire to harness that significance to the engineering of social reconciliation. On one level, the proposal, in emphasizing consumer, economic and community-enhancement benefits of the stadium/conflict center combination, advocates a neutral space; yet in doing so, effectively depoliticizes the debate. On the level of spectrality, however, the Maze Masterplan appears to acknowledge the spectral potential of the site, its multitude of encrypted meanings in both political camps, and simultaneously attempts to contain that power, to rewrite its ambivalence toward a seemingly politically "neutral" end.

Yet the Maze site, its tie to the memory of the Troubles, and the political significance of its proposed transformation, are far from neutral. Two tendencies to memory and the memorialization of conflict diverge here. Unionist politicians, in particular, have spoken out against the "enshrining" of terrorism through the preservation of the H-Blocks. In direct opposition to the Executive, including First Minister and Democratic Unionist Party (DUP) leader Ian Paisley Sr., the DUP's Nigel Dodds declared vociferously that Unionists would never support the proposal if the conflict transformation center was retained.

It is quite clear now that the price for Sinn Féin support for the Maze project including the stadium is a shrine to IRA terrorism. However it is
dressed up, whatever spin is deployed, the preservation of a section of the
H-Blocks—including the hospital wing—would become a shrine to the
terrorists who committed suicide in the Maze in the 1980s [during the
republican hunger strikes].[24]

During the first Question Time held by the new Northern Ireland Secretary (Shaun Woodward), the DUP's Sammy Wilson insisted that the Minister "be aware of the total opposition by unionists to the provision of a
shrine to hunger strikers at the Maze — something which is already happening and which is being promoted by Sinn Féin."[25] The Northern Ireland Finance Minister Peter Robinson (also a Democratic Unionist
member) acknowledged, "I think there's a very strong opinion within the
unionist community that they don't want to have anything on that site
which would glorify terrorism."[26] For many Unionists, the proposed "common ground" for the stadium and the conflict center amounts to Republican blackmailing—future social and economic development is held
hostage by the ghosts of the Troubled past.

Republican opinion, voiced by Deputy First Minister Martin
McGuinness (Sinn Féin), maintains that far from perpetuating the contentious memory of the Troubles, a conflict transformation centre would,
in fact, harness the past to the education of the present. Equating the site's
significance to South Africa's Robben Island or Dublin's Kilmainham Jail
(both now museums and interpretative centers), it is claimed that the
preservation of such symbolically commemorative sites allows for memory itself to be transformative. Razing the site, or destroying the old prison
buildings, "would run totally contrary to everything that we are trying to
do in terms of attracting people to our country to learn from what is
clearly a whole new experience for us."[27] For Edwin Poots (DUP Minister for Culture, Sport, and Leisure), The proposal represents a compromise, an acknowledgement of the past that does not remain tied to it: "We
can't say that some part of the site has to be preserved and then build
around that — the opportunity is there to build for the future, not to build
for the past."[28]

For both Unionists and Republicans, the ghosts of the Troubles are
symbolically tied to the Maze. However, none of the contentious options
of the debate — neither stadium versus museum, nor stadium, shopping
mall and conflict transformation center — offers to resolve the troubling
remains of memory. In both Unionist and Republican discourses, the preservation of a symbolic site is explicitly linked to the preservation of memory. For Republicans, the memory of the Troubles can be deployed in a

positive, transformative direction; for Unionists, such ghosts must be exorcized to prevent the past from continually troubling the present. Those who fear the ghosts of the past as disruptive, destabilizing, and even destructive forces are perhaps justified in doing so — the specter is both powerful and problematic — but their attempts at containment through encryption merely re-inscribe this power, even while it enables the (always temporary, always partial) (re)production of a consensual version of history and identity.

In "Dark Legacy of the Maze,"[29] the Maze serves as both a monument to and invocation of the ghosts of the Troubles. "The Maze is closing, but the long shadow of the prison regime will remain to haunt people on both sides of Northern Ireland's conflict."[30] For former Republican prisoner Seanna Walsh, the spectral memory of the Troubles cannot be contained within a defined space: "I don't think the ghosts of the past can be exorcized, and to a large extent I still carry a lot of those ghosts on my shoulder. [...] If they decide to knock the jail down, they'll not exorcize the ghosts."[31] The ghosts of the past remain because they have been experienced. One cannot escape them, but only learn to live with them. Hunger Strike survivor Laurence McKeown suggests, similarly, that the specters of memory refuse to be exorcized through the transformation of physical space:

> I think the idea of just wiping it clean or demolishing isn't the way [...] You don't wipe things away or wipe them clean by trying to deny that they existed. [...] Nor do I think that by retaining some place, like an element of Long Kesh, you keep on the ghosts of the past. I think what you do is allow a space for those ghosts to quietly disappear.[32]

Yet, for McKeown, the space "for ghosts to quietly disappear" is created slowly, by allowing the memory of the past to be acknowledged and reconciled to the present.

The argument for burial suggests that the return of the ghost must inevitably necessitate a repeat of history — as in *Hamlet*, its ghostly demands cannot and will not be ignored. Derrida refutes this. Ghosts are not simply transported or transmitted from the past, whole and unchanged.

> For an inheritance is not transmitted automatically but is reappropriated. To follow the spirit [...], to obey its injunctions, is not to repeat the formula mechanically, as if it were already finished, but it is actively to reaffirm its significance, for the latter must be produced or reproduced anew from the perspective of an interpretation which reveals what remains living in it.[33]

For both Walsh and McKeown, the prison (what remains) acts as a symbol — both of their involvement in the Hunger Strikes and of the wider conflict. In this way, it is also intricately and intimately tied to the memory of those events. The Maze is the site where the memory of the strikes and the Troubles is encrypted: the attempt to contain the disruptive potential of the past is always necessary yet always already impossible.

The article "Maze Must Shed Its Dark Legacy"[34] reiterates concern over the imminent "dangers" of a conflict center being appropriated as a "republican shrine," especially in the wake of the 25th anniversary commemorations of the Hunger Strikes. While some — including the Northern Ireland Office, Stormont Executive and Maze Consultation Panel — profess that the common ground created by a shared stadium/conflict center location would overcome the divisions of the past, meshing past with future and allowing both sides of the community the opportunity to (re)tell and remember their history, this position is itself considered contentious, particularly by those in the Unionist and Loyalist sector. "Representatives of loyalist paramilitaries have made it clear that they have no desire to have the past revisited by perpetuating the legacy of the Troubles through a conflict centre."[35] In this perspective, the physical reminders of the past will continue to trouble the present (and the future) until and unless they are erased.

> The prison is identified with a dark, sinister side of life in Northern Ireland, and the cherished aim of permanent peace and stability would best be served if the entire site was razed. Then, and only then, would the atmosphere be right [...] to proceed with a national sports stadium.[36]

In an article for the *Belfast Telegraph* ("Layers of Our Troubled History"), the partial demolition of the Maze is presented as a transition point for Northern Irish history:

> History comes in layers. The digger that began tearing down the wall was parked on a Second World War runway, the wall cutting across it. The rubble created will be crushed and re-used on-site as filler, obliterating most surface traces of the prison and the airfield that preceded it.[37]

The article's "layered" imagery is suggestive of archaeology, the excavation of successive layers of history to reach an original, empirical, truth. Traditional archaeology is linear, it reads history in straight lines, yet claims that past history can be "obliterated," torn down to make way for the new, transformed utterly. Here Foucault's concept of archaeology provides a critical counterpoint:

> This term [archaeology] does not imply the search for a beginning; it does not relate analysis to geological excavation. It designates the general

> theme of a description that questions the already-said at the level of its
> existence: of the enunciative function that operates within it, of the discur-
> sive formation, and the general archive system to which it belongs. Archae-
> ology describes discourses as practices specified in the element of the
> archive.[38]

The Foucauldian interpretation of archaeology, as the tracing of a *discon-
tinuous* history, intersects with the spectral — that which disrupts all
attempts at linearity and total narratives. From a spectral perspective, the
demolition of the wall creates an intersection of past, present, and future.
Rather than providing strata that simultaneously obscure and transcend
the past, memory as spectral insists that each successive layer further troubles the present. While the "surface traces" are torn away, the dust of the
past remains to compose the building blocks of the future. This beneath-
the-surface, as Foucault's archaeology illustrates, cannot be destroyed even
when removed from view. What remains of the prison are *remains*: as in
a gravesite, the coded memories of the past are continually buried,
exhumed and re-interred in the context of the present.

Sinn Féin MLA and Vice-Chair of the Maze Consultation Panel Paul
Butler, who during the Troubles had served time in both the Maze and
Magilligan prisons, attended the demolition along with the panel's chair,
DUP Minister Poots. The two politicians found the first gap in the perimeter wall for photo ops, where Butler spoke of "integrating the past into
the future."[39] For the politically-minded, it seems appropriate that two
men, who decades earlier would have been irreconcilable, should find their
common ground on a transformed Maze site.

The article highlighted this image of two former enemies united
amidst an historic transformation where the divisive past has the potential to give way to a shared future:

> In a way that will happen. When the site becomes a shopping centre,
> homes, and maybe a new sports stadium, the rubble will probably form the
> base of new roads around the place — letting people move freely, instead of
> keeping them in.[40]

From wall (as containment) to road (as travel, transition, commerce, and
tourism), the imagery here links back to the Simon Calder quotation at
the beginning of this essay. The road implies a journey, a progression, a
social, political and cultural evolution. The wall suggests the ghosts of the
past restlessly circle the confines of the prison yard. Tourist attraction
claims for itself the ability to make "the world a better place."

Yet, while the rubble of the wall is transformed, it still retains its
backwards pull. The encoded memory is not broken but rather re-encoded.
The "layers of history" do not merely obscure and replace each other, but

function to reinterpret and remember what has gone before. In this way, the transformation of the Maze site represents, in spectral form, what Derrida terms a "conservative rupture." It is, in Duncan Greenlaw's interpretation of Derrida:

> A historical break that keeps what it gives up. In this "logic of repression that still retains what is denied, surpassed, buried," the undesirable or irrational constellations of the past are not superseded, but only displaced within new systems of historical comprehensions. They continue to haunt us.[41]

The liminal space created and occupied by the Maze reproduces and reiterates an undecidability between "holding on" and "letting go"—with political implications for both Unionists and Republicans.

Conclusions: Troubling Memory

The memorialization of the Troubles, as exemplified by the mural and the Maze,

> far from determining the locus in which it speaks, is avoiding the ground on which it could find support ... [it] is trying to operate a decentring that leaves no privilege to any centre ... it does not set out to be a recollection of the original or a memory of the truth. On the contrary, its task is to **make** differences ... it is continually making **differentiations**, it is a diagnosis.[42]

In a corresponding way, Duncan Greenlaw deploys Derrida's concept of "impossible mourning" as a tool to hold open commemorative spaces of political possibility:

> Derridean readings of commemoration as "impossible mourning" lead not to political dead ends or conclude with easy formulations of a post-colonial ambivalence that go nowhere. [...] [Instead] commemorative acts "show that a complete work of mourning can be recognized as impossible without settling on hopelessness or disconsolation, and that the reiterative possibilities of a language of mourning are already being employed as strategies of resistance and revision."[43]

The potential of transforming the Maze site is not merely to create neutralized space nor to enshrine past conflict in the present, but more significantly to hold past, present and future in balance, to "keep to the difference."

> To keep to the difference [...] is to perform a balancing act between possibilities [...] in which troubling memory coincides with the peace of forgetting [...]. As a method of containing difference within sameness, presenting the past, and forgetting the disruptive and haunting force of the dead who

cannot be contained, it permits the subject to feel sovereign [...]. It provides the foundation — illusory but necessary — that lets them dare to begin.[44]

The interplay (implicitly or explicitly conflictual) between commemorative discourses of the Troubles exemplifies a process of incomplete mourning or memorialization — that is, a continual reiteration of memory as a necessary counterweight to foreclosure. Belfast's changing murals and the transitional meaning of the Maze site illustrate "the paradox where memory coincides with forgetting, where recognition of the other (or the past) as unassimilable [sic] is a co-requisite of the desire to assimilate and be rid of it."[45] Both hover on the line between memory and forgetting; both must struggle with ghosts through the assimilation of the past and its transcendence.

The gap in the wall, represented both by the demolition of the Maze as breached containment and by the repainting of murals as blank, transitional space, permits a reiteration of the spectral memory of the past. Even as it creates a physical and temporal boundary, the space of transition and transformation becomes liminal — in-between, neither past, present, nor future. The wall in transition thus remains a gateway to constructive possibilities. In this way, "the ambiguities and contradictions within commemorative discourse are productive of reconfigurations of the past in the service of a different, and previously unimagined, future."[46] As the shifting meanings of Northern Ireland's murals and the re-signification of the Maze site illustrate, the complex and conflicting memories of the Troubles continually demand, like restless ghosts, to be addressed, reconfigured and reproduced, despite, or because of, the powerful paradox of conflict memory.

NOTES

1. This chapter makes use of research and theoretical concepts developed in my doctoral thesis, with particular reference to chapter 1: "Ghosts of 1916: Spectropolitics & the Haunting of Irish History" and chapter 4: "Hunger to Remember: Commemorating & Contesting the 1981 Hunger Strike."

2. Jonathan Safran Foer. *Everything Is Illuminated* (London: Penguin), p. 3.

3. Jenny Edkins, *Trauma & the Memory of Politics* (Cambridge: Cambridge University Press), p. 16.

4. Source: "Terror Murals UK's Top Attraction," BBC News Online, 6 August 2007. URL: http://news.bbc.co.uk/2/hi/uk_news/northern_ireland/6933170.stm. Accessed 17 September 2007.

5. Jacques Derrida, *Specters of Marx* (London: Routledge), foreword xix.

6. Ciaran Carson, *Belfast Confetti* (Newcastle-Upon-Tyne: Bloodaxe), p. 69.

7. See, for example, World Famous Black Taxi Tours (http://www.belfasttours.com/), Belfast Political Tours (http://www.belfastpoliticaltours.com/) or the Northern Ire-

land Tourist Board website (http://www.discovernorthernireland.com/ museums_tours.aspx), which also offers links to similar tours in Derry/Londonderry.

8. Source: http://www.belfastpoliticaltours.com. Accessed 3 November 2007. Original emphasis.

9. "Tourism Takes Hold in Northern Ireland," BBC News Online, 26 February 2007. Source: http://news.bbc.co.uk/2/hi/business/6037525.stm, 26 February 2007. Accessed 10 October 2007.

10. *Ibid.*, BBC News Online, 26 February 2007.

11. Source: http://www.northernireland.gov.uk/news-ofmdfm-100707-deputy-first-minister, 10 July 2007. Accessed 3 October 2007.

12. Source: http://www.gvrt.org/index_files/culture.htm. Accessed 1 November 2007.

13. See Jonathan McCormick, CAIN Mural Directory Albums 55: 1923 & 40: 1392.

14. "Best Mural 'Marks New Beginning,'" BBC News Online, 16 May 2006. Source: http://news.bbc.co.uk/2/hi/uk_news/northern_ireland/ 4774581.stm. Accessed 12 October 2007.

15. Owen Bowcott, "Re-painting History," the *Guardian*, 2 May 2007. Available online at: http://art.guardian.co.uk/art/visualart/story/0,,2070360,00.html

16. *Ibid.*, *Guardian*, 2 May 2007.

17. Derrida, *Specters of Marx*, p. 109.

18. *Ibid.*, p. 97.

19. *Ibid.*

20. Melanie McFayden, "The Legacy of the Hunger Strikes," *Guardian Weekend* magazine, 4 March 2006, p.48.

21. Maze/Long Kesh Masterplan and Implementation Strategy, Introduction, subsection 10.

22. *Ibid.*, Masterplan, Introduction, subsection 3.

23. *Ibid.*, Masterplan, Key Issues, subsection 2.24.

24. "DUP Mixed Messages Over Stadium," BBC News Online, 22 June 2007 Source: http://news.bbc.co.uk/2/hi/uk_news/northern_ireland/6229886.stm. Accessed 18 August 2007.

25. "Maze Will Not be Terror Shrine," BBC News Online, 25 July 2007. Source: http://news.bbc.co.uk/2/hi/uk_news/northern_ireland/6916048.stm. Accessed 18 August 2007.

26. "Robinson Open-Minded on Maze Site," BBC News Online, 21 July 2007. Source: http://news.bbc.co.uk/2/hi/uk_news/northern_ireland/6909243.stm. Accessed 18 August 2007.

27. "Maze Must Keep Status," BBC News Online, 7 July 2007. Source: http://news.bbc.co.uk/2/hi/uk_news/northern_ireland/6279442.stm. Accessed 18 August 2007.

28. "Maze of Ideas for Jail's Future," BBC News Online, 16 February 2004. Source: http://news.bbc.co.uk/2/hi/uk_news/northern _ireland/3493587.stm. Accessed 10 October 2007.

29. "Dark Legacy of the Maze," BBC News Online, 27 July 2000. Source: http://news.bbc.co.uk/1/hi/northern_ireland/854011.stm. Accessed 26 July 2007.

30. *Ibid.*, BBC News, 27 July 2000.

31. *Ibid.*

32. *Ibid.*

33. Pierre Macherey, "Marx Dematerialized, or the Spirit of Derrida," in Michael Sprinker, ed., *Ghostly Demarcations: A Symposium on Derrida's Specters of Marx* (New York, 2008), p. 19.

34. "Maze Must Shed Its Dark Legacy," *Newsletter*, 12 May 2006.

35. *Ibid.*, *Newsletter*, 12 May 2006.

36. *Ibid.*

37. Chris Thornton, "Layers of Our Troubled History Laid Bare as the Maze Walls Come Tumbling Down," *Belfast Telegraph*, 30 April 2007.

38. Michel Foucault, *The Archaeology of Knowledge* (London, 1969, 1972), p. 131.

39. *Belfast Telegraph*, 3 April 2007.

40. *Belfast Telegraph*, 3 April 2007.

41. Duncan Greenlaw, *Borders of Mourning* (Bethesda, MD, 2004), p. 200.

42. Foucault, *Archaeology of Knowledge*, pp. 205–06.

43. Greenlaw, *Borders of Mounring*, foreword xi. Greenlaw here references Derrida.

44. *Ibid.*, p. 125.

45. *Ibid.*, p. 167.

46. *Ibid.*, foreword xi.

Manufacturing Memory at Gallipoli

Bruce C. Scates

No sooner had the Great War ended than Australians began the task of reinventing it. Popularizing the memory of war preoccupied a generation of novelists, poets and journalists: in the 1920s alone, several hundred titles appeared bearing the acronym ANZAC (hereafter Anzac).[1] For a time it seemed we would write as many books about Gallipoli as the memorials springing up across our landscape. *An Anzac Muster*, by William Baylebridge, is but one of these titles. It is a series of soldiers' tales, told "in a soldierly way," a ripping, slightly Rabelaisian yarn, calculated to popularize the memory of war and secure a mass readership.

By far the most intriguing of these narratives is the tale of Pat McCullough, a "digger" (an "Australianism" for soldier) aptly nicknamed "the prophet." McCullouch is wounded and knocked unconscious in a last desperate bid to take the Turkish trenches. Our soldier awakes to find the fighting has ended and Gallipoli's landscape cleansed of war altogether. On ragged slopes, once battered by artillery, are fields of crops and olives. On the peaks of the peninsula, where "snipers crawled" and men "toiled" and "killed," stand hotels, monuments and "all the paraphernalia of sightseers." Even the hallowed beach, site of the Anzac landing, had become its own "antithesis": here "where [once] men had laughed and cursed and swum and died" stood a picturesque pier, a comfortable hotel and swarming crowds of day-trippers.

Gallipoli, it seems, has been quietly conquered by tourists: "men clad in holiday attire" and women dressed in the latest summer fashion, "girls of all ages." And as with so many a tourist site, Gallipoli's history was now packaged and commodified. McCullough watched as "guides for the battlegrounds" plied speeches and patriotism, Anzac museums were stocked with souvenirs, and (since the visitors were "mostly Australian") pubs lined the route of every pilgrimage. "The dry throat," Baylebridge dryly noted, was "notably out of fashion in this later Anzac." McCullough's dream ends as he slips down another ravine and is again knocked unconscious. Our last image is his bandaged body, tended by a nurse on a hospital ship. The prophet, it seems, was only dreaming.[2]

And yet Baylebridge's prophecy has proved alarmingly accurate. Once a site of bitter fighting, Gallipoli has in recent years been colonized by tourism. Dawn services at Anzac (marking the historic moment of the Landing) now attract crowds of many thousands. The peninsula may not yet be lined by hotels but more young Australians camp there every Anzac Eve than all the soldiers who came ashore in those first few days of fighting. As Baylebridge's text suggests, the popularization of Gallipoli, and ultimately its remaking as a site of battlefield tourism, began well before the backpacker invasions of the 1990s. This essay will compare and contrast travelers from the 1920s with the pilgrimage industry of today, consider the creation of what is often called a "commemorative landscape" and ask whether Australians' deep desire to remember that war has been compromised — even cheapened — by tourism. The literature surrounding war and memory is vast, complex and often problematic. Far from being fixed, unified or predictable, the memory of war has often been described as contingent, malleable and dynamic: "socially and politically mediated as well as historically and culturally imbedded." It is also, in Pierre Nora's celebrated phrase, inherently selective, highlighting certain aspects of the past, "forgetting" or "distilling" others. The popularization of war memory offers (as the introduction notes) a rich field of historical inquiry. It also obliges the historian to step beyond the familiar terrain of the archives and engage with the memory of war as it is lived, imagined and spoken. Accordingly, this paper draws on a detailed survey of today's travelers to Gallipoli, their emotionally charged and highly subjective testimony set at the complex intersection of collective and individual memory.[3]

Sites of Memory, Places of Pilgrimage

Perhaps the Peninsula was always destined to be a place of pilgrimage. The "memory work" (as historians have called it) began on the day of the Landing. It was not just that this was Australia's first major military engagement, or that rough untried Anzac troops had proved themselves "worthy sons" of the Empire. The landscape itself seemed to provide the stuff of legends, the rugged slopes held at such terrible human cost, the battles fought in the shadow of Troy and on the shores of the Aegean. The legend grew larger throughout the 1920s as one soldier's reminiscence after another (Baylebridge's included) evoked Gallipoli as the birthplace of a nation and Anzac became akin to a "secular religion." As early as 1930 officers seconded to the Imperial War Graves Commission predicted their lonely outpost in the Dardanelles would one day be a site of both tourism and pilgrimage. "Soon Helles would boast Turkey's largest airport," one declared, "and every Anzac Day the beaches will swell with visitors."[4]

In the postwar period Gallipoli was remade to greet them. In 1923 the Turks were forced to surrender ownership of the entire Anzac area. Nominally, they retained sovereignty over the site, but the battlefield itself, from the ridges down to the beaches, was ceded to the Empire. It was a compact unprecedented in war, claiming territory not for the living but for the dead, driven by a deep-set anxiety that graves so distant from home might be desecrated or forgotten. More than that, the landscape became the dead's memorial. On the Western Front, the policy was often one of "concentration." Soldiers' remains were gathered up from No Man's Land and interred in vast sprawling cemeteries.[5] At Anzac, men were largely left "where they fell ... so that the site of their graves would mark their heroism." Their bodies would blend with the ground Australia "held," every ridge, every gully harnessed in a dramatic gesture of remembrance. The gullies were planted with gum and wattle, Australianizing a landscape that technically belonged to Australia.[6]

The first visitors to Gallipoli, then, would have found this commemorative landscape strangely familiar: popularizing Gallipoli worked with all the most potent ingredients of memory. Travelers trod a well-worn path across the ridges, retracing soldiers' footsteps but also reliving their stories. A succession of cemeteries marked the old front line: Quinn's, Courtney's, the Nek, these were not empty abstract place names, they echoed with memory, with the saga of the Landing. The wild gorse and sun-bleached clay was, many noted, a landscape similar to Australia, and at least one would-be grazier did a quick calculation of just how many sheep per acre the country might actually carry. Old soldiers spoke of what many called their "homesickness for Anzac"; somehow Australians had come to belong there. And here we confront the first great paradox of Anzac tourism. From the 1920s to today, Australians travel across the globe to return to what they see as a part of Australia.[7]

These early journeys were undertaken in a fervent spirit of pilgrimage. It was not just that most Gallipoli travelers had some association with the dead who were buried there. They subscribed to what Pat Jalland has called a Victorian view of death and bereavement: to see and tend a loved one's grave was "a vital part in the process of mourning." All sought relics from the battlefield — badges, buttons, bullets and the ubiquitous pressed poppy became treasured mementos of their journey. And the journey itself mirrored the pattern of pilgrimage since time immemorial. Diaries, letters, even tattered family albums, convey the sense of a "quest," a journey "out of the normal parameters of life [and] entry into a different other world," a visit to a landscape saturated with meaning and a return home to an everyday world, exhausted but renewed by the experience.[8]

Photographs offer insight into the emotional world of pilgrimage; they also suggest how sites like Gallipoli, accessible to the few who could afford to travel, could also be popularized for the many. From the end of one world war to the beginning of another, a steady stream of travelers' accounts helped to visualize the battlefields. Newspapers commissioned special correspondents to inspect the work of the Imperial War Graves Commission; books with titles like *Ship of Remembrance*, *A Glance at Gallipoli*, *Crosses of Sacrifice*, and simply *Pilgrimage* beckoned their readers on an imaginary journey. All featured photographs of battlefields and cemeteries, enabling readers to imagine not just a loved one's grave but also the landscape that claimed him.[9] In a sense these early pilgrims became proxy mourners, and nowhere is that more clearly seen than in Sarah Irwin's journey to Gallipoli.

One Family's Journey: A Community of Loss

Sarah's son George went missing at Gallipoli in August 1915. Last seen plunging into the Turkish trenches at Lone Pine, his body (like so many of McCullouch's comrades) was never recovered from the carnage. The testimony of the men who survived offered little comfort to families like the Irwins; memory, like the battle itself, had a merciless quality. George died many times in the course of a single Red Cross inquiry. He was shot, bayoneted, or in that sparse but eloquent soldier imagery, "knocked over," as he climbed the parapet. Long before the Gallipoli campaign was over its memory was fractured, disputed and open to contestation:

> I have interviewed so many boys who were with mine in the enemy trench and were blown up that I have ... come to think that he might have been in one of these explosions, and been carried to some hospital suffering from loss of memory ... [I've been] told ... there were a number of cases like this.

So Sarah Irwin continues to "hope," "pray" and imagine until the very end of the war, as indeed, did so many others like her: "I have never been able to think of him as dead. I feel he is still living somewhere. I write regularly to Turkey, [and] I will keep on trusting and hoping, until this dreadful war is over...."[10]

Twelve years after his death, Private Irwin's parents finally make their way to Gallipoli. In the blistering heat of September, the Irwins climb to the summit of Lone Pine and Australia's Memorial to the Missing. Unable to lay the body of their son to rest, they take a rubbing of all that is left of him, a name. Photographs published in the Sydney press captured that moment of "communitas" for many a mourning family back home in Australia. Mrs. Irwin, whose long search for her son has finally ended, is crumpled at the base of the memorial. Her face hidden from view, her hands limp and motionless, her eyes fixed on George's name as it is traced out before her. Beside her rests a formal wreath of paper poppies (carried by the pilgrimage party) and her own ragged posy of freshly picked flowers. It was no coincidence that the Irwin's pilgrimage was reported so fully in the media, that photographs of the couple, bent with grief at Lone Pine, were so widely circulated. Their loss came to symbolize that of a generation, the name they touched might have been any name. Therein lay the paradox of pilgrimage, a private act of personal devotion laid the basis for a community of bereavement and belief. Pilgrimage popularized memory for the many.[11]

Historians of war and memory might look at the Irwin's journey in a number of different ways—what can we read into the space of remembrance? In the work of Benedict Anderson and Eric Hobsbawm, we see what has been called a state-centered approach. Commemoration at Gallipoli was, as we have noted, an elaborate ritual of national identification, framed by the cultural templates of official memory. Memorials like the one raised at Lone Pine served a conservative political purpose: they are grand, imperial, patriotic statements, they sanitized the grim experience of death and killing, transformed the killing field into neatly manicured cemeteries, and subsumed private loss in the narrative of nation.[12]

But was that entirely true of Gallipoli in the 1920s? When Mrs. Irwin stumbled across the shingle at Anzac Cove, the beach was still cluttered with debris; the hills she climbed were as steep and unforgiving as on the day of the Landing; Lone Pine itself was ringed by subsiding dugouts and trenches, in the tangled brush and sodden clay human bones, perhaps the bones of her own boy, worked their way insistently, obscenely to the surface. And those who would subsume private grief with the publicly sanctioned memory of war do well to ponder the Latin roots of that word "monument." It literally means "something that reminds us." As Mrs. Irwin gazed on the name of her boy, chiseled in the long lists of the missing, King and Country were probably far from her mind; indeed, in all her correspondence to the Red Cross, George is addressed as "my boy," "my child," "my son," seldom as a soldier. He belonged, it seems, to a family, not to an Empire.

The work of Jay Winter and the so-called "social agency school" offers a finer appreciation of what Winter has called the languages of mourning. Indeed, in Irwin's case we have a whole vocabulary of grief and bereavement. There is the sharp pang of loss, the flood of soldier witness accounts, years of denial, hope and anguish, but finally the memory of war settles into the gentler task of remembrance. Families, Winter tells us, moved on, trauma was converted into misfortune, the haunted image of blackened, decomposing bodies is replaced by the clean, white enduring stone of their memorials. In this light, Sarah's pilgrimage to George's memorial was a way of transforming private pain to public remembrance: "a means [Winter tells us] of passing through mourning, separating the dead from the living, beginning to live again."[13]

But that passage from melancholia to mourning was never certain, never easy. In Sarah's case, for instance, grief had a restless, relentless, volatile character. Like the mourning mothers of any of a dozen countries, she sifted ceaselessly through George's belongings, the letters, photographs, muddied shred of uniform that came home without him. She relived that bitter moment of loss every time she read that cruelly inconclusive soldier testimony. Perhaps Mrs. Irwin accepted George's death when she took that rubbing of his name at Gallipoli — her "private loss" (as Christine Moriarty would have it) "publicly sanctified," but that very same ritual could be read as denial, a refusal by the living to part with the dead, a longing still to hold him.[14] The way that Mrs. Irwin's story resists incorporation into the greater narratives of collective memory, prompts us to consider the equally problematic memory of Gallipoli today.

Gallipoli Dreaming: The Backpacker's Pilgrimage

The revival of Anzac pilgrimage has both surprised and perplexed Australian historians. Once we believed the memory of the Great War would die out with the last of the "Diggers," the last of the Irwins. Contrary to all our expectations, the Anzac mythology and with that the pull of the Peninsula has grown ever stronger. The numbers involved are little short of astounding. In the 1920s the occasional cruise ship skirted Gallipoli; now (in an age of mass tourism) convoys of buses ferry tens of thousands to the beaches. In Australia, at least, there are few more compelling instances of the popularization of war memory. Once a rite of passage for the privileged few, a Gallipoli "pilgrimage" is now a part of what is often dubbed the "backpacker itinerary," as much an "event" as running the bulls in Spain or Oktoberfest in Germany. Unlike the Irwins, few of this most recent generation of Gallipoli travelers have any direct family association with the campaign. Indeed, with the death of the last Anzac veteran, the war has passed beyond living memory. How, then, do we account for the resurgence of Anzac pilgrimage, a popularization of war memory on a scale even Baylebridge would have found incredible? A changing political climate, structural shifts within the travel industry, the memory boom of the late twentieth century, the wanderlust of the young, and the experience of expatriation all help to explain it.[15]

Though Australians are apt to claim Gallipoli as their own, we should begin by acknowledging that this commemorative frenzy is really part of a worldwide phenomenon. The memory boom has been in full swing for decades. It was fueled in part by a deep nostalgia for the past, a search for traditions in a society without ritual, a longing for something fixed and familiar in a world where change tears old certainties asunder. In this understanding, memory becomes a crucial site of identity formation. It is a way of deciding who we are and positioning ourselves in time, an assertion of national identity in an age of rampant globalization, "defining our place in a complicated and changing world." The "Anzac mythology," as it came to be known, stands at the center of this popularization (and valorization) of war memory. Like the assertive nationalism of the 1920s, it celebrates the sacrifice of young Australians who went to war and affirms their part in the making of a distinctive Australian identity. But unlike the Irwins' generation, Anzac no longer serves an Imperial ideology. To the contrary, young Australians actively remake the memory of war, condemning Britain's mismanagement of the campaign and positioning the "diggers" as the victims rather than the heroes of Empire. The lure of that "Anzac mythology" for the young, its potent blend of nationalism and nostalgia, regret and adulation, is nowhere better seen that than in the testimony of young travelers.[16]

An Australian expatiate on a "two year work stint," Lisa sailed through the Greek islands, "did Egypt in a week" and "settled awhile in London." But Gallipoli was always what she called "a target destination":

> [It's] the camaraderie and patriotism of so many young Australians and New Zealanders abroad [that is] the main reason for [going there]. We are all such a long way from home ... and you tend to really cling to anything that reminds you of your roots. That explains why we all live together (all 19 of us in a 5-room house!).... Going to Gallipoli is the expression of this national pride, [it's] the "done thing" for any ... Aussie or kiwi back packer. [It reminds you just who you are].[17]

Katie's remarks were very similar, linking the lure of Gallipoli to the heritage of what she called a shared Australianness. A pilgrimage to Anzac, she declared, "gives you something to tie yourself to while you are travelling overseas—gives you an identity of who Australians are and what has influenced our culture." The values long associated with the campaign — mateship, courage in adversity, strength and Stoicism — were values the young were prepared to believe in. They provided what Ben Anderson has called a sense of "shared history," that crucial element in the construction of "an imagined community."[18]

Much the same sentiments are echoed in Gallipoli visitors' books, even in the same cemetery registers long ago signed by the Irwins. For many, the Peninsula marked Australia's baptism of fire, our first major military engagement as a nation, a chance to demonstrate courage and fortitude, "mateship" and determination. That the campaign was a failure made the Anzac mythology all the more compelling. "Our soldiers" had scaled impossible cliffs and clung there, carving a nation's name on the ridges. The very landscape seemed, as one visitor wrote, "a legend."[19] One after another, young pilgrims pay homage to what they called their "brave ancestor"; women and men alike celebrated the feats of long dead soldiers. "You are all heroes," wrote Sarah from Glen Waverly, "TO ALL WELL DONE" the next lines bellowed in capitals.[20] In testimony like this we see the inherent dangers of the memory boom and the mythmaking that so often attends it. Walking Gallipoli is a quest to recover a personal connection with a vanishing heritage: "A search [as Nora puts it] for one thread in the social fabric of the past which will permit direct contact with the irrevocably dead past." And it highlights the distinction between what David Lowenthal has called heritage and history — the former "an exclusive myth of origin and continuance," the latter "a critical spirit of inquiry" that refuses "to substitute an image of the past for its reality."[21] As these visitors' narratives testify, the urge to commemorate is often deeply ahistorical.

Of course, the state has played a key role in shaping the way war at Gallipoli was and is remembered. Indeed, it often generates the "myths of origin and continuance" Lowenthal referred to. The opening of a new commemorative site to mark the 85th Anniversary of the Landing was but one in a procession of state-sponsored commemorative landmarks. In 1965 the diggers first returned en masse to Gallipoli's shore; they returned again in 1975, 1985 and 1990, fewer in numbers but formidably reinforced by politicians and the media. In all these pilgrimage productions, the state has played a crucial role, shaping a commemorative culture in much the same way it once fashioned the form of Gallipoli's cemeteries. When Lisa and Katie visited Gallipoli, the landscape was marked by interpretive plaques and panels, a few raised by private agencies but most sponsored by the Australian, New Zealand or Turkish government. Their time there was structured around carefully orchestrated ceremonies. Fragments of war documentaries are screened through the long night of Anzac Eve. At once didactic and entertaining, they inform a tired and shivering audience of the "true meaning of Anzac." Morning breaks with the Dawn Service, speeches by politicians, war veterans and dignitaries eventually giving way to a minute's solemn silence. The military underpins this commemorative performance. Bands of uniformed men and women escort state officials to designated sites and frame the entrance to chosen memorials; catafalque parties march their melancholy tribute to the war dead; and service bands play hymns, requiems and "Waltzing Matilda." In most cases the young witness this in awe, respect, even admiration. Several reflect on the history they were taught at school and register a new appreciation of what it means to be Australian. Others, like Heather, carefully record the highlights of state-sponsored remembrance in their e-mails:

> The sky ... change[d] colour from black to dark blue then to midnight blue, then the RAAF band cranked up. We sang hymns and said prayers.... The best and most moving speech for me came from Gary Beck [,] director of the War Graves Office. He talked about how it was that time of the morning in 1915, when all our Aussie blokes landed on ANZAC Cove at Dawn with 40kg packs on there (sic) backs, soaking wet ... and expecting to be ... somewhere totally different [not facing this] ridiculous terrain. He really put it all into perspective. Then came the wreath laying followed by more speeches.[22]

These ceremonies invited Heather to enter into an emphatic relationship with those who lived the past, "to imagine their experiences and feelings, mourn their suffering and deaths and celebrate their triumphs." It was, she concluded (and without a hint of irony), "a fantastic feeling."[23]

The "fantastic feeling" at Gallipoli owed much to the changing ecology of war remembrance, the third crucial element in the renewed popularization of Anzac. "The power of the present," as Jan-Werner Müller astutely observed, "shapes remembrance of the past" and in recent years a changing political climate has effectively refocused the historical memory of war. Indeed, one can date this rehabilitation of the "Anzac mythology" from the end of Australia's involvement in Vietnam. Up until the early seventies, young Australians were conscripted to fight that deeply immoral and deeply divisive war — ironically they now gather to commemorate the Great War, a war just as immoral and just as divisive. They can do so (in part) because the public memorialization of that war has changed and nowhere is that more apparent than in Australian film and literature. In the wake of Vietnam, a number of historical dramas—from Bert Facey's best-selling autobiography to the epic cinema of Peter Wier's Gallipoli—reinterpreted the campaign as an odyssey of youth and a great Australian tragedy. A shifting political climate and the need to claim Australia's place in a changing world order encouraged the old association of war, "mateship" and nationalism. One cannot underestimate the role media and politics has played in popularizing this perspective on Gallipoli, asserting what Timothy Snyder has called "sovereignty over memory." As young travelers like these walk across Anzac, they traverse a cinematic as much as an actual landscape: throughout the "Anzac Season" Peter Wier's *Gallipoli*, depicting Diggers' deaths under the callous command of the British, is screened every night, in every backpacker hostel in Çannakale.[24]

Weir's *Gallipoli* is above all else the saga of a journey and mass tourism, one that may well be the most important element of all shaping the popularization of war memory and the character of commemoration at Gallipoli. Entries in the visitor's book tell us much about these journeys: here commemoration is commodified, an "event" that glamorizes war memory for a restless generation of Australians. Few of the young who descend on Gallipoli for those few days each year come directly from Australia.[25] Most reach the Peninsula near the end of a rambling world tour and many belong to the huge expatriate community that now nestles in the heart of London. Visiting Gallipoli is a chance (as many put it) "to touch base," to "make connection" with a site long eulogized and much imagined. Anzac Cove, thought Gabby, was "worth 16 months on the road"; "You ain't a real Aussie until you've been to the Rock and Gallipoli" declared "always an Aussie" from London.[26]

And on Gallipoli "the best thing" was the ceremonies. Visitors described the Dawn Service and the Australian National service to follow it as "very emotional," "very moving," and (stumbling into those sensational expletives of youth) "awesome," "amazing," "Brilliant."[27] Gillian from Manly, New South Wales, thought it "one of the most moving and memorable days of my life." Several were "lost for words" and others perhaps should have been—"Nice One!" scribbled Con From Lockleys, South Australia.[28]

Like any tourist destination the peninsula is carefully packaged by the industry; selling the memory of war to travelers hungry for authenticity. Recruitment posters have been cleverly re-crafted: the image of an Anzac straddles the Dardanelles Straits, issuing his cooee call to a new generation of travelers. At Eceabat, ("port" of the Gallipoli ferry) the Boomerang

Cafe bakes its Anzac biscuits; at Çannakale (transformed overnight to a back packer village), enterprising street stalls sell their Gallipoli tea shirts. In the 1920s, as we have seen, every effort was made to sacrilize Gallipoli's landscape, preserving every ridge and gully as a battlefield memorial. Now Gallipoli takes the appearance of a theme park, recreated trench lines are artfully woven with barbed wire, No Mans Land occupied by larger than life soldier statues. In all this, one sees what the Canadian historian Graham Carr has called an "ersatz experience" of memory. Though young travelers walk the beach and climb the ridges "standing where the soldiers stood and seeing it with [their] own eyes," the sanitized landscape of Gallipoli bear no real resemblance to war's reality. And of course the terror of the campaign, the fear, pain and stench of war, defy the most enterprising travel agent's power of reconstruction. History, it seems, has been held to ransom by tourism, the memory of war popularized to the point of forgetting.[29]

The Decline of History?

Australian historians have been quick to condemn the so-called Gallipoli revival. Several have linked it to an inward-looking and chauvinistic nationalism; most deplore the crass commodification of the past all too often evident in the backpacker experience.[30] But the popularization of war memory is not far from a simple hegemonic process. As the tussle of entries in visitors' books suggests, some praising the feats of warrior ancestors, others bemoaning the waste of life in a "pointless war," there is no simple consensus in our collective memory of the campaign. Indeed, one wonders if "the field of memory" at Gallipoli is not as troubled and contested as the battlefields themselves.[31]

Far from privileging Australian sacrifice, Turkey's loss looms large in modern memory. Indeed, discovering the number of Turkish dead changed the whole configuration of history. "I don't ever remember being told at school," Mel complained. "What we learnt I think was very one sided. Being in Turkey makes you realise that they were fighting for their country and in their country we were the enemy." Unlike Baylebridge's generation, many young Australians believed their countrymen were "sacrificed" for a cause "that had nothing to do with them." Appalled by the loss of Turkish as much as of Australian life, Naomi would write simply "shame" in Lone Pine's Visitors' Book.[32] And for some the tragedy of war went well beyond the old complaint that "we were cannon fodder for the British." Within a day of arriving on the Peninsula, Priscilla ceased to see the fighting "from an Australian point of view":

> On Gallipoli ... there are the graves of so many nations, I really felt the personal tragedy of war and thinking about the experience of ... these men transcended nationalities. I thought about human loss, human bravery, etc not purely Australian. My visits made me feel sorrow for these people, all they never got to experience, the loss their families would have felt. It made me examine my life in a different way.[33]

Priscilla's testimony alerts us again to the paradox of Anzac pilgrimage — a rite of "Australianness" transcending a narrow sense of nationalism. The beaches that witnessed the Landing and with it the mythic narrative of nation, now set the scene for a much more personal kind of history. As they walk the cemeteries of Anzac, the young note the ages on the epitaphs: these lives which "ended before they even began" could well have been their own. Young women thought of the boys they loved and journeyed with, young men imagined mates and of course themselves in some shallow grave on the Peninsula. A surprising number wrote with great tenderness of the same mothers they were so keen to escape back home in Australia.[34]

Nor should we dismiss the popularization of war memory at Gallipoli as a crude commercial imperative of the tourism industry. While "the meaning" of Gallipoli varied with every traveler, every young backpacker I surveyed insisted this was "not just a stopover." Anzac was a "historic landscape," charged with stories they have grown up with, suffused (as Lisa noted) with memory, myth and legend. Many described "being there" as a "spiritual" experience, and Anzac Day on Anzac Cove "as close to a sacred day as Australians ever get." Gallipoli seems to have satisfied a hunger for ritual and "meaning" in the hearts of these restless travelers; it involves a search for transcendence in an age as secular as our own. And the word pilgrimage sprang to the lips of those who surely do not often use it. Kate F had left Newcastle fifteen months before and spent most of her time working in London. Like the young folk she traveled with, she felt compelled to go to Gallipoli.

> KATE F: today when we were walking around and that I just had tears in my eyes the whole time ... it was really really moving and its, its like a Mecca basically, like a pilgrimage for Australians.
>   SCATES: Pilgrimage is a big word
>   KATE F: Well, look around you, there's a fair few people here and you don't get that many people outside of Australia coming together [for nothing]. I think to me it's a spiritual thing, definitely. I didn't come here to party. I came here to commemorate what they did, what they did for us ... I think that's the majority of people as well.[35]

"What they did for us" was a recurrent phrase in the responses to my survey. No less than for the Irwin's generation, these young pilgrims felt a sense of debt to those who had fought and died. Interestingly, the sacrifice of one generation became conflated with that of another. As a child, Katie "used to stay with [her] Grandfather." On Anzac Day, "he'd go off to the Dawn Service in Melbourne," returning quiet, distant, somehow a stranger. "I now understand why ["Pop"] used to go and I hope one day to make it to the [Melbourne] service to honour him and the men and women who fought with him."[36]

Sometimes "Pop" was actually present. A surprising number of backpacker respondents met up with families on the Peninsula; a few traveled from one commemorative site to another, crisscrossing the Mediterranean in a journey through generational memory.

> I was travelling with my Grandparents, father, uncles, aunty, cousins, friends and boyfriend [Sarah reported]. It was amazing to be there with people who are so special to you ... My grandfather was based in Crete in WWII, and the family continued the trip from Turkey to Crete to remember his fallen friends.[37]

No less than the pilgrimages of the 1920s and 30s, these were family journeys; "History with a capital H" made meaningful through a "personal connection" with the past, a convergence of collective and individual memory.[38]

Family Journeys

The vast majority of young travelers who make that journey to Gallipoli have no direct family association with the campaign but family, in the 1920s as today, explains the reason for many a pilgrimage. Alongside backpackers scrambling across the ridges one will often see what might be called "family pilgrims," the children and grandchildren, nieces and nephews of men who fought (and often died) in battles ninety years ago. Their visits to the cemeteries of the Great War are at once "a personal quest" and "a family obligation," a chance, as one respondent put it, to address "the terrible unresolved grieving process of [that whole generation] who could never afford to go there." Many carry battered diaries across the Peninsula, walking in the footsteps of men who died generations ago. And in an age of Internet, most are amateur historians. The recent digitization of all Australian service records has placed family history within reach of a keyboard, popularizing and personalizing the memory of war in ways unthinkable to past generations.[39]

At one level, these pilgrims long to be connected with an event so much larger than themselves, the Great War that shaped and marred a century. At another, their sense of the past is "personal," "local" and "familiar." Their Gallipoli is also a family memory, pieced together with the fragments of fading diaries or letters, shreds of tattered uniform, half remembered tales told "by long dead relations." Pilgrims related what they called the relics of a young man's life, the photographs "hung above the telephone" of an endlessly grieving grandmother, the medals prized by children each Anzac Day, the grim collection of personal effects ("one pipe, one belt ... one damaged wristwatch"), the final letters (beginning always with "I regret to inform you") folded carefully in a family bible. In one case a respondent in his seventies insisted that his uncle had never really left them: every Sunday the uniform that came home without him was tenderly set out on the hallway table.[40] All these items, these material links to the past, were treasured and revered by pilgrims' families. They could be touched, handled, fashioned into what one man called a "collage" of memory. And like the stories of the men themselves, these artifacts are passed on, from father to son, generation to generation.

> I have my father's medals from both world wars. Uniform badges and battalion colour patches ... My children and grand children all know about the Anzacs and the fact that their grandfather and great grandfather was an Anzac. My son will eventually take possession of all these items and will eventually leave them to his son.[41]

Clearly, men still have a proprietary interest in the mythology of Anzac. Many of these family pilgrims had themselves served as soldiers, many were named after uncles lost on the Peninsula or "buried at sea." Most had grown up with the wounds of war, "nervy uncles" crying into the night, fathers strangely unfamiliar, great aunts who grieved away a lifetime. Often the "horrors" of history "shadowed" several generations, scaring fathers, brothers, sons. Conrad's brother had been lost on HMAS *Sydney*, his stepbrothers died in the Middle East, his father was "permanently disabled by four years overseas," and his mother's first husband had been killed in 1917. Yet another family member had been killed in Vietnam. Going to Gallipoli or the Western Front was a way of "honouring all these men," a chance to "admire," "salute" and "mourn them."[42]

But this was also a journey made by women. In the 1920s it were grieving wives and mothers who led the first pilgrimages to Gallipoli; today their daughters and grand daughters walk Gallipoli still. Rosalind's story is typical of many. Her family, from a small town in rural Tasmania, lost four sons to war; "ravaged by death and grief" her family remembers them still.

> My grandmother died at age 98 [she wrote] an amazingly strong, intelligent and inspirational woman to me. She spoke of [her] brother Roly ... in reverent hushed tones and usually only when I asked. In telling her stories

she would recite in almost breathless and sacred fashion the place-names that had been common household usage during the war — Poziers, Pass-chendaele, Amiens, Villers-Bretonneux. Roly was an original 25 April Anzac who saw most of the war until he died in the re-taking of Villers-Bretonneux three years to the day of the Gallipoli Landing ... when the ... Minister brought the news to the family home, my grandmother ... sat stony-faced in the sitting room ... [Like a whole generation, she was] hard-ened by that war.[43]

When Rosalind journeyed to Gallipoli, she did so in search of Roly's mem-ory, rambling the same ridges her great uncle had scaled in 1915. And her pilgrimage finally ended at Roly's grave at Villers-Bretonneux, "the first relative in my family to ever visit it." Rosalind pressed a posy of Tasman-ian wildflowers into the cold muddy earth and spoke back to history: "I lay this here for my grandmother and all in my family." The salience of memory links such pilgrims to past generations, their enduring family narratives (to borrow Louisa Passerini's term) renewing, replenishing, remembering. All expressed that need to run their fingers across a name, their name, chiseled softly in stone.

Conclusion

How, then, should we interpret the mass migration back to Anzac, a pilgrimage more popular than even Baylebridge could imagine? A num-ber of social commentators have seen the return to Gallipoli as a return to more conservative values.

What is going on [Anne Coombes asks] when thousands of young people make a pilgrimage to a remote foreign shore ... where hundreds of thou-sands of young men were persuaded to fight for Britain's Empire [?] Now a new generation is being deluded, encouraged to commemorate these futile deaths instead of examining what caused them, expressing awe when they should be expressing outrage.[44]

But history is never as simple as journalism. For many of these young travelers, Gallipoli is not foreign or remote at all. It is central to their ram-bling itinerary of Europe, an "imagined landscape" that evokes a sense of home, going there (as many put it) "touches base" with Australia. Nor is their response to "that place of human slaughter" as simplistically patri-otic as many observers imagine. The deaths on the Peninsula are described as futile as well as heroic, awe is expressed but so too is outrage: with over a hundred thousand dead, Turkey surely shares Australia's sorrow. Com-memoration at Anzac is complex, ever changing and much contested and popularizing the memory of war need not sanitize its tragedy. Nor should we overlook the older lineage of this new wave of Anzac pilgrimage. For many, Gallipoli is no less a sacred place than it was for the Irwins' generation; young men still mourned and still remembered are buried deep in its gullies and high on its windswept ridges. It may well be that these pilgrims seek "an emotional engagement with the past" and of course battlefield tours are a profitable subset of the whole heritage industry. But these were often also haunted journeys, undertaken with all the fervor of pilgrimage and a deep sense of obligation to what many called "a lost generation." Can we really dismiss such emotions as simply "invented" or attribute them "to a prurient interest in second hand gore" or "a bizarre aspiration to misery"?[45] Over ninety years since the Day of the Landing, Gallipoli remains a part of how Australians see themselves. But now, perhaps, it also teaches us the folly of empires, the need for reconciliation and the human cost of war.

NOTES

1. ANZAC was originally the acronym of the Australian New Zealand Army Corps, but it also came to represent a place (the site where Australian and New Zealand troops landed at Gallipoli), a group of servicemen (initially those who served in the campaign) and a mythology or legend. In each case, the meaning of Anzac is contextualized by the narrative to follow. This paper was first delivered to the Popularization of War Memory symposium convened at the University of Calgary in November 2007. My warm thanks to all the participants and organizers for their helpful comments and to Rae Frances, Michael Keren and Holger Herwig in particular.

2. William Baylebridge, *An Anzac Muster* (Sydney, 1962). This is a revised version of the 1922 English edition. All references appear in Chapter 26.

3. John Gillis, ed., *Commemorations* (Princeton, 1994); Alan Borg, *War Memorials From Antiquity to the Present* (London 1991), p.15; Pierre Nora, "Between History and Memory," *Representations* 26 (1989). For useful surveys of recent literature see J. Winter & E. Sivan, eds., *War and Remembrance in the Twentieth Century* (Cambridge, 1999); T.G. Asplant Graeme Dawson and Michael Roper, *The Politics of War Memory and Commemoration* (London, 2000); Jan-Werner Müller, ed., *Memory and Power in Post-War Europe: Studies in the Presence of the Past* (Cambridge, 2002). These surveys were gathered as part of an Australian Research Council funded inquiry into the history of Australian pilgrimage. For a detailed discussion of their scope and methodology (and the relationship between individual and collective memory) see Bruce Scates, "In Gallipoli's Shadow: Pilgrimage, Memory, Mourning and the Great War," *Australian Historical Studies* 33 (April 2002).

4. Raphael Samuel, *Theatres of Memory* (London, 1994); Ellis Ashmead-Bartlett, *The Uncensored Dardanelles* (London, 1916); C.E.W. Bean, *The Story of Anzac*, vol. 1 (Sydney, 1922). For useful inquiries into the invention of the Anzac tradition see Alistair Thomson, *Anzac Memories: Living with the Legend* (Melbourne, 1994); Graham Seal, *Inventing Anzac: The Digger and National Mythology* (St Lucia, 2004); and Ken Inglis's classic study, "The Anzac Tradition," *Meanjin* 100 (March 1965); Cyril Hughes, "Gallipoli: Our War Graves," *Reveille*, 28 February 1930.

5. For the fraught negations surrounding Gallipoli see Bruce Scates, *Return to Gallipoli: Walking the Battlefields of the Great War* (Cambridge, 2006), ch. 2; also Lausanne

Conference Proceedings, League of Nations Archives, Geneva, 949.9:063; Frederick Kenyon, *War Graves, How the Cemeteries Abroad will be Designed* (London, 1918); Philip Longworth, *The Unending Vigil: A History of the Commonwealth War Graves Commission* (London, 1967). There was also an effort to preserve some of the smaller cemeteries on the Western Front, but concentration of cemeteries became a bureaucratic necessity.

6. A.G. Hampson, *Where the Australians Rest* (Melbourne, 1920), p. 54; T.J. Pemberton, *Gallipoli Today* (London, 1926). For an engaging inquiry into the creation of these commemorative landscapes see Bart Ziino, "A Distant Grief: Australians, War Graves and the Great War," PhD thesis, University of Melbourne, 2003.

7. On soldiers returning see, Scates, *Return to Gallipoli*, ch. 5; also Ken Inglis' classic, "Gallipoli Pilgrimage 1965," *Journal of the Australian War Memorial* (April 1991); C.E.W. Bean to John Bean, 3 February 1919, Letters concerning Australian Historical Mission 1919, Australian War Memorial, 38, 8042/49; *Sydney Mail*, 25 April 1931.

8. Ian Reader and Tony Walter, *Pilgrimage in Popular Culture,* (London 1993), pp. 3, 63; Victor and Edith Turner, *Image and Pilgrimage in Christian Culture,* (Oxford 1978).

9. "The Graveyards in Gallipoli," *Manchester Guardian,* 4 March 1924, clipping in the Commonwealth War Graves Commission Archives, Maidenhead; Ian Hay, *The Ship of Remembrance Gallipoli — Salonica* (London, 1926); C.L. Head, *A Glance at Gallipoli* (London, 1931); J.C. Waters, *Crosses of Sacrifice: The Story of the Empire's Million War Dead and Australia* (Sydney, 1932); Lt. Col. Graham Seton Hutchison, *Pilgrimage* (London, 1935); see also various photographic accounts published for a popular market, "General Aspects: Pilgrimages," Item 4, Liddle Collection, University of Leeds.

10. Sarah Irwin to Vera Deakin, 16 March 1917, 4 August 1918; Pte. G. R. Irwin, Red Cross Wounded and Missing Enquiry Bureau Files, Australian War Memorial, 1 DRL/0428.

11. *Sydney Mail,* 20 October 1926; 25 April 1931; on the significance of naming, see Thomas Laquer, "Memory and Naming in the Great War," in Gillis, *Commemorations,* pp. 125–6; Daniel Sherman, "Bodies and Names: The Emergence of Commemoration in Interwar France," *American Historical Review* 102 (April 1998): 455; Leonard V. Smith, Stephane Audoin-Rouzeau, Annette Becker, eds., *France and the Great War* (Cambridge, 2000), p. 167; Joanna Bourke, *Dismembering the Male: Men's Bodies, Britain and the Great War* (London, 1996).

12. E. Hobsbawm and T. Ranger, *The Invention of Tradition* (Cambridge, 1983); Benedict Anderson, *Imagined Communities: Reflections on the Origins of Nationalism* (London, 1983); for the conservative dimensions of this "cult of remembrance," see "Name upon Name: The Great War and Remembrance," in Roy Porter, ed., *The Myths of the English* (Cambridge, 1992), pp. 137–161.

13. For the language of loss see Winter's path-breaking study, *Sites of Memory, Sites of Mourning: The Great War In European Cultural History* (Cambridge, 1995), p. 7; Jay Winter, "Forms of Kinship and Remembrance in the Aftermath of the Great War," in Winter and Sivan, *War and Remembrance in the Twentieth Century,* ch. 2; J.M. Winter, "Communities in Mourning," in Frans Coetzee and Marilyn Shevin-Coetzee, eds., *Authority, Identity and the Social History of the Great War* (Oxford, 1995), pp. 326, 337.

14. Catherine Moriarty, "The Absent Dead and Figurative First World War Memorials," *Transactions of the Ancient Monuments Society* 39 (1995); "The Material Culture of Great War Remembrance: Review Article," *Journal of Contemporary History* 34 (1999); Ashplant, Dawson and Roper, *The Politics of War memory,* ch. 1; investigation of memorials continues to be an area of inquiry and debate: Alex King, *Memorials of the Great War in Britain: The Symbolism and Politics of Remembrance* (Oxford, 1998); Ken Inglis, *Scared Places: War Memorials in the Australian Landscape* (Melbourne, 1998); William Kidd and Brian Murdoch, eds., *Memory and Memorials: The Commemorative Century* (London, 2004). Rewarding work has also emerged from the field of Holocaust/Shoah studies, generating a literature all of its own: E.T. Linenthal, *Preserving Memory: The Struggle to Create America's Holocaust Museum* (London, 1997); Saul Friedlander, "His-

tory Memory and the Historian: Facing the Shoah," in Michael S. Roth and Charles G. Salas, eds., *Disturbing Remains: Memory, History and Crisis in the Twentieth Century* (Los Angeles, 2001), pp 277–9.

15. This is a summary of detailed analysis in Scates, *Return to Gallipoli*, pp. 101–2, 173–4, 193–6, 213–4.

16. Scates, "In Gallipoli's Shadow"; Geoff Eley, "Foreword" to Martin Evans and Ken Lunn, eds., *War and Memory in the Twentieth Century,* (Oxford 1997); Tessa Morris-Suzuki, *The Past Within Us: Media, memory, History,* (London 2005), p. 23.

17. Questionnaire completed by [henceforth Q.] Lisa B. (Cairns Qld).

18. Q. Katie H. (Brunswick East Vic.); Anderson, *Imagined Communities;* see also David Glassberg's "Public History and the Study of Memory." *The Public Historian* 19 (Spring 1997): 32.

19. Lone Pine Visitors' Book (henceforth LPVB) Simone H. (Newcastle, NSW) 25 April 1998; Matt J (No Home Town Provided, Qld) 25 April 1998; Nathan T (Melbourne Vic) 25 April 1997.

20. LPVB Gerard McC (Corogulac, Vic), 27 April 1998; Sarah T. (Glen Waverly, Vic.) 25 April 1998; Larrie H. (North Avoca, Vic.) 25 April 1998.

21. Pierre Nora, *Realm of Memory: The Construction of the French Past,* (New York 1998), p. 626; David Lowenthal, *Possessed by the Past* (New York 1996), pp. 128, 102; see also the forum entitled "Collective Memory and Cultural History: Problems of Method," *American Historical Review* 102 (December 1997).

22. Scates, *Return to Gallipoli,* chs. 4, 8; Heather L., email correspondence to the author dated 1 May 2002.

23. *Ibid.*; Morris-Suzuki, *The Past Within Us,* p. 22.

24. Jan-Werner Müller, "Introduction: The power of memory, the memory of power and the power over memory"; Timothy Snyder, "Memory of sovereignty and sovereignty over memory, Poland, Lithuania and the Ukraine, 1939–199," in Müller, ed., *Memory and Power,* pp. 1–59.

25. Q. John McG. (Camperdown NSW).

26. LPVB Gaby (Rockhampton Qld) 25 April 1998; Don K. (London, UK) 25 April 1998; Scates, *Return to Gallipoli,* 194-, 213–14.

27. LPVB Indecipherable, (Scarborough WA) 25 April 1998; Rebecca S. (Sydney NSW), 25 April 1998; Sara? A. (Burwood, Vic) 25 April 1998; Mt (Blacktown NSW) 25 April 1998.

28. LPVB Gillian M (Manley, NSW) 25 April 1998, Shelley S (Melbourne Vic), Toby, (Lismore, NSW) 25 April 1998; Con P. (Lockleys, SA) 25 April 1998.

29. Graham Carr, "War, History, and the Education of (Canadian) War Memory," in Katherine Hodgkin and Susannah Radstone, eds., *Contested Pasts: The Politics of Memory,* (London 2003), p67; Scates, "This is not a day for posturing," *Age,* 25 April 2006.

30. Mark Mckenna and Stuart Ward, "Writing the Past: History, Literature and the Public Sphere in Australia," http:www.humanitieswritingproject.net.au/mckenna.htm accessed 1 February 2007; Marilyn Lake, *Memories, Monuments and Museums: The Past in the Present* (Melbourne, 2006), pp. 56–7.

31. Jaques Le Goff, *History and Memory* (New York, 1992), pp. 55–6.

32. Q. Mel M. (Brisbane Qld); Andrew W. (Erskineville NSW); Naomi B. (Woy Woy NSW).

33. Q. Kerry D. (Sabina Qld; Priscilla E. (Strathfield NSW).

34. Q. Jacqueline M. (Dromana Vic.); Priscilla E. (Strathfield NSW); Annabel W. (Gold Coast Qld); Josh C. (no home town provided).

35. Q. Barbara A. (Roseville NSW); Interviews with David K. (Adelaide SA); Kate F. (Newcastle NSW), Gallipoli, 25 April 2000.

36. Q. Katherine S (Melbourne, Vic).

37. Q. Sarah S (Melbourne Vic).

38. Roy Rosenzweig and David Thelan, *The Presence of the Past: Popular Uses of History in American Life* (New York, 1998), p. 126.

39. Q. Edwin G (Wollongongm NSW), Anon, (NHTP).

40. Q. Jim V. (Eastwood NSW); Ross M. (Canberra ACT; Terry S. (North Sylvania NSW); John C. (Redfern NSW); John B. (Cargo NSW).

41. Q. Peter R. (Scarborough Q'ld); Robert F. (Melbourne); for meaning invested in artifact, see Sue Georgevits, "Places of the Heart: Personal Narratives of the Past through the Objects People Keep," *Oral History Association of Australia Journal* 22 (2000), pp. 72–7; Paul Ashton and Paula Hamilton, "At Home with the Past," *Australian Cultural History* 22 (2003): 27–8.

42. Q. Frank P (Mitcham Vic), James M. (Cottesloe); TE N. and HT N. (Blacktown NSW); Conrad P (Rockhampton Q'land).

43. Q. Rosalind T. (Melbourne Vic); for the gendered dimensions of early pilgrimage see Scates, *Return to Gallipoli*, ch. 3.

44. Anne Coombes, *Sydney Morning Herald*, 25 April 2000; I thank Brad West for drawing my attention to this article.

45. Dan Todman, *The First World War: Myth and Memory* (London 2005).

Commemoration and Consumption in Normandy, 1945–1994[1]

Sam Edwards

In May 1984, having recently witnessed preparations for the fortieth anniversary of D-Day, an outraged American high school teacher wrote to the tourist authorities in Normandy to protest against the "commercial opportunism" he and his students had seen as they wandered along the Norman coast, an opportunism he deemed "reprehensible." The teacher continued,

> from the beaches of Arromanches to the tourist shops of the villages of Calvados, one saw everywhere the spectacle of the merchants of tack. One can expect to see this summer t-shirts of the landings, military flags, postcards, small plastic soldiers, miniature tanks: perhaps one will also see chocolate land mines or sugar-almond machine guns?[2]

As these comments make abundantly clear, this teacher was less than impressed by the activities of many Norman communities. And while he was willing to admit that the "commercial exploitation" of historic sites was not something uniquely French, such exploitation seems to have been a particular affront in this instance because the veterans shortly to return, veterans who had previously paid for the beaches with "their blood," were now being asked to part with their dollars. In short, a "sacred" landscape had been profaned by the pursuit of profit. Similar criticisms were often to be heard over the next twenty years. In 1994 a regional newspaper actually declared that the return of thousands of veterans for the fiftieth anniversary of D-Day had led to "*un débarquement de produits*,"[3] while the national daily *Le Figaro* went so far as to suggest that a "souvenir war" had broken out on the beaches of Calvados and La Manche.[4] Writing shortly after this "war," one scholar even questioned whether "instead of 'commemorating' the events of 1944, is not such indulgence in consumerism an excellent formula for forgetting the real nature of life in 1944, dominated as it was by shortages of everything, the black market, civil war, bombardments, fear and danger?"[5]

To be sure, it is certainly tempting to dismiss the production and consumption of souvenirs, as well as the development and expansion of commercial tourism, as being antithetical to *commemoration*, a term often connected with rather solemn acts of mourning. Indeed, Nathan Bracher keeps good company when he contends that an "indulgence in consumerism" is best understood as an act of *forgetting*. George Mosse took a rather similar line (for entirely understandable reasons) when he argued that the presence of analogous activity in Europe after 1918 served to "trivialize" memory(s) of World War I; Mosse even made explicit use of the binary opposites noted above when he claimed that the "conflict between the sacred and the profane was an inevitable result of the process of trivialization."[6] Comparable concerns have also been raised elsewhere. At the Civil War battlefield of Gettysburg, for example, criticisms have long been made of commercial activity. Back in 1888, during the 25th anniversary of the battle, the *New York Times* even commented that "nowhere else in the wide world is the art of squeezing [that is, 'exploiting' battlefield tourists] so thoroughly understood and so harshly practiced as at Gettysburg."[7]

Although we should be sensitive to the resentment that such "squeezing" may provoke, and although it is entirely understandable that those who experience (or seek to examine) the trauma of war may feel aggrieved by recent "commemorative excess,"[8] an interpretation which establishes the commercial (profane and trivializing) and the commemorative (sacred and transcendent) as opposites does, nonetheless, risk simplifying the processes at work. Thus, this paper examines the post–1945 "memory work" of Norman communities and American veterans' groups to appreciate just how the presence of the "merchants of tack" has come to be. In doing so, I conclude that rather than being merely an example of exploitative opportunism indicative of a culture of forgetfulness, the growth of battlefield tourism towards the end of the twentieth century represents but another stage in a set of developments which have, in Normandy at least, fused commemoration with commerce. Acts of consumption (that is the purchase of *objects* as well as travel to, and experience of, specific *places*) thus became, within the processes of contemporary memory production, acts of commemoration. For in the market place of memory, the product would be the past.

The Structures of Commercial Commemoration

To understand the interaction of commemoration and commerce increasingly evident in recent years, indeed to understand what Michael Kammen has referred to as the "commercialization of memory," we first need to consider that which took place in the immediate post-war period.[9] In so doing, two issues draw our attention.

First, efforts to establish areas of Normandy for commemoration *and* consumption became evident just a few months after the war's end. For example, a scheme to memorialize the American army's victorious procession through France, but which was also designed to promote regional tourism, was launched by a former French liaison officer with the U.S. military as early as February 1946. Indeed, the officer in question — Guy de la Vasselais — explained, in correspondence with several French mayors, that although he intended that this scheme, later named the "Voie de la Liberté" (Liberty Highway), should pay "homage" to the "traditional fraternity" of the Franco–American armies, he nonetheless hoped to do so with structures of an economically "useful character," especially considering the "difficult situation" in postwar France. So attractive were the possible benefits hinted at by Vasselais that a "battle" even broke out among rival mayors in the department of La Manche, all of whom argued that their commune should be included in the route the "Voie" was to take, a route which was to be signposted by over one thousand kilometer markers (or "*borne*" in French). Moreover, as a commemorative project designed to aid regional recovery, considerable time was also devoted to developing various commercial "spin-offs." Among these spin-offs, for example, was a commemorative Michelin map detailing the route of the "Voie"; the publication of a special edition of a French magazine entitled "Tourism and Holiday"; a cycling race along the "Voie"; and the production of a commemorative documentary film. Regional authorities even identified the impetus behind such projects as being the potentially lucrative tourist market represented by the 400,000 American troops who had passed through Normandy during the course of the war.[10]

Similar attempts both to memorialize and to market the recent past were also to be found elsewhere in Normandy. Residents of Ste. Mère Église, for example, a town which had been at the center of the fighting on 6 June 1944, began exploring the possibility of constructing two tourist "circuits" designed to link local commemorative sites as early as March 1946, even going so far as to consider the new infrastructure, such as roads and rail connections, which these circuits would require.[11] Meanwhile, at the national level, 1946 saw the French government enact legislation to ensure the protection of the D-Day beaches, legislation designed to rec-ognize the historical significance of this landscape while also aiding regional tourist initiatives. In fact, the organization quickly established in Normandy to take advantage of this legislation — the Comité du Débar-quement (Landings Committee) — explicitly acknowledged the compati-bility of these aims when it defined two of its principal objectives as being the "commemoration" of the Allied "landings" and the "development of tourism in the landing zones."[12]

The second issue of significance to emerge in the immediate postwar period concerns the extent to which many of the initiatives designed to target American tourists were also undertaken with the knowledge and support of veterans' groups. Indeed, the American Legion, the Veterans of Foreign Wars and the Disabled Veterans' of America (the three biggest veterans groups in the United States) all attended the dedication of the first "borne" of the Voie de le Liberté at Ste. Mère Église in 1947.[13] Else-where, many other veterans' groups had begun their own efforts to com-mercialize the wartime past. By 1949, for example, and at the very same moment during which they were also erecting monuments on the D-Day coast, organizations like those for veterans of the 1st and 4th Infantry Divisions were already selling a range of commemorative products, among which were to be found various types of jewelry as well as souvenir pho-tograph albums.[14] To be sure, such goods might be conveniently labeled as "kitsch." Yet they were nonetheless advertised as objects which provided a physical, tangible connection to the past, and this was a connection which had apparently been demanded by the veterans themselves. The July 1949 issue of *The Bridgehead Sentinel* (periodical of the Society of the First Infantry Division), for example, included an advertisement for a cig-arette lighter prefaced with the words "We are again able to meet your demand for the Beautiful Zippo lighter," while a few months later the same periodical carried a similar advertisement for a signet ring, this time introduced with the lines "At last! We can meet your demand for a Soci-ety ring."[15] A year subsequent, in 1950, the idea that the sale of souvenirs was a *service*, rather than merely an exercise in exploitation, was made even more apparent after the editor of *The Bridgehead Sentinel* received a letter from a disgruntled veteran accusing the Society of the First Divi-sion of unscrupulous "money grabbing." In response, the *Sentinel* pub-lished the following, indignant, retort from the Society's Executive Secretary:

> We do not ask nor expect a member to purchase any article, if he cannot afford to do so; we do ask, and rightfully expect all members, who can afford to purchase a similar article elsewhere, to make their purchase

through the Society and thus SUPPORT THE SOCIETY. These articles are EXCLUSIVE to you. Only the man who was privileged to wear the BIG RED ONE may, with propriety, display them.[16]

In this view, therefore, the production and consumption of 1st Division merchandise was an act of support, if not indeed an act of commemoration, for the goods on offer were, they claimed, designed for public *display*.

Building on the success of these commercial operations, by the early fifties some veterans' groups were also able to offer their members organized tours of the European battlefields, and these provide yet more hints of the developing connection between commemoration and consumption. In 1951, for example, one veteran noted that after attending a moving ceremony of remembrance on a Normandy cliff-top, he then wandered into the nearby villages to buy some souvenirs.[17] A few years later, a European tour by veterans of the 1st Infantry Division included what were undoubtedly emotional visits to the battlefields of Normandy and the Ardennes, but it also included shopping trips to "top tourist areas" such as London, Paris and Brussels.[18] Crucially, the consumption of all these "products," be they souvenir jewelry or a European holiday, was explained as an act of homage, of commemoration. As *The Bridgehead Sentinel* declared in 1951: "Support the Society, within your financial means, by purchase of the various items advertised in BHS, all of which are designed to further the prestige of the Big Red One [the division's nickname]."[19]

Within a decade after 1945, therefore, commemorative activity in Normandy had already become infused with a commercial dynamic. The *bocage* and beaches of Calvados and La Manche had been marked by numerous monuments to battle, but at the same time these landscapes were also set aside for future tourism, an activity that John Urry has described as representing the "consumption" of time and space.[20] Likewise, veterans' organizations had erected memorials to their dead, but they were also more than content to sell their members commemorative merchandise and battlefield tours that combined commemoration of the past with purchasing in the present.

That such developments had taken place is, of course, unsurprising if we consider the precedents that had been established at other locations in earlier times. Jim Weeks, for example, has ably demonstrated the extent to which it was commercial activities which helped construct and establish the historic significance, if not indeed the sanctity, of the Civil War battlefield of Gettysburg.[21] Similar suggestions have been made by D.W. Lloyd with regard to World War I battlefields of the Western Front that were constructed as "sacred" while the war was still being fought, later documented in tourist guidebooks, and then visited by thousands of "pilgrims," often as part of a Thomas Cook tour.[22] The emergence in Normandy of what might be termed "commercial commemoration" was not, therefore, particularly unusual.

Yet, despite the energetic work of those such as Guy de la Vasselais, the scale of this activity was, in the postwar period, still rather limited. Indeed, while those master mapmakers— Michelin — had produced a tourist guide of the Normandy battlefields as early as 1947, the number of visitors, especially returning American veterans, seems to have remained relatively small. After an exhaustive trawl through regional press coverage one French historian has even suggested that the tenth anniversary of D-Day in 1954 was actually rather "discreet,"[23] while elsewhere a local Normandy paper concluded that the ceremonies accompanying the thirteenth anniversary in 1957 were "very simple."[24] The situation remained much the same over the next thirty years. There were, to be sure, the occasional moments of heightened interest. Despite increasingly strained diplomatic relations between Washington and Paris (partly provoked by a resurgent Gaullist nationalism) the twentieth anniversary of D-Day in 1964 was attended by several thousand American, Canadian and British veterans, not to mention numerous "allied" dignitaries.[25] Five years later, in 1969, American veterans were again well represented, with the National Guard Association sending a delegation of over 1,500 members.[26] But even these large-scale events were then followed by a period of commemorative inactivity. In fact, amid an economic depression partly caused by an international fuel crisis, the thirtieth anniversary of D-Day in 1974 seems to have been, in relative terms, a real low point. One scholar has even suggested that commemorative activity in Normandy was actually "in retreat,"[27] while the lack of British media interest in the anniversary actually prompted at least two people to write letters of complaint to the London *Times*.[28] Even in 1976 an officer in the National Guard Association could say of the annual D-Day commemorations that "in all the countries involved ... interest starts to wane."[29] However, by the 1980s circumstances were changing.

Back to the Past

The causes of the resurgent American interest in World War II that first emerged toward the end of the 1970s and then gained pace in the early 1980s, have been well studied. More than one scholar has suggested that this period witnessed an increasing anxiety in western culture connected to the social, political and technological changes associated with the "postindustrial" and "post-modern" age, an anxiety which then prompted many people to ponder the certainties (at least as they saw it) of a past from which they felt cast adrift. Or, to put it rather more succinctly, "Disenchantment with today impels us to try to recover yesterday."[30] Elsewhere, other scholars have identified the "globalization" of the past twenty years as a cause of this "anxiety." After surveying an impressive array of literature on this subject Emily S. Rosenberg, for example, surmises that as political and economic boundaries have collapsed, and as people have become more mobile, "the yearning for localized roots and fixed identities ... grows." Returning to the past, therefore, might be understood as an attempt to "buttress ever tenuous identities."[31] In short, the nostalgia prevalent in western culture during the last twenty years, what J. Winter has termed a "memory boom," should be understood as a response, among other things, to a contemporary sense of discontinuity felt at both an individual and a social level.[32]

With regard to the increased activity of American veterans after 1980, however, we must also consider some other issues. First, the significance of life-cycle should not be discounted. Ulric Neisser, for example, has suggested that in later life many people experience a surge of memories (a reminiscence "bump") connected to adolescence and early adulthood which is, of course, the very period during which many veterans of World War II had served.[33] Second, those American veterans who encountered this experience in the early 1980s did so within a historical moment which was ready and willing to hear their stories. Indeed, just a few years after defeat in Vietnam, as well as the social unrest with which it became synonymous, the Reagan Administration (which took office in January 1981) sought to offer a "New Beginning,"[34] and establish a "New Patriotism" by, as one historian has put it, reversing direction in order to "lead America back to its past."[35] And no past was more attractive, or appealing, than World War II, especially 6 June 1944, a day when, according to one recent examination of this Reagan assault on history,

> there were no unanswered questions or moral ambiguities ... our young martyrs liberated Europe from the macabre stranglehold of the diabolical Hitler. Period. American GIs gave their lives so others could be free. D-Day was clearly America's finest hour — and Reagan knew it.[36]

In other words, the events of D-Day seemed to have a moral clarity, and, just as important, a victorious conclusion that was absent in the American present.

But this return to the war years was not only American. In France too, Henry Rousso has suggested that the 1980s also witnessed a "forties revival," although the causes and dynamics of this revival were, to be sure, rather different.[37] Briefly put, after nearly two decades of "repressions" during which the controversies of the war (defeat, occupation, collaboration) were, in Rousso's words, "exorcised" by Charles De Gaulle in an attempt to "bestow on France an invented honor," the late seventies and early eighties witnessed an era of "obsession" in which references to World War II "became a constant of the cultural scene."[38] These references did, of course, frequently call forth the very controversies that De Gaulle had sought to repress and deny. But other, less problematic, wartime events also received renewed attention, with the government of François Mitterand (like Reagan in Washington) devoting considerable time and energy to planning and organizing the ceremonies for the fortieth anniversary of D-Day in 1984.

Finally, this return to the war years, both French and American (and of course British and Canadian), was also made possible by the economic prosperity of the 1980s and 1990s, a prosperity particularly significant to many recently retired veterans who now found they had the time and money to revisit their youth. Indeed, Winter has identified the affluence of recent years as crucial to the "memory boom," for "dwelling on memory is both a matter of disposable income and leisure time."[39] We should not be surprised to find then that within such a context many ex-service organizations in the United States experienced a period of rapid growth. For example, the Eighth Air Force Historical Society gained 14,000 new members between 1975 and 1984.[40] The periodical *Splasher Six* of another American veterans' group explicitly identified the changed circumstances by proudly proclaiming in 1983 that "World War II is back in fashion."[41]

Beginning in the 1980s and continuing into the 1990s, therefore, a variety of circumstances— psychological, political, cultural, economic — had combined to produce the perfect environment in which the already established structures of commercial commemoration could flourish.

The Commercialization of Memory

Among the first signs of this flourishing were renewed attempts to mark and preserve the landscapes connected to the D-Day past, attempts that had, as we would now expect, both a commemorative and a commercial rationale. Between 1980 and 1986, for example, a local Norman community, together with American veterans, campaigned to have the battlefield of Pointe du Hoc (scene of a celebrated D-Day assault by American Army Rangers) restored to its former wartime condition to ensure that future generations of tourists could wander among the ruins.[42] Moreover, the mayor of a nearby community initiated a scheme to have a new memorial erected on this battlefield because, as he wrote to one Ranger veteran, "thousands and thousands of visitors come and return, every year, to meditate in this high inspiring spot of the History of the Normandy landing," and consequently he wished to "keep visitors informed on the number and names" of those Americans killed.[43] By 1984, such a memorial had been successfully established and it was duly unveiled that June by President Ronald Reagan who was in Normandy for the 40th Anniversary commemorative events.

Of course, these years also saw many other communities in Normandy help Allied veterans' groups to construct memorials, while these structures, like that at Pointe du Hoc, were then incorporated into commercially produced tourist guidebooks. In the run-up to the 40th Anniversary in 1984, for instance, the departmental authorities of La Manche even published an information brochure (for distribution on both sides of the Atlantic) providing details of the commemorative events due to take place as well as information about other sites of interest.[44] Among these sites were military cemeteries, various privately established museums and the locations of some of the numerous memorials to be found throughout La Manche, all of which were marked on an accompanying map which suggested possible routes that the discerning tourist might like to take.

A decade later, during the preparations for the 50th Anniversary, the same local authorities organized another program of commemorative events, this time under the direction of a specially created committee entitled "Association Liberté 44." According to the members of this committee, no doubt conscious that for many veterans 1994 would be the final opportunity for a "return," the commemorative events marking the 50th Anniversary were to offer a "profound" message to inhabitants and visitors alike. With this in mind, and drawing on the experience of June 1984, considerable time was devoted to planning the means by which such a message would be communicated. Among the ideas discussed were the signposting of historic sites, a concert of solemn hymns celebrating "liberty" and, of particular interest to us here, the sale of various "*produits*" such as chewing gum and playing cards. Significantly, given the views expressed by the American high school teacher ten years previous, "Association Liberté 44" justified the sale of such goods by explaining that these were items carried ashore in the bags of American soldiers on D-Day and thus were, in the words of an advisory report, "symbols of our memory."[45] Elsewhere, the commercial tint to the events of June 1994 is also apparent in a contemporary newspaper report which remarked that while the 50th Anniversary was certainly going to take a "commemorative aspect," it was also an "occasion to reinforce local tourism."[46] Two year previous, in July 1992, regional authorities in La Manche had even reminded their tourist offices that the upcoming anniversary represented an important occasion for the "promotion of international tourism."[47]

Meanwhile, in the same years during which authorities in La Manche and Calvados were advertising Normandy as a destination for battlefield tourists, several veterans' groups were also engaged in developing and expanding their commercial activities. The Society of the First Infantry Division, for example, which had always maintained close links to communities along the D-Day coast, organized a battlefield tour to coincide with the fortieth anniversary in 1984. The tour was so popular that a waiting list had to be drawn up for those who failed to get tickets.[48] Many other veterans' groups encountered similar enthusiasm. Indeed, the scale of interest in the fortieth anniversary is amply demonstrated by the fact that a group of American veterans who wished to visit Normandy a month *prior* to the "main event" still found that all local accommodations were fully booked.[49] So busy was Normandy in the summer of 1984 that some veterans' organizations were still returning *en masse* as late as September.[50] Similar scenes were also witnessed ten years later. In fact, by 1994 veterans were returning so frequently and in such numbers that they generated literally hundreds of articles in the local Normandy press.[51] Moreover, just like the trips made by veterans in the 1950s and 1960s, these visits did not only include journeys to battlefields and other commemorative sites; they also involved excursions to popular tourist destinations such as London, Paris, Caen, and Bayeux.

At this point, however, our attempt to identify, and account for, the existence of such a thing as "commercial commemoration" encounters a problem. For, although these battlefield tours might appear to be perfect examples of what Urry has referred to as the "consumption of culture," it was not quite that simple.[52] Indeed, by the 1980s these journeys were frequently described both by press and veterans as "pilgrimages," a term which would seem, at first glance, critically to undermine any attempt to fuse the commercial with the commemorative. After all, pilgrimage is often understood to involve the pursuit of the sacred, an act which, by definition, must be clearly demarcated from the "profanities" of commercial tourism. Tony Walter, for example, has persuasively argued that the trips undertaken by British veterans to the battlefields of the Western Front in the 1920s can, and should, be defined as pilgrimages because they focused on a moment of "catharsis" at a destination deemed "sacred," for example the grave of a friend.[53] As well, for many American veterans and their families traveling to the beaches of Normandy was not merely an act of sightseeing or of cultural "consumption." Rather, in the words of Bruce Scates, who has examined similar activities at the World War I battlefield of Gallipoli, such trips were a "reckoning" with the past, with memory.[54] As early as 1951, for example, one veteran published an account of just such a reckoning in *The Bridgehead Sentinel* that included the following description of a commemorative ceremony held overlooking Omaha Beach:

> Then we were thirteen men remembering little things that happened on
> June 6, 1944, bowing our heads in silent prayer after we had placed a
> wreath on a monument to men we had lived, fought and nearly died with.[55]

The somber nature of journeys such as this can also be identified in the words and actions of later "pilgrims." In 1969, for example, one American veteran explained after returning to Normandy, "It hits me in the stomach ... I've got buddies lying here. I really didn't think it could hurt me so hard after 25 years."[56] Several years subsequent, in 1984, an article about the 40th Anniversary events likewise referred to the sight of a veteran who was visibly moved by the "emotion born of memory."[57] Similar sentiment was again echoed in 1994 when *Le Figaro*, reporting on the commemorative activities surrounding the 50th Anniversary, suggested that it would be "the occasion for an emotional pilgrimage [by veterans] to the places of the battle of Normandy."[58] The emotional intensity of these occasions is perhaps best summed up though by the words of one veteran who returned to Normandy in 1982: nearly forty years had passed, but it was still only just "soon enough."[59]

Such statements rightly demand that we remain sensitive to the pain, fear and tears that formed the very center of these battlefield tours. At the same time, however, the use of the "pilgrimage" metaphor to describe the European trips of American veterans also offers us a means to refine our integrated framework and, in so doing, reconsider the role and function of material goods in recent commemorative activity. For the pilgrimages of the medieval period were well known to contain a mixture of God's time and the Merchant's time, a point made explicit by the sale and purchase of "relics."[60] While these objects were, of course, supposed to be "sacred," they were often deemed to be profanities of questionable authenticity by medieval church authorities. Nonetheless, they were bought by pilgrims who sought to take a piece of the sacred, a piece of their journey, home. Similarly, within the structures of contemporary memory production, structures which had long established the Norman landscape as something to venerate and consume, memorialize and market, the sale of souvenirs—mainly to veterans at first but also, in more recent years, to later generations of "pilgrims" to the past — represents, we might suggest, a point of contact between the commemorative and the commercial, the "sacred" and the "profane," the past and the present. Diane Barthel, commenting on similar activities elsewhere, has even argued that although such merchandise might appear mundane and worldly (or perhaps even "tacky"), they also have the ability to "hint at something beyond"[61]; indeed, they may also be understood as "technologies of memory" or what one French historian, surveying the commercial flurry which surrounded the fiftieth anniversary of D-Day, referred to as commemorative "gadgets."[62]

Whatever expression is favored, all these concepts proceed from the idea that the commercialization of memory, a commercialization which has become increasingly prevalent over the last twenty years, should not just be understood as indicative of an uncaring, exploitative and profaning "amnesiac" culture. Rather, as Marita Sturken has argued, such commercialization is best understood as representing the "generation of memory in new forms"[63] because we live, she continues elsewhere, "in a society in which commercialization and marketing tactics are so pervasive, in which the boundaries of art, commodity and remembrance are so easily traversed, and in which merchandise is so often grassroots-produced that it no longer makes sense, if it ever did, to dismiss commodities as empty artifacts."[64] In this formulation, therefore, commercially produced commodities are understood to be "objects through which memories are shared, produced and given meaning."[65] With this is mind, it is interesting to note that during the 40th Anniversary of D-Day in 1984, the "big-seller," at least according to the local Normandy press, was not, in the end, "chocolate land-mines," but rather a history of the Allied invasion published in both English and French, a type of commodity which is surely well positioned to aid in the production of "cultural meaning."[66] Moreover, the ability of such commodities to be more than the sum of their parts is hinted at in the very name we give them, and the very word which I have already frequently used: souvenirs. This word was, ironically, brought into the English language by soldiers returning from France after 1918. While it has often become synonymous with "tack," it nonetheless has a rather arresting translation. In French it simply means "memory."

If, therefore, the sale of various types of goods is central to the means by which contemporary consumer cultures engage in the production of memory(s), particularly considering that the late twentieth century became, as Lowenthal has famously asserted, the age of the "Heritage Industry,"[67] it is surely unsurprising that so many Norman communities, not to mention American veterans' groups, increasingly placed mementos and merchandise at the very centre of their *commemorative* operations.

In 1986, for example, Ranger veterans even sought to have a small museum built on the battlefield of Pointe du Hoc so that visitors, of which there were over 500,000 between June and September of that year alone, could be guided around the "sacred" landscape before then having the opportunity to purchase a piece of the past.[68] As one veteran explained with regard to this project, which was to involve substantial redevelopment of the battlefield site:

> As visitors come in to see what the Rangers did at Pointe du Hoc, they should have to park only once to see the museum, obtain brochures, to purchase souvenirs and to tour the battlefield... If the privately owned and operated souvenir stand is still in operation, that person could be interested in a joint venture with us [....][69]

To the veterans' disappointment, however, this project was not undertaken as the owners of the battlefield — the American Battle Monuments Commission — refused permission to construct such a museum for fear of the strains it would place on their rather limited funds, and because they believed, unlike many old soldiers, that such a development would be inappropriate on a memorial landscape. Nonetheless, the point is that it was the very people who might be expected to resent the commercial exploitation of *their* past — veterans — who had, in this instance, explicitly encouraged such activity in an attempt, it would seem, to market their memories to later generations. Moreover, Ranger veterans were not alone in seeking to ensure that tourists wandering among the ruins of war were provided with a selection of souvenirs. When the head of tourism in La Manche replied to the accusations of exploitation made by our American high school teacher, he even retorted that not all the enterprises to be found up and down the Norman coast were the work of cynical scheming locals. Rather, he explained that many of the "commercial" museums purveying the "tack" which our teacher found so disturbing had actually been established, like that planned by the Rangers, at the insistence of American veterans' groups.[70]

Conclusions: Commemoration and Consumption

Some of the commercial activities present in Normandy in the 1980s and 1990s have provoked understandable criticism from those who feared that the sanctity of the past had been profaned. Some undoubtedly do view battlefield tourism and the sale of commemorative merchandise as cynical opportunism best understood as evidence of contemporary disregard for, rather than veneration of, the events of June 1944. Yet, although we would certainly be amiss to suggest that these activities were always sensitive to the past they popularized, and although we must surely accept that attempts to commercialize memory are inextricably tied to the pursuit of profit, such activities must also be understood as a process, and a product, of the dynamics of commercial commemoration. These dynamics have ensured that in the social production of memory the "sacred" and the "profane," pilgrimage and tourism, the "transcendent" and the "trivial," monuments and mementos, are not simply opposites and that they are not necessarily antithetical. On the contrary, they are "knit into a helix."[71] Little wonder, then, that during the 60th Anniversary of D-Day in 2004 a Zippo lighter could be commercially produced and distributed to American veterans as a "sacred," indeed commemorative, object. For the key ingredients in this piece of merchandise, this piece of what some might consider "tack," were grains of sand taken from one of the D-Day beaches, a beach that American troops had christened "Bloody Omaha."[72]

NOTES

1. The research for this paper was generously provided by the Economic and Social Research Council (U.K.) and the United States Army Military History Institute. The author would like to thank Dr. Stephen Constantine, Dr. Patrick Hagopian, Emma Vickers and Sarah Rose for commenting upon drafts of this paper.

2. T. Challman to Comité Départemental de Tourisme, 1 May 1984, File: 40e ann. Revue de presse (1983–1984), Entry: 1095 W 91, Archives Départementales de la Manche (hereafter ADM). Author's translation.

3. *Libre Service Actualie*, No. 1392, 7 April 1994. See "Revue de Presse, 1994," held in the archives of Le Mémorial du Caen.

4. *Le Figaro*, 16 March 1994.

5. N. Bracher, "A Time to Remember," *Contemporary French Civilization* XII (Summer/Fall 1995): 141–42.

6. G. Mosse, *Fallen Soldiers: Reshaping the Memory of the World Wars* (Oxford, 1990), pp. 126–56, esp. p. 152. Mosse's argument that the war kitsch which emerged in 1920s Europe had its part to play in reducing the brutality of the battlefield to something 'manageable,' and thus something which could be contemplated again is surely beyond doubt. My point here, however, is to suggest that this process of "trivialization" is not the *only* result of memory commercialized and consumed.

7. *The New York Times* 16 July 1888, quoted in J. Weeks, *Gettysburg: Memory, Market and American Shrine* (Princeton, 2003), p. 73.

8. G. Eley, "Finding the People's War: Film, British Collective Memory and World War II," *American Historical Review* 106: 818.

9. See M. Kammen, *Mystic Chords of Memory: The Transformation of Tradition in American Culture* (New York, 1986), p. 655.

10. See the correspondence between Le Commandant G. de la Vasselais and Le Préfet de la Manche, in 1946 and 1947, File: "1948 — Voie de la Liberté," Entry: 1004 W 917 (I12), ADM.

11. See "Rapport de L'Ingenieur," 26 March 1946, File: "Archives du Cabinet du Préfet," Entry: 1012 W 341, ADM.

12. S. Barcellini, "Diplomatie et Commémoration. Les Commémorations du 6 Juin

1984: Une Bataille de Memoire," *Guerres mondiales et conflits contemporains* 186 (1997), p. 122.

13. Vasselais to le Préfet de la Manche, 9 July 1947, Entry: 1004 W 917 (I12), ADM.

14. See, for example, *The Bridgehead Sentinel*, July 1949.

15. *The Bridgehead Sentinel*, July 1949; and *The Bridgehead Sentinel*, October 1949.

16. *The Bridgehead Sentinel*, January 1950.

17. *The Bridgehead Sentinel*, January 1951.

18. *The Bridgehead Sentinel*, July 1952.

19. *The Bridgehead Sentinel*, January 1951.

20. J. Urry, *Consuming Places* (London, 1995), pp. 1–30.

21. Weeks, *Gettysburg*, p. 8.

22. D.W. Lloyd, *Battlefield Tourism: Pilgrimage and the Commemoration of the Great War in Britain, Australia and Canada, 1919–1939* (Oxford, 1998), esp. pp. 101–30 and pp. 140–46.

23. P.L. Pizy, "Commémorations du Débarquement de la Bataille de Normandie à travers la journal Ouest France (1954–1994)," unpublished French MA dissertation, p. 95.

24. *La Reveil*, 8 June 1957. Author's translation.

25. See *The New York Times*, (international edition), 6–7 June 1964.

26. See memo to General Greenlief, 23 November 1976, File: "Normandy Commission/Travel Programs, 1974 and later," Entry/Box: "Normandy," National Guard Library (hereafter NGL), Washington, D.C.

27. Pizy, "Commémorations de Débarquement," p. 97.

28. See *The Times*, 13 June 1974 and 20 June 1974.

29. Memorandum to General Greenlief, re. Normandy visit, 23 November 1976, File: Normandy Commission/Travel Programs, 1974 and later, Entry/Box "Normandy," NGL.

30. D. Lowenthal, *The Past is a Foreign Country* (Cambridge, 1990), p. 33.

31. E. S. Rosenberg, *A Date Which Will Live: Pearl Harbor in American Memory* (London, 2003), p. 117.

32. See J. Winter, *Remembering War: The Great War Between Memory and History in the Twentieth Century* (London, 2006), pp. 17–51.

33. U. Neisser and L.K. Libby, "Remembering Life Experiences," *The Oxford Handbook of Memory* (New York, 2000), p. 318.

34. Kammen, *Mystic Chords*, pp. 645, 652.

35. H. Johnson, *Sleepwalking Through History* (New York, 1992), pp. 157–58.

36. D. Brinkley, *The Boys of Pointe du Hoc: Ronald Reagan, D-Day, and the U.S. Army 2nd Ranger Battalion* (New York, 2005), p. 12.

37. H. Rousso, *The Vichy Syndrome: History and Memory in France since 1944*, translated by A. Goldhammer (London, 1996), p. 127.

38. Rousso, *Vichy Syndrome*, p. 132.

39. Winter, *Remembering War*, pp. 38–39.

40. Memorandum, J. Woolnough, Eighth Air Force Historical Society, no date, File: 8AFHS Correspondence, 1983, Entry: Box 42, Eighth Air Force Archive, Special Collections Library, Pennsylvania State University.

41. *Splasher Six*, 14 (Winter 1983), p. 2.

42. See File: "Pointe du Hoc Monument, Priv. Spons, Foreign and Other Govt. Facilities Maintenance (FAM) 5–7," Entry: 45, Box 6, Record Group 117 (hereafter RG 117), National Archives and Records Administration II (hereafter NARAII), College Park, Maryland.

43. L. Villiers, Mayor of Criqueville-en-Bessin, to L. Lommell, Chairman, D-Day Committee, Pointe du Hoc, 10 July 1981, File: "Pointe du Hoc Monument, Priv. Spons," Entry: 45, Box 5, RG 117, NARAII.

44. See Entry: 1095 W 91, 40e ann. Revue de presse (1983–1984), ADM.

45. See files relating to "Association Liberté 44," in particular entries: 1366W1; 1366W2; 1366W3; 1366W4; 1366W5. ADM.

46. *Ouest France*, 26 April 1994.

47. Office Départementale du Tourisme de la Manche to les Présidents d'OT/SI de la Manche, 16 July 1992, Entry: 1366 W 2, ADM.

48. See *The Bridgehead Sentinel*, Spring 1984.

49. E.R. Reed to "Calvados Tourisme," 26 January 1984, File: 40ème Anniversaire du Débarquement, Entry: 1095 W 90, ADM.

50. See, for example, *La Manche Libre*, 21 September 1984.

51. 773 articles about D-Day commemorations were published in *Ouest France* in 1994. See Pizy, "Commémorations du Débarquement," p. 87.

52. Urry, *Consuming Places*, esp. pp. 129–51.

53. See T. Walter, "War Grave Pilgrimage," in I. Reader and T. Walter, eds., *Pilgrimage in Popular Culture* (London, 1993), p. 82.

54. B. Scates, "In Gallipoli's Shadow: Pilgrimage, Memory, Mourning and the Great War," *Australian Historical Studies* 119 (2002): 1–2.

55. *The Bridgehead Sentinel*, June 1951.

56. *Pittsburgh Post-Gazette*, 6 June 1969.

57. *Ouest France*, 14 June 1984.

58. *Le Figaro*, 16–17 April 1994.

59. Quoted in S. Ambrose, *D-Day June 6, 1944: The Climactic Battle of World War II* (London, 2002) p. 447.

60. Weeks, *Gettysburg*, p. 27.

61. D. Barthel, *Historic Preservation: Collective Memory and Historical Identity* (New Brunswick, NJ, 1996), p. 138.

62. For "technologies of memory," see M. Sturken, *Tangled Memories: The Vietnam War, the Aids Epidemic, and the Politics of Remembering* (London, 1997), pp. 9–12. For a discussion of the 50th Anniversary "gadget," see R. Desquesnes, "1994: Échos des Commémorations en France," *Contemporary French Civilization*, XIX (Summer/Fall 1995): 157–58.

63. Sturken, *Tangled Memories*, p. 2.

64. *Ibid.* pp, 11–12.

65. *Ibid.* p. 9.

66. *Ouest France*, 7 June 1984.

67. D. Lowenthal, *The Heritage Industry and the Spoils of History* (Cambridge, 1998), pp. 1–30.

68. See J.W. Donaldson, American Battle Monuments Commission to L. Lommell, 16 March 1987, File: "Pointe du Hoc Priv. Spons," Entry: 45, Box 6, RG 117, NARAII.

69. L. Lomell to J. W. Eikner, 1 December 1986, File: "Pointe du Hoc Priv. Spons," Entry: 45, Box 6, RG 117, NARAII.

70. M. Leprieur to T. Challman, 22 May 1984, 1095 W 91, ADM.

71. Weeks, *Gettysburg*, p. 8.

72. *Ouest France*, 14 March 2004.

Nuclear War and Popular Culture

Arthur G. Neal

There are many reasons that war memories occupy a prominent place in modern consciousness. During the course of the twentieth century, the number of people who died violently is greater than for any previous century in the history of mankind (Elliot, 1972). In the first half of the twentieth century, social life was shattered by two major world wars. If both civilian and military casualties are included, the fatalities from World War I exceeded 18 million. The loss of life stemming from World War II was approximately 62 million. An additional 6 million people were annihilated in the Holocaust of Nazi Germany, and a comparable number of killings resulted from purges in the Soviet Union. Single bombing raids during World War II produced an estimated 100,000 fatalities.

The rules of engagement changed dramatically during World War II. Modern warfare became "total war," and as a result the civilian casualties exceeded those of military personnel (Aaron, 1955). The civilian toll of the war was around 37 million, while the military fatalities numbered about 25 million. Modern warfare had become much more than armies meeting on the field of battle. The total population of the countries at war was defined as the enemy to be exterminated.

The prevailing concept of "total war" permitted disregarding the restraints of morality, custom and international law. "Total war" required the mobilization of entire populations and drawing civilian infrastructures into the war effort. The widespread killing of civilians grew out of the assumptions that the factories producing the implements of war could not function if enough civilians were killed. But more importantly, the assumptions held that the country would become so demoralized from massive civilian fatalities that it would lose its capacity for continuing the war.

The above assumptions turned out to be unwarranted. Instead of weakening civilian morale, policies of democide tend to intensify hatred and to stiffen the determination to resist (Rummel, 1999). The defeat of the German army in the Battle of the Bulge made it evident that Germany would lose the war. Yet the resistance continued even after the Allied forces had crossed the Rhine River and pursued their advance toward Berlin. The Germans continued fighting until the Americans and the British met the Russians at the Elbe River. Within the context of tenacious German resistance, the British initiated massive urban area bombing. In retrospect, this strategy came to be symbolized in the persisting controversies over the saturated firebombing of the cities of Dresden and Hamburg (Knell, 2003).

Under the command of General Curtis LeMay, massive firebombing attacks were launched against Japanese cities. The civilian fatalities of a single incendiary attack on Tokyo may have exceeded those of the devastation of the atomic bombing of Hiroshima. While the full scope of the motives for conducting such attacks remains somewhat obscure, the justifications were for weakening the capacity of the Japanese to resist and to hasten the date of surrender. Given the tenacity of Japan in pursuing the war, there was little reason to believe their resistance would be any less than that of the Germans with a foreign invasion of their homeland (Craig, 1997).

The dropping of nuclear bombs on the cities of Hiroshima and Nagasaki was an outgrowth of the concept of "total war" that had been elaborated during World War II. Whether these two cities were suitable military targets was never in question. The subsequent symbolism of the mushroom cloud over Hiroshima became deeply etched into modern consciousness as an indication of the potential consequences of future warfare. To the military, Hiroshima verified the proposition that a technologically advanced war machine could defeat a less sophisticated and primitive one (Gibson, 1988). Yet to others, Hiroshima provided a model of what can be accomplished with the mobilization of personnel and resources for achieving some specified task.

Pearl Harbor stands alongside Hiroshima as two primary lessons from history in the American consciousness. Pearl Harbor is remembered for the disastrous consequences of the lack of military preparedness at a time that preparedness was necessary. The trauma of the Japanese attack was intensified by the failure to develop an adequate awareness of the importance of the wars in Europe and Asia for their own national security. Americans came out of World War II with a determination to never again be caught unprepared militarily. Pearl Harbor also became the master symbol of the preemptive strike. Americans lost their innocence in a world that had become more interdependent.

In the analysis that follows, attention will be directed toward the continuity of the symbolism of Hiroshima and Pearl Harbor in the fears and anxieties underlying American collective memories. With the passing of time, these memories came to be characterized by mythmaking and Cold War preoccupations with the worst-case scenario (Clarke, 2006). The realities of nuclear war were prominent themes in popular culture for several decades following World War II. Justifications for national policies in the war on terrorism drew heavily upon memories of Hiroshima and Pearl Harbor.

The Bombing of Hiroshima

Daily activities around the world were disrupted by the news bulletin announcing on 6 August 6 1945 that the city of Hiroshima had been destroyed by an atomic bomb, a new weapon of historically unprecedented proportions. The city of Hiroshima was demolished and the fatalities far exceeded the number that had been expected. Three days later a second bomb was dropped on the city of Nagasaki. Approximately 150,000 lives were lost from the two aerial assaults using nuclear weapons. The bombing of Hiroshima and Nagasaki had provided Americans with the opportunity both to avenge Pearl Harbor and to end the war. The survivors at Hiroshima and Nagasaki were faced with serious psychological problems from seeing their social worlds instantly vaporized by a weapon about which they had no prior knowledge (Seldon and Seldon, 1989).

The bombing of Hiroshima sent a clear message to the rest of the world. The Americans had developed an awesome weapon and had demonstrated a willingness to use it if they saw it in their own best interests to do so (Takaki, 1996). This was the message sent to the Soviets on what the United States would do if their more than a hundred divisions in Eastern Europe were used to overrun the rest of Europe. The overall message seemed to be that an end had come to traditional forms of warfare for resolving international disputes among adversaries.

On the fiftieth anniversary of the end of World War II, the Mayor of Nagasaki noted in his speech that the nuclear bombing of Japanese cities by the Americans stood alongside the Nazi Holocaust as the two major atrocities of the twentieth century. Robert Jay Lifton and Eric Markusen (1990) had previously made a similar observation in their analysis of *The Genocidal Mentality*. Both the Nazi Holocaust and the bombings of Hiroshima and Nagasaki provided dramatic illustrations of what human beings are capable of doing to each other. As defining events of the twentieth century, these historical episodes have taken on symbolic meanings that have given them a prominent place in the universality of basic human concerns.

Following the end of World War II, there initially was hope for creating some mechanism for international control over nuclear weapons. The need was evident since it would only be a matter of time before nuclear capability would proliferate among the nations of the world. The debates among Americans over the international control of nuclear weapons, however, were fraught with a basic contradiction (Bundy, 1990). Americans had a monopoly over nuclear weapons and were unwilling to give up that control voluntarily. Given the atmosphere of suspicion and distrust between the United States and the Soviet Union, there seemed to be no reasonable basis for banning nuclear weapons as instruments of war.

Levels of anxiety intensified in the early 1950s when President Harry S Truman announced the initiation of a crash program to develop the hydrogen bomb. He saw this as a necessary step for keeping ahead of the Soviets in the Cold War. Instead of generating an increased sense of national security, the announcement only intensified collective awareness of the possibilities of new forms of destruction. Some of the scientists who worked on the Manhattan Project had second thoughts about their contribution to the development of weapons of mass destruction. J. Robert Oppenheimer, the "father" of the atomic bomb, was strongly opposed to the development of any weapon with an even greater explosive capability (Bird and Sherwin, 2005).

Many of the scientists who worked on the development of the atomic bomb suffered intense levels of guilt from their contribution to a research project that resulted in the civilian deaths at Hiroshima and Nagasaki. It had become clear that the scientists who developed the bomb were totally disconnected from the government officials who decided what to do with it. Out of their concerns, the Bulletin of Atomic Scientists created the "Doomsday Clock" to inform the world of the time remaining prior to destruction (McCrea and Markle, 1989). When the Soviet Union exploded its first atomic bomb, the hands on the clock were moved to "three minutes to midnight." When the United States and the Soviet Union tested new thermonuclear devices within six months of each other in 1953, the doomsday clock was moved to "two minutes to midnight."

The Threat of Nuclear War

Throughout the Cold War, memories of Pearl Harbor and Hiroshima provided the guiding metaphors for military strategies on each side of the

Iron Curtain. Airplanes and missiles had provided new opportunities for the rapid delivery of nuclear weapons to an enemy nation. The surprise attack on Pearl Harbor and the destruction of Hiroshima provided visions of potential nightmares in an uncertain future. Vast resources were put into military budgets by both the United States and the Soviet Union to prepare for a war that could put an end to civilization as it was known and understood.

Military strategies were devised on each side of the Iron Curtain to assure that neither side could launch a preemptive strike on the other without provoking a comparable retaliatory response. Retrospective judgments hold that it was a balance of terror that provided the primary source of political stability over the subsequent four decades (Gaddis, 2005). But it was a form of stability that was promoted at the risk of a major catastrophe though a quick and inappropriate launch of a retaliatory response on the basis of an accident or some other form of false information.

The doctrine of "mutually assured destruction" (MAD) was a deterrence theory which held that the threat of annihilation from a retaliatory response would keep each side from launching a nuclear attack. Mutual adherence to this doctrine resulted in the escalation of an arms race in which neither side could rest assured that their military capability was adequate. Each adversary was required to invest vast resources into the development of nuclear weapons and increasingly efficient delivery systems. As a result of the threat of nuclear war, men and women throughout the modern world became primarily spectators of a drama that could result in a war being fought and over before they hardly realized that it had started.

The tensions stemming from the threat of nuclear war grew out of a series of questions that could not be answered with confidence. Is nuclear war inevitable? How will a nuclear war start? Will there be any advanced warning, or will it start suddenly and unexpectedly? Will it be possible to survive a nuclear war? The uncertainty of answers to these questions precluded determining the seriousness of the nuclear threat. For most people, the threat of nuclear war was gradually muted as forms of denial and repression were developed (Lifton and Mitchell, 1995). Some Americans downplayed the threat of nuclear war by developing attitudes of fatalism: "Since there is nothing we can do about the world situation, why worry about it."

Others took a more direct approach and were concerned with surviving nuclear war. Rather than a fatalistic resignation in the face of nuclear war, it was believed that individuals could take matters into their own hands (Popkess, 1980). Accordingly, during the fifties and sixties some

Americans constructed fallout shelters in their back yards. An even larger number concluded that they did not wish to survive a nuclear war. The shelters were bunker-like constructions covered with several feet of dirt and stocked with a sufficient supply of food and water to survive for several days after a nuclear attack. When asked what they would do if neighbors attempted to force their way into their shelter, the answer was frequently "we would just have to shoot them."

Several scientists elaborated on the concept of a "nuclear winter" and maintained that there would be no survivors of an all-out nuclear war. The debris released into the atmosphere from the explosions of a nuclear war would alter the earth's climate by blocking out rays from the sun. A rapid drop in temperature would soon result in heavy snowfall covering the millions of burned bodies in metropolitan areas. Drastic environmental changes would occur as temperatures dropped to severely low levels. The plant and animal life on which humans depend for food would be extinguished (Ehrlich, et al., 1984).

By being caught up in the doctrine of "mutually assured destruction," the race was on for not only developing increasingly effective weapons, but also for increasing the efficiency of delivery systems. While history had demonstrated that wars were won by technologically more efficient war machines, there was nothing in historical precedent for demonstrating a need for further technological efficiency if we already had an "overkill capacity" for eliminating every man, woman, and child on this planet (Lifton and Markusen, 1990).

Nuclear War in Popular Culture

Since a nuclear war had not yet occurred, no one actually knew what the effects would be. Thinking about nuclear war could only take us into the realm of fiction and mythmaking (Chaloupka, 1992). It was for this reason that popular culture filled the gap by drawing on symbolic representations of what could happen. In novels, popular music and movies the theme of nuclear war was evident throughout the Cold War years. Prominent in images of nuclear war were such notions as "doomsday," "Armageddon," "the apocalypse," "total destruction," and "a lifeless planet." Such images conveyed the implication that there would be no survivors of a nuclear war. The earth would join the other planets of the universe on which life had never developed or been extinguished.

The themes in science fiction about survivors of nuclear war mirrored the sentiments of the nation. Total annihilation has its limits in the development of a plot. It could only represent the ending, rather than the beginning of a story. Scripts with the theme that a few people would survive a nuclear war permitted giving free reign to the imagination in portraying what life would be like under these circumstances. The environment typically confronted was one of wasted cities, burned bodies and the destruction of civilization. The survivors of nuclear war were also portrayed as suffering from physiological mutilations and deformities (Porter, 1993).

The lessons from Hiroshima had suggested that much more was involved in nuclear war than the deaths resulting from the explosion itself. The acute radiation aftereffects at Hiroshima and Nagasaki were grotesque. Symptoms of "the invisible contamination" included severe diarrhea, ulcerations of the mouth, bleeding gums, skin cancer, high fever, loss of hair, low white cell blood count, and damage to the central nervous system. There was also evidence that exposure to high levels of radiation would have gruesome effects on future generations. Children and grandchildren would be born with genetic abnormalities, and deleterious mutations would occur (Lifton, 1967).

Given the prevailing culture of the Cold War (Whitfield, 1991), the psychological atmosphere reflected pervasive anxiety and fear. Yet, it would perhaps have been pathological or incapacitating to dwell on what could happen. The worst-case scenario (Clarke, 2006) would have been doomsday. No one could rest assured that he or she had a realistic grasp of what the probabilities actually were. These were the conditions promoting dark humor as a means of dealing with the absurdity of nuclear war.

While individuals could not make realistic assessments of the prospects of nuclear war, the songs and music of the Cold War years drew freely on underlying fears and anxieties. The following is a casual list of song titles drawn from the many ways in which popular culture expressed the dangers of nuclear war:

"After the Bomb"	"Christmas at Ground Zero"
"The Earth Dies Screaming"	"Einstein A-Go-Go"
"Fallout Theory in Practice"	"Mutually Assured Destruction"
"Nagasaki Nightmare"	"Eve of Destruction"

In the late 1950s and early 1960s the satirical songwriter Tom Lehrer composed several lyrics that promoted nervous laughter in the listener. One of his lyrics started, "So long Mom/ I'm off to drop the bomb/ So don't wait up for me." The song ended with the lines "I'll look for you when the war is over/ An hour and a half from now." Another of Lehrer's songs emphasized the democratic principle of human mortality: that all human life on this planet would be extinguished within a relatively short period of time. This would include women as well as men, the rich as well as the poor, and all other people regardless of social characteristics. His ode to the end of the world was titled *We Will All Go Together When We Go*. Drawing on the repetition of old revival hymns, lines in the song included "Oh, we will all fry together when we fry/ We will all bake together when we bake/ We will all burn together when we burn/ We will all go together when we go."

The connection between tragedy and pleasure has been well recognized in the theater from the days of Ancient Greece to modern times (Nuttall, 2001). However, the pleasure people derive from tragic events remains primarily at the latent level (Portman, 2000). The open expression of happiness as a response to suffering is gruesome and unthinkable. But when people gather in small groups to reflect on tragic events, there is a certain amount of pleasure derived from the shared experience. Some sense of unity grows out of sharing sadness and being jointly involved in reflecting on the implications of tragic events for personal lives and for the human condition. Through sharing crisis and tragedy, lonely and isolated individuals become temporarily integrated into a local community.

A primary example of the blending of extraordinary tragedy with humor was the 1964 film *Dr Strangelove or: How I Learned to Stop Worrying and Love the Bomb*. One of the many memorable images from the film includes the demented Dr. Strangelove unable to keep his mechanical arm from flying into a Nazi salute. The subject of the film was the extinction of life on earth. The fail-safe procedures designed to prevent nuclear war by accident resulted in bringing it about. A crazed American General, Jack D. Ripper, had decided that the time had come to go "toe to toe with the Russkies" and put an end to the communist menace.

The catastrophic myth of "mutually assured destruction" as deterrence was dramatically and relentlessly exposed. The American president, portrayed by Peter Sellers, had his hands full in calming the Russians since there was no way of recalling the bomber wing. Unknown to the Americans, the Russians had developed "a doomsday machine" that would automatically be activated by any preemptive nuclear strike on the Soviet Union. Another memorable image of the movie was Slim Pickens riding astride the H-Bomb all the way down. The movie ended with the mushroom cloud symbolizing Armageddon and the World War II song by Vera Lynn, "I'll Be Seeing You in All the Old Familiar Places."

Of the hundreds of movies about nuclear war, only a few succeeded in the use of humor. Most drew on the dark, morbid and apocalyptic character of nuclear war. This was reflected, for example, in the movies *On the Beach*, *Fail Safe* and *The Day After*. Each of these depicted the intrusion of nuclear war into the lives of ordinary men and women. Several assumptions about everyday social living were shattered (Browne and Neal, 2001). There was no longer continuity from one generation to the next. There was no longer a connection between what people deserve and what they get out of life. Social norms were no longer effective in regulating conduct. The outcome of events was no longer predictable, and social time was no longer durable and continuous.

The 1957 movie *On the Beach* focused directly on a nuclear war between the Soviet Union and the United States. It depicted the disruption of everyday life in Australia as a small group of people waited for the end. The rest of the world had been destroyed and a radioactive cloud was moving toward Australia. The last of the survivors were innocent victims of an accidental war and were doing the best they could with the resources at their disposal as they waited for the inevitable end. Although Australia did not provide a direct target for any of the nuclear bombs, global winds carried the deadly fallout to all parts of the planet. Audiences left the theater with a lump in their throats as they confronted the darkest of their fears and as they identified with the characters in the movie who were engaged in making plans that could never be carried out.

During the year of the Cuban Missile Crisis, 1962, Eugene Burdick and Harvey Wheeler published the novel *Fail Safe*. Two years later it was made into a movie featuring Henry Fonda as the President of the United States. An accidental nuclear attack had been launched against the Soviet Union, and the country and the world were faced with the risk of a nuclear apocalypse. The absurdity of the Cold War was dramatized in the necessary decision of the American president to drop an atomic bomb on New York City to compensate for the accidental bombing of Moscow.

The 1983 movie *The Day After* was an American-made film that aired on the ABC network. Its disturbing content discouraged advertisers, but achieved tremendous ratings success. The movie depicted a military escalation of World War III that resulted in both the Americans and the Russians launching a full-scale nuclear war. In subsequent evaluations of the movie, military theorists observed that the movie portrayed a very realistic possibility during the Cold War. The film was intended to counter the popular idea that nuclear war would result in a simple and instant end of the world. Instead, it emphasized the grisly details of radiation poisoning, a large number of casualties, overwhelmed hospitals, chaotic governance, and inadequate food supplies.

The primary plot of the movie highlighted struggles in the aftermath of nuclear war by residents living in Lawrence, Kansas, and Kansas City, Missouri. Nearly 100 million Americans watched *The Day After* in its first broadcast, making the film one of the most successful in broadcast history. It served as a stimulant for antiwar activists, and was discussed by scientists and other experts in subsequent television programs. As a result of its traumatic content, ABC opened several hotlines with counselors available to calm disturbed viewers. Psychological counselors were made available to students in Lawrence, Kansas, who found the movie disturbing. The film was subsequently made available for international audiences. Following the perestroika reforms under the leadership of Mikhail Gorbachev, it was shown in 1987 on Soviet television.

In combination, the novels, movies, music, and other forms of popular culture addressed the many contradictions inherent in the Cold War. These included the ethical neutrality of scientists and technicians, the uncertainty inherent in developing risky technologies, the doublespeak of preparing for war in order to achieve peace; and spending vast resources on the development of weapons that no rational person could ever use (Broderick, 1991). The absurdity also consisted of ideological extremism and an unwillingness to seek a solution or negotiate a compromise. We now know that at no time did the Soviet Union consider launching a preemptive strike on the United States. At no time could either side achieve a clear military victory by launching an attack on the other.

11 September 2001

With the breakup of the Soviet Union and the tearing down of the Berlin Wall, the prospect for a new and peaceful world order seemed promising, but was short-lived with the terrorist attack of 11 September 2001. Terrorists had commandeered four commercial airplanes that were loaded with highly explosive jet fuel. Two of them crashed into the World Trade Center, one into the Pentagon and the fourth in a field about eighty miles southeast of Pittsburgh. The nation was caught unprepared and the collective response was one of shock, disbelief and incredulity.

War memories of both Pearl Harbor and Hiroshima played a major part in the response of Americans to the terrorist attack. It became evident that war memories are mediated by cultural ways of making sense out of extraordinary events. The news media made comparisons with the surprise Japanese attack on Pearl Harbor. The number of fatalities in New York was compared to those at Pearl Harbor. War memories are mediated by cultural ways of telling stories. The emerging stories about 9-11 included references to "Our Second Pearl Harbor," another "Day of Infamy" and "This Generation's Pearl Harbor." Both in newspaper headlines and in subsequent political attempts at war mobilization, comparisons were made between 9-11 and Pearl Harbor. Differences between the two events were either ignored or minimized in the news media.

While there were no immediate references to nuclear war, the subsequent national discourse included frequent references to the historical precedent of Hiroshima. In his State of the Union address in January 2002, President George W. Bush applied the terms "rogue nations" and "axis of evil" to Iraq, Iran and North Korea. These designations were based on the claim that these countries were developing nuclear weapons as a central component of their military arsenals. The term "weapons of mass destruction" moved to center stage in the American culture of fear.

Intelligence reports suggested that Iraq was actively involved in the production of weapons of mass destruction and that these weapons could be made available to terrorists. In an address to the United Nations, Secretary of State Colin Powell sought endorsement for air strikes and a ground invasion of Iraq. Inspectors from the United Nations had failed to find any evidence of weapons of mass destruction in Iraq and the proposed plan for an invasion was rejected. Condoleezza Rice, National Security Adviser, responded to the uncertainty by observing that we could not wait for the definitive evidence "provided by a mushroom cloud" before taking decisive action. In spite of opposition from European allies, the United States implemented its plans for a preemptive strike against Iraq.

In their book *Hiroshima in America*, Robert Jay Lifton and Greg Mitchell (1995) noted that in exploding atomic bombs over Hiroshima and Nagasaki, Americans frightened themselves more than anyone else. Attempts to overcome a fear of nuclear weapons and to establish a sense of "national security" have become American preoccupations for more than sixty years. This is apparent in the American national defense budget that has continued to increase until it now exceeded that of nearly all other countries of the world combined. Yet the United States was defenseless against the terrorist attack of 11 September 2001.

The fear of nuclear weapons falling into the hands of terrorists took the form of what Lee Clarke (2006) called the "worst case" scenario. Terror and catastrophe came to occupy central place in both popular imagination and in policy formation. The preemptive strike against Iraq was based on assumptions about the motives, intentions and plans of an enemy nation. Why wait for another Pearl Harbor in which an enemy might use weapons of mass destruction against the United States? The "forceful interrogation of enemy combatants" (torture of prisoners of war) was justified on the grounds that they might have knowledge of a planned nuclear attack on an American city (Dershowitz, 2002).

Under conditions of modernity, collective memories are characterized by uncertainty and by recognizing that social order is always fragile and subjected to disruption in unexpected ways. Both triumphs and tragedies become deeply embedded in both popular culture and in public policy. Novels, movies and other forms of popular culture are grass roots approaches to the contradictions inherent in modern social life. In contrast, policy formation is a top-down approach to what is presumed to be the overriding priorities of the nation. The symbolic meanings of Hiroshima provide the raw materials for shaping both American national identity and the culture of fear. These meanings may be thought of as echoes from the past drawn upon to symbolize the prospects and the limitations of social living for both current and future generations.

References

Aaron, Raymond. *The Century of Total War.* Boston, 1955.

Bird, Kai and Martin J. Sherwin. *American Prometheus: The Triumph and Tragedy of J. Robert Oppenheimer.* New York, 2005.

Broderick, Mick. *Nuclear Movies.* Jefferson, NC, 1991.

Browne, Ray B. and Arthur G. Neal. *Ordinary Reactions to Extraordinary Events.* Bowling Green, OH, 2001.

Bundy, McGeorge. *Danger and Survival: Choices About the Bomb in First Fifty Years.* New York, 1990.

Chaloupka, William. *Knowing Nukes: The Politics and Culture of the Atom.* Minneapolis, 1992.

Clarke, Lee. *Worst Cases: Terror and Catastrophe in the Popular Imagination.* Chicago, 2006.

Craig, William. *The Fall of Japan.* New York, 1997.

Dershowitz, Alan M. *Why Terrorism Works: Understanding the Threat, Responding to the Challenge.* New Haven, CT, 2002.

Ehrlich, Paul R., Carl Sagan, Donald Kennedy, and Walter Orr Roberts. *The Cold and the Dark: The World After Nuclear War.* New York, 1984.

Elliot, Gil. *The 20th Century Book of the Dead.* New York, 1972.

Gibson, James William. *The Perfect War: The War We Couldn't Lose and How We Did.* New York, 1988.

Gaddis, John Lewis. *The Cold War: A New History.* New York, 2005.

Knell, Hermann. *To Destroy a City: Strategic Bombing and Its Human Consequences in World War II.* Cambridge, MA, 2003.

Lifton, Robert Jay. *Death in Life: Survivors at Hiroshima.* New York, 1967.

Lifton, Robert Jay and Eric Markusen. *The Genocidal Mentality: Nazi Holocaust and Nuclear Threat.* New York, 1990.

Lifton, Robert Jay and Greg Mitchell. *Hiroshima in America: Fifty Years of Denial.* New York, 1995.

McCrea, Francis B. and Gerald E. Markle. *Minutes to Midnight: Nuclear Weapons Protest in America.* Newbury Park, CA, 1989.

Nuttall, A. D. *Why Does Tragedy Give Pleasure?* New York, 2001.

Popkiss, Barry. *The Nuclear Survival Handbook: Living Through and After a Nuclear Attack.* New York, 1980.

Porter, Jeffrey L. "Narrating the End: Fables of Survival in the Nuclear Age." *Journal of American Culture* 16 (1993): 41–47.

Portman, John. *When Bad Things Happen to Other People.* New York, 2000.
Rummel, Rudolph J. *Statistics of Democide: Genocide and Mass Murder Since 1900.* London, 1999.
Seldon, Kyoto and Mark Seldon, eds. *The Atomic Bomb: Voices from Hiroshima and Nagasaki.* Armonk, NY, 1989.
Takaki, Ronald. *Why the Decision to Use the Atom Bomb.* New York, 1996.
Whitfield, Stephen J. *The Culture of the Cold War.* Baltimore, MD, 1991.

The Cult of Heroic Death in Nazi Architecture

Holger H. Herwig

"Architecture is the language of the *Volk*," its letters carefully laid "stone upon stone." With these words architect Wilhelm Kreis explained the vast circle of "castles of the dead" that he designed for Nazi Germany's fallen warriors. The *Totenburgen* were to memorialize and to popularize "for eternity" the "sacrificial deaths" of the Wehrmacht's soldiers. They were to transcend individual, ephemeral "earthly lives" and through cycles of ritual days of remembrance to serve as collective shrines and pilgrimage sites for a new "religion." They were to evoke memories of the glory of ancient and medieval times, and to "speak" to future generations of great unselfish deeds. They were to memorialize and popularize a "new architectural order," one that would every generation rejuvenate the German *Volk* and reintegrate it into the Nazi "closed communal inner order." They were to preserve, purify and make eternal the collective body. They were to be a constant reminder of the dominance of the nation over the individual, the dialectic of war and architecture in stone. The *architectura militans*, in Adolf Hitler's words, was to be the eternal "Word in Stone."

Hitler and Speer

At an exposition of the "new" German architecture at Munich in January 1938, Hitler lectured Yugoslavian Prime Minister Milan Stojadinović on the close tie between history and architecture. "Every great epoch finds its final expression of value in its building projects. When peoples internally experience great times, they also want to give these external forms. Their [message] is then more convincing than the spoken word: It is the Word in Stone!"[1] Historians, a quarrelsome lot at the best of times, agree on two issues: Hitler's personal interest in and influence on architecture; and his obsession with death.

The notion of "Hitler the artist" or "Hitler the architect" runs like a red thread through the man's life. At the height of "his" war in the East in May 1942, he commented: "If this war had not come about, he would certainly have become an architect, perhaps—yes, indeed most certainly—one of the top architects, if not *the* top German architect...."[2] Gerdy Troost, widow of Hitler's first master architect, Paul Ludwig Troost, understood the tie between power and architecture. The new "German architecture," she argued, was "a part of the German revolution" of 1933. Its monumental buildings represented "National Socialism ... cast in stone"; its hard granite firmness paid witness to firm faith in the new "racially-secure" German *Weltanschauung*; and its staunch pillars represented Hitler's bulwark against "Bolshevist cultural nihilism." Using the Führer's words, Troost concluded that it was "Germanic *Tektonik*."[3]

Hitler abhorred traditional German military monuments because of their over-ornamentation and lack of originality. All too often, he argued, they consisted of little more than "potentates high up on horseback with plumed helmets billowing."[4] Or of romantic *Kitsch*, a term that he applied especially to the navy's U-boat memorial on the Kiel Bight with its soaring brass eagle perched high on a semicircle of red Weser sandstone.[5] To him, these monuments merely venerated the individual and as such offered no "moral" or "lesson" to the nation at large. Architecture had to serve a purpose, it had to have an integrating function for the new society that Hitler hoped to forge through war.

In deciding on a style for their architecture, Hitler and his *amanuensis*, Albert Speer, faced a dilemma. On the one hand, by reaching back to antiquity for their models, they wanted to make the connection between Athens, Sparta and Rome and the Third Reich. On the other hand, they felt the urge to connect their creations to a heroic Germanic past.[6] To square the circle, on the one hand they forbade public reference to their designs as being "Greek" or "Roman" or "Hellenistic" or even "classical"; while on the other hand, they searched for suitable terms such as "new," "German," "racially driven" (*rassebedingt*), or "stemming from the depths of the German *Volk*." In the end, the term "new Germanic style" was as close as they came to a single, satisfying designation.[7] The point was that their architecture had to be new, innovative, fresh, and original—while of course it was not.

Speer and his disciples did not plan in a vacuum. They kept a close eye on the Soviet Union, where plans were revealed for a new heroic Soviet capital from the drawing boards of the architects B. M. Jofan, V. G. Hlfreich, and V. A. Shtschuko, complete with a super-broad parade street and a Soviet Palace. As well, they followed developments in Washington, D.C.: the graceful classical forms of the Supreme Court, the Thomas Jefferson Memorial, and the National Gallery of Art; the Greek colonnaded Lincoln Memorial; and the "stripped classicism" of the Federal Reserve Building. Finally, they studied Benito Mussolini's designs for a new city "Roma al Mare" and a massive plan for "E '42," the site for the twentieth anniversary of the March on Rome.[8] But the Soviet model was too "plebeian"; the Roman plans too "modernist"; and the American architecture just too "American" for Hitler.

First off the drawing boards were designs for the five so-called "Führer cities" whose cores Hitler ordered Speer to tear down and to rebuild. Those for Berlin were the most revealing of the Führer's style. They were to be classical, gargantuan and "eternal." The new world capital, "Germania," Hitler had already written in *Mein Kampf* in 1925, was to radiate the "magic of Mecca and Rome."[9] Its centerpiece was to be a six-kilometer long "*via triumphalis*," a "Great Street" more than twice the length of the Champs Élysées in Paris and wider than the Avenida del Libertador in Buenos Aires. A Triumphal Arch at least twice as large as its Parisian model and a Congress Hall seven times the size of St. Peter's in Rome were to be fitting monuments for the new "master of the world." The 290-meter high Congress Hall for 150,000 spectators, at Hitler's insistence, was to be crowned by a giant eagle clutching a globe, "whose possession," Speer later recalled, "Hitler did not seek merely symbolically."[10] The Führer deemed "his" gigantic Congress Hall, which was to function as a hall of worship with cult significance, to be "worth more than three wars won."[11]

With regard to war memorials, Hitler as early as 1925 had designed a mammoth Triumphal Arch for Berlin; its attic severy was to have chiseled in granite the name of each of the 1.8 million German soldiers who had died in World War I. For Hitler, this gargantuan granite mausoleum was to be *his* triumphal arch, it was to be associated with *his* person, and the immense total would include *his* name. In short, Hitler the "unknown soldier" personified. Future generations of heroic German warriors would march under "the bridge of traditions" in constant reminder of the "sacrificial deaths" that had made it possible.[12] And it was "to give back to every single German a sense of self-confidence." All memorials that Hitler planned to build would scream out to his subjects, "We are not inferior, but on the contrary, we are absolutely equal with every other people."[13] It was an obvious reference to his fervent desire to erase "the shame and stain" of defeat and revolution in 1918.

Wilhelm Kreis

There was also a starker symbolism of death yet to come, and it was to be closely associated with the name Wilhelm Kreis (1873–1955). Best known for having designed some fifty "Bismarck Towers" and the Monument of the Battle of Nations (1813) at Leipzig before the Great War, Kreis by 1933 was the doyen of German architects and president of its august academy. In a strange twist of fate, when Kreis in 1933 applied for membership in the NSDAP, his official family records came back stamped "previous Jewish religion" and his application rejected. His Protestant wife's blood line was deemed to be "one-quarter Jewish" due to a maternal Jewish grandmother. Kreis was stripped of the presidency of both the Dresden Academy of Art and the Union of German Architects.[14] Yet, in the sometime nebulous world of National Socialist racial practices, Kreis was soon thereafter admitted to membership in the NSDAP — largely on the recommendations of Speer and Troost. In fact, Kreis had on several occasions met privately with Hitler at the Obersalzberg and as early as 1936 — that is, three years before the outbreak of World War II — had presented the Führer with his first sketches for setting the "heroic cult of death" into stone.

Initially, Hitler entrusted Kreis with designing a giant Hall of Soldiers (*Soldatenhalle*) as the centerpiece for Berlin's new north-south grand axis. It was to be 250 meters long, 100 meters wide, and 80 meters high. Visitors would enter a granite barrel-vaulted "national room of celebration" — twice the size of a football field — and then descend a 20 × 40 meter staircase to an inner 90-meter-deep burial crypt, a "pantheon" for Germany's great captains.[15] The vast hall, flooded by natural light streaming in through a pillared front, was to represent a hybrid form of a medieval cathedral. The crypt, with its triple naves modeled on the one at the Marienburg honoring the Teutonic Knights, would evince an aura of pressing grief and "solemn" sadness. As Kreis' fellow architect, Friedrich Tamms, argued:

> It shall be a place in which the German people will become aware of the limits of their earthly lives, a place of admiration, remembrance and worship, ... a sacred shrine, a new true German cathedral, born of the sacrifices of those who gave their dearest so that the future may live.

And whereas the past had always honored its fallen warriors posthumously, the *Soldatenhalle* was designed for those who had not yet died, "an overt invitation to die a hero's death."[16] Kreis thus sought to bind together in ocular form the great military captains from Germany's past, present and future. The Hall of Soldiers was to be a temple of victory and sacrifice for the New Germany, a propagandistic expression of heroic death through-out the ages. Interestingly, Kreis in early 1939 also designed a "world war museum" on Berlin's main parade street, Unter den Linden — for a world war that had not yet even begun!

From the start, Hitler and Speer saw the obvious connection between architecture and great-power status, one that they took over from the architects of the French Revolution. Gargantuan scale was to be applied so that the great monuments of the past would shrink to insignificance when compared to the Third Reich's "masses of concrete and stone." At the height of the Sudetenland crisis of 1938, the Führer informed Reich Minister Hans Frank, the future head of the General Government in Poland, "I am building for eternity — because, Frank, ours will be the last Germany."[17] When Speer showed his father, also an architect, the plans for the new German "Führer cities," the elder Speer was somewhat less enthusiastic. "You have all gone completely mad!" he blurted out.[18]

In March 1941, on the eve of the attack on the Soviet Union, Hitler appointed Kreis to the position of "General Architectural Counselor for the Construction of German Warrior Cemeteries."[19] Thereby, he entrusted Kreis with what was to become the crowning glory of the new *Drang nach Osten*: a chain of granite and stone "castles of the dead" (*Totenburgen*[20]) along the invasion route of Operation Barbarossa and the conquered *Lebensraum*, one that would evoke memories of the Teutonic Knights who first had brought "culture" to the "barbaric" Slavic East. Kreis was respon-sible for his creations only to Hitler.

Germanic Tektonik

Hitler and Kreis, both veterans of the Great War and both seething that the Allies, unlike Germany, had been allowed to construct vast mon-uments to the dead of the Great War, shared a fascination with sacrifice and death. For them, Horace's famous comment, *dulce et decorum est pro patria mundi*,[21] bound ancient Rome via medieval Germany to Nazi Ger-many. Indeed, Hitler and Kreis were anxious (at least privately) to con-nect the Third Reich to antiquity; they sought to carve in stone "the German inheritance of the spirit of ancient Hellenic culture."[22] They had studied the prehistoric cairns of the Teutons, the Spartan warriors' ceme-tery at Thermopylae (480 B.C.), the Roman Emperor Trajan's (53–117) monument at Adamklisi, and the Gothic Emperor Theodoric's (454–526) tomb at Ravenna.[23] Moreover, they remembered how the Romans had built celebratory trophies on the borders of their empire, both to com-memorate military triumphs and to warn off would-be attackers.

This was precisely the model to be followed for the new *architectura militans*. Kreis envisaged a ring of *Totenburgen* around the perimeter of a future Germanic Europe. He described these "castles of the dead" in lyrical-heroic words. "From the cliffs of the Atlantic coast, great architectural works, directed against the West, will arise as an eternal memorial to the liberation of the Continent from its dependence on Britain." They would symbolize "the unification of Europe under the leadership of the German master race." In the East,

> towering fortresses, high and mighty, and surrounded by the cemeteries of a warrior nation of Germanic blood, will rise as a symbol for the mastering of the chaotic powers of the eastern steppes by the disciplined might of the Germanic forces of order — which, as so often in the past two millennia, has secured the existence of Western Civilization against the destructive storm floods from Central Asia.[24]

To prepare the way, a monstrous wave of destruction and "deportation" was to be launched. Starting in Poland and moving east, "everything ugly, unclean, aimless" was to be "removed" to create a pure "German" environment. All architectural "deformities" and "defects" were to be destroyed. In their stead would come a new "unity of politics and architecture," a new "political form of life which speaks out of a building."[25] At the height of the Allied air assault in World War II, Hitler caustically commented that the Allies at least were saving him the costs of tearing down the old Prussian capital!

In June 1941 Reichsführer-SS Heinrich Himmler ordered the Reich Main Security Office to draft a thirty-year "Generalplan Ost." Completed in May 1942, it called for the eventual "deportation" of 31 to 45 million Slavic so-called *Untermenschen*, their places taken by about 10 million settlers of "Aryan" stock from Germany as well as Denmark, Holland, Norway, and Sweden. A series of "racial belts" of soldier-settlers was to be established to keep out the "storm flood of Asia for all time."[26] The crowning glory of this "Eastern Colonization" was to be Kreis' "castles of the dead," stone monuments to a heroic race of Germanic warriors who had died in this "second crusade" against the Slavs. As Himmler put it in January 1941, "When people are silent, the stones speak. By means of the stone, great epochs speak to the present.... Buildings are always erected by people. People are children of their blood, are members of their race. As the blood speaks, so the people build."[27]

Kreis and his staff by early 1943 had completed thirty-six pen-and-ink designs for the *Totenburgen* of this new "war of liberation."[28] They were to be stone expressions of new Germanic conquests; to exude an aura of invincibility; to tie the Third Reich to the glory of both ancient and medieval times; and to be simple and yet majestic. They were to be of local stone (granite and marble) and incorporated into existing landscapes, to be sited away from everyday traffic routes and yet accessible to the public. Hitler's directive had been clear: "We will win this war, but we can only secure this victory through our building."[29]

Along the southern borders of the New Germanic Empire, the mastaba[30] memorial graves and pyramids at Giza served as the model for the Panzer Memorial in North Africa: a square base of a pyramid with sloped pylons and an open top crowned with eagles on all four corners. Palms were to imbed the "heroic landscape" into a heroic past — and to reveal the distant reach of the German armed forces (*Wehrmacht*). Kreis developed a similar stone design for the monument on the banks of the Struma River in southern Bulgaria, this time with burning funeral pyres stationed at its four outer corners. For the heights of the Vitosha massif south of Sofia, he designed a round stone tower resting on a fortress-like base topped with a burning pyre, surrounded by eagles on the corners of the base. The Pergamon Altar in Berlin was the model for the double-winged, Doric colonnaded Ceremonial Square with an Egyptian obelisk supporting a giant "hero warrior," entitled simply "at the foot of Mount Olympus." A replica of a medieval stone gate was to guard one of the passes in Macedonia.

In Poland, just outside Warsaw astride the Vistula River, a dark, round, medieval brick fortress with crenellated walls and supported by a ring of ten lesser towers was to commemorate the battle for the Polish capital in 1939. At Kutno, just north of Łódź, a towering square triumphal arch with eternal flames lit on each corner would stand watch over the region of the Bzura River and ward off future "barbarian" invasions emanating from the East. Its massive center altar was to feature a giant granite sword with its tip pointed up — the logo of Hitler's publisher, Franz Eher.

In the Far North, ancient Norse stone cairns were the models. Norway was to receive several *Totenburgen*. For the sloping banks of the Ofot fjord at Narvik, Kreis designed a "megalithic stone circle," topped by a stone fortress with an arcade of Greco–Roman design. In its center he placed a massive stone Egyptian revival obelisk, upon which stood a giant Siegfried-like warrior-hero representing the three German armed forces. For the Norwegian capital, Oslo, Kreis sketched a "Germanic-Norse circle of stone" resembling ancient Norse mausoleums. The central platform carried a "German eagle" perched high atop a stone Egyptian obelisk. Its stone and wood were to link myth and memory of an ancient Germanic past to the Third Reich. The Warrior Memorial at Trondheim was to consist of a squat, square stone tower. Behind it, two Hellenistic halls of honor featuring a giant sarcophagus were to pay homage to the German warrior-soldiers who had given their lives first to take and then to hold Norway.

By far the grandest project was to be a gargantuan pyramidal conus of stone above the Dnieper River in Ukraine, simply entitled "In the Interior of Russia." It was to symbolize "the re-conquest of European culture from Bolshevism."[31] The surrounding Russian steppe was first to be cleared away to accord future visitors a sweeping panoramic view from the monument into the newly-conquered *Lebensraum*. Based on Artemisia's "mausoleum" at Halicarnassus (today Bordum, Turkey), it was to be the greatest of all the *Totenburgen*, an "eternal" reminder of the winter battles in the Soviet Union.

This crowning edifice to the "heroic sacrifices" of the "Germanic East Army" was to consist of concentric "Germanic stone circles" hewn out of rough granite. The base, with its 280-meter circumference, was to soar 165 meters into the sky, then to taper off to a 13-meter-high peak, crowned with an eagle clutching a globe — like Hitler's Congress Hall in Berlin. Four pillared portals would support gigantic lions. Funeral pyres would burn day and night. Smaller mounds would pay homage to the fallen soldiers of allied nations, their "armed warriors" standing on "national shields." A broad stone stairway was to sweep the visitor several hundred meters up from the river to the monument's interior. Open arches midway up the cone would flood a massive round granite floor altar plate (under which Kreis planned to collect earth from the conquered Russian lands) with indirect sunlight. The "rush of wind" that would howl through the seven layers of crypts Kreis planned for the conus would be a constant reminder of the "spirits of the fallen."[32] It was to be the prototype for countless other *Totenburgen*, leading future pilgrims from a "stone mound of sacrifice" on the Volga River up to the western slopes of the Ural Mountains. The dialectic of war and architecture set in stone.

Kreis went out of his way to link his Dnieper monument to death. Poets, musicians, sculptors, and architects, he recalled, throughout the ages had "dedicated their best cultural works to death." "Heroic persons" who were prepared "to sacrifice their lives for the fatherland rather than to yield to the enemy" deserved a heroic final resting place so that successive generations could honor their great unselfish deeds. That warrior class was to be covered by "sacred soil, the earth, the mother of all beings." And by deserving stone monuments. "Great as the earth, simple and [yet] noble is to be the form of these stones, proud also, as we are of these dead."[33] In short, "castles of the dead" to be admired for "eternity."

Hitler was well pleased with Kreis. In 1943, on the architect's seventieth birthday, the Führer bestowed upon Kreis the nation's highest civilian decoration, the Eagle Shield of the German Reich, as due reward for the "heroes' memorials of this war."[34] Less clear is what monetary reward Kreis received for his morbid designs. If his honoraria between 1938 and 1941 just for the new "Party Forum" in Dresden—135,000 RM (today $675,000)—are any indication, Kreis must have been well paid, indeed.[35]

From whence had come Kreis' obsession with venerating death? His nephew Helmut Arntz has provided clues.[36] During his student years at Munich (1892–94), Kreis had become smitten with Richard Wagner's *Der Ring* in general, and with *Die Walküre* in particular. The "Valkyrie" was an epic centered on the betrayal, death and burial of Siegfried. Act II climaxed with the "Annunciation Death" scene after the slaying of Siegmund, and it ended with the apocalyptic "Ride of the Valkyries." From that point on, Kreis became obsessed with everything pertaining to *Wal* ("those who are left dead on the field"): *Walhall, Walküre, Walstatt, Wal-Termini,* and *Wal-Burgen.*[37] Hence, what could be more alluring for Kreis than to commit to stone this fascination with ancient Germanic *Wal* in the form of *Wal-Burgen*, heroic "castles of the dead"? They would perpetuate for "eternity" that ancient heroic saga of sacrifice and death — and burial. Indeed, as his world crashed about him in 1945, Kreis referred to the end of the Third Reich in Wagnerian terms: "the *Götterdämmerung*," or "Twilight of the Gods."[38] That opera had ended with Hagen cowardly thrusting his spear into Siegfried's back; and with Brünnhilde ordering a funeral pyre into which she committed Siegfried's magic ring before joyously plunging into the flames herself, thereupon to join her beloved Siegfried in Valhalla.

"Architectural Order"

A few words of a comparative nature on the meaning of the National Socialist architectural "cult of heroic death" are in order. It is all too easy to dismiss it as mere symbols of Hitler's megalomania or as too "futuristic" for serious study.[39] What if, God forbid, Hitler had won the war and completed these projects? How would we then today be analyzing his creations? In fact, Hitler saw himself as building within and upon a solid tradition — that of Rome. If Speer foresaw that Hitler wanted to build for a grandiose "eternal" future, so Vitruvius had appreciated that Augustus was building on a massive scale for "eternal" greatness. Both Romans and Nazis used architecture of "colossal dimensions to overawe and intimidate." Both used "architectural order" in the form of "gridiron town plans," "axial symmetry," and "hierarchical placement of state structures within urban spaces" to reinforce their social and political order.[40]

According to Gerdy Troost, Hitler's monumental architecture was to function as an integrating factor. By its very gargantuan proportions and its rugged simplicity, Hitler had stated already in 1937, it was "for centuries to come" to be a symbol of "the proud sense of unity" among the German people, the outward expression of a new "closed communal inner order," one that would for "eternity" erase "all earthly social differences," read Bolshevism.[41] Every new building, Troost trumpeted in 1943, represented the "powerful, united leadership" of the Führer. Every "noble stone of every mighty wall" was an "expression of the roots of power that had rejuvenated the German people." Thanks to this "belief in building," the German *Heimat* had been melded into "an ordered and rank-and-file unity."[42] In a state defined by a neo-feudal order of competing organizations and offices, it remains an open question to what degree Troost was also appealing for a more harmonious future political "inner order."

In the realm of public finances, both Rome and Nazi Germany used plunder and loot to cover the vast expenditures required for the *opera publica*. Just as Trajan financed his great Forum with plunder (*manubiae*) from the Dacian wars and Julius Caesar (and after his death Augustus) realized their grandiose building plans with plunder from Gaul, so Hitler planned to build and to finance his triumphant arches, congress halls, stadiums, and *Totenburgen* with booty from German-occupied Europe. The marble and granite quarries of Croatia, Denmark, France, Greece, Italy, and Sweden, Hitler and Speer had calculated in the 1930s, would not suffice for the Third Reich's "Redesign Plans." Thus, on the morrow of his invasion of Russia, Hitler joyously informed Speer that in the East they would "get the granite and marble" needed for their constructions, "as much as we want."[43] In August 1942 the Führer fairly drooled over the prospects of plunder before three of his favorite *Gauleiter*: "Timber we [will] have in abundance. Iron in limitless quantities, the greatest manganese-ore deposits in the world; oil — all is awash in it! German manpower deployed there; O Dear God!"[44]

Most darkly, both Rome and Nazi Germany used slave labor to build their stone temples. Speer had viewed this practice firsthand when he visited Syracuse. Only after the war did he lament "the Greek prisoners of war who dug out the caves of Syracuse 2000 years ago," the "heritage of cruel centuries."[45] Thus, the Nazis established many of their early forced labor camps near stone quarries from where the rough-hewn stones for the Third Reich's architectural wonders came under the auspices of the German Earth and Stone Works (*Deutsche Erd- und Steinwerke*).[46]

With specific reference to Kreis' *Totenburgen*, they were designed, as George Mosse has argued, to display "the dominance of the nation over the individual."[47] Rather than individual graves with the names of the dead inscribed on single crosses, as was the case with most soldiers killed between 1914 and 1918, the "castles of the dead" were to be massive stone fortresses designed to stress the collective. The "fallen heroes" were to be buried in each of the mausoleums from the Atlantic to the Urals, from North Africa to northern Norway, in anonymous mass graves sited in mammoth crypts under massive stone altars. Each *Totenburg*, what philosopher Elias Canetti has called "a heap of dead" (*Haufen der Toten*), would thus become a "united entity" (*Einheit*).[48] In other words, Martin Luther's hymn, "A Mighty Fortress is Our God," set in stone.

Historian Detlev Peukert has argued with regard to Nazi ideology that the "ephemeral body of the individual" was to be fused into the "potentially immortal body of the *Volk* or race"; that is, it was to become part of a new "holistic national entity."[49] This split between the individual and the national "body" not only explained the "borderline experience of death" but also "reintroduced a language for negotiating the fact of death." The fleeting nature of individual existence and individual death was "secondary" to the "eternal life" of the *Volk*. In practice, Nazi racism sought to secure "the immortality of the racially pure *Volk*" by way of a "crusade against life." In this way, the collective body was preserved, purified and made "eternal"— in the case of the *Totenburgen*, in stone. Put differently, Hitler's idealized *Volksgemeinschaft* was to be celebrated and made manifest in death.

One could also argue that the "castles of the dead" were to serve as a tool of social cohesion to replace religion in the Third Reich — perhaps a conscious (or even subconscious) replacement for Michelangelo's suffering *Pietà*— and thus constitute shrines designed to project the image of a common heroic warrior fate and to instill the belief in an afterlife that unites all believers.[50]

Conclusion

We can only speculate as to the future ritual functions of the monuments, since none were built and the war was lost. But given Nazi pageantry associated with the fallen party members of the "Beer-Hall Putsch" of 1923 at Munich, with the party rallies at Nürnberg, and with Hitler's birthday parades at Berlin, it is highly conceivable that the *Totenburgen* would have became shrines and pilgrimage sites. Cycles of civic ritual days of remembrance — much as with Memorial Day, or Armistice

Day, or Tombs of the Unknown Soldier with which we in the West are familiar — would undoubtedly have brought school children, Hitler Youth, party members, women's groups, veterans, and the like, to these sites, both to remember the dead heroes and to rededicate themselves to Party and Reich. The political function of the *Totenburgen* in many ways was a parallel to Joseph Goebbels' infamous "total war" rallies as well as to his propaganda films. In Kreis' words, "architecture is the language of the *Volk*," its letters carefully laid "stone upon stone." The monument, he stated, "tells and sings" and thereby "carries the observer along with it." It was not "cerebral" but of the soul of the *Volk*.[51] And it was "eternal." Even centuries later, when the granite might succumb to the forces of nature, Speer slyly suggested to Hitler, the monuments would still have great value as heroic "ruins."[52] Rome and the Third Reich linked even in decay.

As far as Hitler's architect of the "cult of heroic death" goes, the final verdict remains mixed. On the one hand, it is too far fetched to see in the *Totenburgen* simply an architectural expression of Nazi racial theory and doctrine. Kreis' life-long obsession with and constant reference to "Semitic" models— such as the Giza pyramids, the Egyptian mastaba, and the Etruscan and Numidian *Tumuli*— were hardly in line with "Aryan" mythology. On the other hand, Kreis as late as 1953 on the occasion of his eightieth birthday selected two "castles of the dead," the Panzer memorial in North Africa and the Dnieper monument in the Soviet Union, for a special exhibition of his life-long work. By then, the nature of Germany's barbaric war of racial extermination in the East was well known.

What remains of all the Third Reich's architecture? Some of Speer's projects can still be seen. In Berlin, part of the present Ministry of Foreign Affairs is housed in the former Central Bank of the Third Reich; and the current Ministry of Finance is sited in Hermann Göring's former Air Force Ministry. In Nürnberg, the Zeppelinfeld (minus eagles and swastikas) and the Stadium (now a truckers' storage facility) remain. In Munich, some of the former "Führerbau" complex still borders the Königsplatz. Perhaps most incredibly, Robert Tischler, a Kreis predecessor, unveiled the last of the *Totenburgen* first at Tobruk (1954–55) and then at El Alamein (1956–59)— at a time when he was well into his seventies. His postwar projects downplayed the national and the heroic and instead substituted Christian iconography (Crosses and Stations of the Cross).[53] Francisco Franco's massive *Valle de los Caidos*, completed in 1959, with its 150-meter-high Cross and 262-meter-long basilica certainly evoked memories of Speer's gigantomania. And the burial chant for its internees, "*Via la Muerte*," certainly paralleled Hitler's and Kreis' obsession with death.[54]

Last but not least, one of the many ironies of the Nazi past is that the largest stone monument in German-speaking Europe today is the mammoth Soviet war memorial in Berlin's Treptow Park, a design with great affinity to Kreis' creations.[55] And for those so inclined, "the word in stone" lives on in the music of Lucisferrato, who in 1998 released a limited edition album on the Russian label Black Dead Rabbit, with one track named "Totenburgen." It is distributed by "Stone Sound [*Steinklang*] Industries." Somehow the macabre always survives.

NOTES

1. *Völkischer Beobachter*, 23 January 1939.

2. Percy Ernst Schramm, ed., *Hitlers Tischgespräche im Führerhauptquartier 1941–1942* (Stuttgart, 1963), p. 323. Italics in the original.

3. Gerdy Troost, *Das Bauen im neuen Reich* (2 vols., Bayreuth, 1943), vol. I, pp. 10, 15, 20, 132, 157.

4. Schramm, ed., *Hitlers Tischgespräche*, p. 329. Entry for 12 May 1942.

5. *Ibid.*, p. 491. Entry for 29 July 1942.

6. See Manfred Hinz, *Massenkult und Todessymbolik in der Nationalsozialistischen Architektur* (Florence, 1982), p. 29.

7. Winfried Nerdinger and Ekkehard Mai, eds., *Wilhelm Kreis. Architekt zwischen Kaiserreich und Demokratie 1871–1955* (Munich and Berlin, 1994), p. 172; Albert Speer, *Neue deutsche Baukunst* (Berlin, 1941), pp. 7–8.

8. See Albert Speer, *Architektur. Arbeiten 1933–1942* (Frankfurt, 1978), pp. 164–74.

9. Adolf Hitler, *Mein Kampf* (Munich, 1939), p. 381.

10. Albert Speer, *Erinnerungen* (Berlin, 1969), p. 525. See also Jochen Thies, *Architekt der Weltherrschaft. Die "Endziele" Hitlers* (Düsseldorf, 1976).

11. Thies, *Architekt der Weltherrschaft*, p. 82.

12. Wolfgang Schäche, "Herrscher Tod. Krieg, Zerstörung, Opfer- und Todeskult in der NS-Architektur," *Daidalos* 38 (1990), pp. 53–56.

13. Speer, *Erinnerungen*, p. 82.

14. Nerdinger and Mai, eds., *Wilhelm Kreis*, pp. 211–12.

15. Speer, *Architektur*, pp. 186–7. See also Robert R. Taylor, *The Word in Stone: The Role of Architecture in the National Socialist Ideology* (Berkeley, Los Angeles, London, 1974), p. 195.

16. Friedrich Tamms, "Die Kriegerdenkmäler von Wilhelm Kreis," *Die Kunst im Deutschen Reich* 7 (March 1943), p. 57.

17. Hans Frank, *Im Angesicht des Galgens. Deutung Hitlers und seiner Zeit auf Grund eigener Erlebnisse und Erkenntnisse* (Munich-Gräfeling, 1953), p. 320. See also Barbara Miller Lane, *Architecture and Politics in Germany, 1918–1945* (Cambridge, MA, and London, 1985), pp. 189–90.

18. Speer, *Erinnerungen*, p. 148.

19. *Völkischer Beobachter*, 17 March 1941; Max Domarus, ed., *Hitler. Reden und Proklamationen, 1932–1945* (Munich, 1965), vol. II/2, *Untergang*, p. 1675. Kreis was also charged with designing some 200 soldiers' cemeteries and all warriors' monuments within the Reich (save for Berlin, Munich and Linz) costing more than 100,000 RM. Bundesarchiv (hereafter BA) Berlin, Circular, Ministry of the Interior, 27 March 1943.

20. The term *Totenburgen* was invented by modern art historians; Kreis simply yet graphically described them as *Kriegerehrenmäler*, "monuments honoring warriors."

21. "It is sweet and fitting to die for one's country."

22. Troost, *Das Bauen im neuen Reich*, vol. II, p. 7.

23. *Ibid.*, vol. I, pp. 40–42; and Taylor, *The Word in Stone*, p. 190.

24. Cited in Hildegard Brenner, *Die Kunstpolitik des Nationalsozialismus* (Munich, 1963), pp. 128–29.

25. *Ibid.*, pp. 139–40. See also Christian Gerlach, *Kalkulierte Morde. Die Deutsche Wirtschafts- und Vernichtungspolitik in Weissrussland 1941 bis 1944* (Hamburg, 1999).

26. See Helmut Heiber, "Der Generalplan Ost," *Vierteljahrshefte für Zeitgeschichte* 6 (October 1958), pp. 289–91, 297–324.

27. SS magazine, *Das Schwarze Korps*; cited in Paul B. Jakot, *The Architecture of Oppression: The SS, forced labor and the Nazi monumental building economy* (London and New York, 2000), p. 114.

28. The following descriptions are from Wilhelm Kreis, *Soldatengräber und Gedenkstätten* (Munich, 1944), pp. 65–66; Kreis, "Kriegermäle des Ruhmes und der Ehre im Altertum und in unserer Zeit," *Bauwelt* 34 (1943), pp. 1–8; Nerdinger and Mai, eds., *Wilhelm Kreis*, pp. 165–67; Meinhold Lurz, "Die Kriegerdenkmalsentwürfe von Wilhelm Kreis," *Die Dekoration der Gewalt. Kunst und Medien im Faschismus*, Berthold Hinz, et al., eds. (Giessen, 1979), pp. 185–97; and Gunnar Brands, "From World War I Cemeteries to the Nazi 'Fortresses of the Dead': Architecture, Heroic Landscape, and the Quest for National Identity in Germany," *Places of Commemoration: Search for Identity and Landscape Design*, Joachim Wolschke-Bulmahn, ed. (Washington, D. C., 2001), pp. 215–56.

29. Cited in Wolfgang Schäche, "Die 'Totenburgen' des Nationalsozialismus," *71 Arch+. Zeitschrift für Architekten, Stadtplaner, Sozialarbeiter und kommunalpolitische Gruppen* (October 1983), p. 73.

30. Oblong Egyptian tombs with sloping sides and a flat roof from the time of the Memphite Dynasties.

31. Hans Stephan, *Wilhelm Kreis* (Oldenburg, 1944), p. 86. Within the confines of his family, the Dnieper monument was sardonically dubbed "Stalingrad." Comment by Kreis' nephew cited in Nerdinger and Mai, eds., *Wilhelm Kreis*, p. 210.

32. Friedrich Tamms, "Die Kriegerehrenmäler von Wilhelm Kreis," *Die Baukunst. "Die Kunst im Deutschen Reich"* (March 1943), p. 57.

33. Kreis, "Kriegermäle des Ruhmes und der Ehre," in *Bauwelt* 34, pp. 1–8.

34. Domarus, ed., *Hitler*, vol. II/2, *Untergang*, p. 1999; Domarus, ed., *Hitler: Speeches and Proclamations*, vol. IV, p. 2772. Dated 17 March 1943. On 11 May 1943 Joseph Goebbels recorded in his diary that Hitler "was very pleased with the constructions of Professor Kreis for the heroes' monuments." Elke Fröhlich, ed., *Die Tagebücher Joseph Goebbels*, Part II, *Diktate 1941–1945*, vol. 8, *April— Juni 1943* (Munich, 1993), p. 273.

35. The Kreis records in the NSDAP files at the Bundesarchiv list an honorarium from Hitler of 30,000 RM for the architect's work in Dresden on 19 January 1938; an accounting tally on 20 January 1941 shows total honoraria for Dresden in the amount of 135,000 RM. BA, DS Wissenschaftler: Kreis, Wilhelm 17.3.1873.

36. In late 2005 Helmuth Arntz transferred the "Kreis-Archiv" from Castle Arntz at Bad Honnef down the Rhine River to the Historisches Archiv der Stadt Köln.

37. Nerdinger and Mai, eds., *Wilhelm Kreis*, p. 210. *Walhall* was "the dwelling of the fallen warriors"; *Walstatt* referred to a battleground; and *Termini* were ancient German "eternal" courts. See Elias Canetti, *Masse und Macht* (2 vols., Hamburg, 1960), vol. I, p. 73.

38. Nerdinger and Mai, eds., *Wilhelm Kreis*, p. 210.

39. Hinz, *Massenkult und Todessymbolik*, pp. 26, 86.

40. Alex Scobie, *Hitler's State Architecture: The Impact of Classical Antiquity* (University Park, PA, and London, 1990), pp. 133–37.

41. Anna Teut, *Architektur im Dritten Reich, 1933–1945* (Berlin, 1967), p. 189.

42. Troost, *Das Bauen im neuen Reich*, vol. I, pp. 10, 20, 132, 157.

43. Speer, *Erinnerungen*, p. 195. Comment of 21 June 1941.

44. Werner Jochmann, ed., *Adolf Hitler. Monologe im Führerhauptquartier 1941–1942* (Munich, 1980), p. 170. Dated 9 August 1942.

45. Albert Speer, *Infiltration* (New York, 1981), p. 211. The German title of the book, *Sklavenstaat*, comes much closer to the truth. Also, Scobie, *Hitler's State Architecture*, p. 130.

46. Thies, *Architekt der Weltherrschaft*, p. 101. See also Jan Erik Schulte, *Zwangsarbeit und Vernichtung. Das Wirtschaftsimperium der SS. Oswald Pohl und das SS-Wirtschafts- und Verwaltungshauptamt* (Paderborn, 2001); and Jaskot, *The Architecture of Oppression*.

47. George L. Mosse, *Fallen Soldiers: Reshaping the Memory of the World Wars* (Oxford, 1990), pp. 85–86.

48. Canetti, *Masse und Macht*, vol. I, p. 73.

49. Detlev J. K. Peukert, "The Genesis of the 'Final Solution' from the Spirit of Science," in Thomas Childers and Jane Caplan, eds., *Reevaluating the Third Reich* (New York and London, 1993), pp. 236, 241–2, 246.

50. I am indebted to my colleague, Dr. Annette Timm, for this observation. See also Michael Rissmann, *Hitlers Gott. Vorsehungsglaube und Sendungsbewusstsein des deutschen Diktators* (Zurich, 2001).

51. Kreis, "Kriegermäle des Ruhmes und der Ehre," in Teut, *Architektur im Dritten Reich*, p. 222.

52. Hinz, *Massenkult und Todessymbolik*, p. 77.

53. Mosse, *Fallen Soldiers*, pp. 86, 215.

54. See Sabine Kraft, "Das Tal der Gefallenen," *71 Arch+*, pp. 76–77.

55. Taylor, *The Word in Stone*, p. 191 n. 33.

The Superhero Comic Book
as War Memorial

Bart Beaty

In her article "Ambiguity as Persuasion," Sonja K. Foss argues that the particular visual features of the Vietnam Veterans Memorial in Washington, D.C., render it accessible to visitors on an affective level regardless of their predisposition with regard to the war. Specifically, she cites five contributing elements: the violation of the conventional forms of the war memorial; the welcoming stance of the memorial created by its physical shape, size and location; the lack of information provided to the visitor; the fact that attention is focused on those who did not survive the war; and the use of multiple referents for its visual components.[1] Foss is undoubtedly correct to highlight the significant ways in which Maya Lin's design for the Vietnam Veterans Memorial broke with the established traditions of the war memorial. Crucial in this regard were the rejection of realist portrayals of combatants, and the minimization of information about the war. The Memorial's V-shaped wall of black granite on which are engraved the names of the 57,930 American men and nine American women who died or are listed as missing during the war envelops the visitor into its space, even as it can overwhelm with the sheer expanse of names of the dead. In that sense, it works to construct a visual reminder of loss, rather than a celebration of the war. Foss argues that the abstract nature of the Memorial renders it ambiguous and open to contestation. To this end, she cites a number of critics of the Memorial who sought to have the design changed, and who successfully sued to have the realist sculpture "Three Fightingmen" and an American flag added to the site.[2] Yet, ultimately, Foss is pulled in somewhat contradictory directions regarding the Memorial, arguing on the one hand that its ambiguity stems from its status as a speech act (all of which are open to levels of interpretation

120

and contestation), and on the other that, through its design, the Memorial is more successful than most in reconciling audiences from diverse backgrounds and political viewpoints to a common emotional response.

The controversy that once engulfed the Vietnam Veterans Memorial can be read as the refusal of some to open monuments up to ambiguous, polyvocal or contestatory meanings. However, several of the more controversial contemporary memorials are not polyvocal, so much as they simply convey a message that is at odds with the triumphalism of traditional memorials. For example, Peter Eisenman's 2005 Memorial to the Murdered Jews of Europe in Berlin was constructed only after the previous winning design by Christine Jackob-Marks had been vetoed by German Chancellor Helmut Kohl. Eisenman's design, which is composed of 2,711 concrete slabs or "stelae," contains no textual information of any kind and itself has been criticized both for contributing to a German "Holocaust industry" as well as for neglecting to memorialize other victims of the Holocaust. Similarly, the World Trade Center Memorial in New York has had the winning design by Michael Arad re-conceptualized by landscape architect Peter Walker in order to reduce its severity. The placement of the names of those who died as a result of the attacks on the World Trade Center has become a source of controversy, with representatives of the New York City Fire and Police Departments insisting on the separation of officers' names from civilians killed, and an indication of the service, badge, rank, and assignment of all fallen officers. Additionally, plans to incorporate a Drawing Center and an International Freedom Center were canceled for having little to do with the events of 11 September 2001, and for the possibility that the instructional centers might include material critical of the United States or its policies.

The apprehension about the instructional centers particularly highlight the important ways in which active participants often wish memorials to minimize the kind of ambiguity that Foss identifies in Maya Lin's work, while the anxieties over the lack of referential specificity in the designs of Eisenman and Arad demonstrate one of the difficulties of allowing memorials to remain under-determined. The process of building dialogue and multi-purposiveness into a memorial carries the possibility of destabilizing the fixed nature of the interpretative project, allowing the possibility that competing and contrasting visions will remain unreconciled, resting beyond the desired limits of the discursive frame. In short, the very polyvocality that is so celebrated in the democratic tradition that informs so many of these memorials becomes a danger in the memorializing process as its ambiguities work to undermine the creation of officially sanctioned meanings.

By contrast, mass mediated popular culture, with its traditional reliance on polyvocality and on rapid processes of generic transformation would seem to be clearly at odds with the dominant traditions of the war memorial. The source of this tension stems first of all from the fact that the dramatic structure of film, television and comic books is largely dependent on the presentation of divergent viewpoints that the text works to resolve. Indeed, the construction of dramatic tension crucially relies on the creation of characters that have conflicting values, goals, or desires, and the resolution of that tension is achieved through the reconciliation of opposing viewpoints either through mutual accommodation or the defeat of one party by the other. By offering up these opposing viewpoints, the popular cultural text is opened as a space for interpretation, contestation and debate. Of course, all texts and all cultural artifacts are subject to interpretation, but popular culture seems to be more open to disparate readings than civic or national memorials, for reasons that have to do with generic constraints. To express things in a reductionist manner, war memorials are historical, while popular culture is topical. From the Arc de Triomphe to the Tomb of the Unknown Soldier, celebrations of military struggle are visually designed to be timeless signifiers, pilgrimage sites that will resonate for generations. Popular culture, on the other hand, has no such mandate and is fascinated by the topical and the novel. Keenly aware that fashions change with the times, popular culture is highly invested in staying on top of fads, and cultural industries are designed for a high degree of flexibility and change so as to be responsive to shifting audience interests and demands. In other words, memorials endure as history while the artifacts of popular culture fade into memory. The difference has as much to do with the physical construction of memorials and with the generic conventions of the civic culture in which they are built and for which they are intended, as it does with popular culture. In the case of the former, the goal is to create something that reflects the official discourse of state and citizenry, a monument that speaks directly to a public sphere in the Habermasian sense. In the case of the latter, its meanings are deliberately open to negotiation and contestation in order to appeal to multiple audiences.

Popular culture artifacts are generally not made of stone or metal, but of far less sturdy materials. Furthermore, they tend not to operate primarily at the level of the symbolic, but as narratives. Indeed, the most commonly prevalent forms of popular culture — film, television, novels, and even music — are media for storytelling and for reflecting on the culture in which they are created. In the drive for topicality, popular culture focuses primarily, some would argue exclusively, on its uses for contemporary audiences, with little regard for the audiences of future generations. This sense of timeliness is one factor that makes the products of popular culture ripe for analysis, since, insofar as they can be read as symptomatic of discursive formations that existed at the time of their creation, they are often regarded as windows into attitudes from the past. Yet at the same time, the formal complexity of popular cultural artifacts undermines their value as memorial objects. Indeed, I wish to argue that a certain hallmark of popular culture — its discursive ambiguity — problematizes the idea of the popular cultural memorial. While some may see this as exclusively the failure of popular culture, I want to stipulate that it is as much, if not more, one of the limitations of memorials. In other words, and despite the claims made by Foss, the memorial's status as a static and weighty object mitigates against an ongoing, fluid construction.

In identifying five features that contribute to the success of the Vietnam Veterans Memorial, Foss provides a guide through which it is also possible to conceptualize the limitations of the popular cultural war memorial project that relies on a narrative structure. In the wake of "9/11" that most triumphalist of American popular culture genres, the superhero comic book, attempted to memorialize the event, but its inherent generic constructions made the task near-impossible. Centrally, the two features of narrative-based popular culture that work to undermine its memorializing possibilities are ambiguity, which is a function of dialogue and dramatic structure, and topicality, which is a sub-function of novelty and innovation. Thus, the conventions of the comic book adventure series require the reinsertion of almost all of the elements that contemporary memorial art eschews: realist imagery, references to ongoing conflicts, and a clearly identified educational component. While the presence of well-known and well-loved popular characters might serve as a welcoming entry point to the memorial, not dissimilar to the comforting role of Lin's V-shaped wall, the need to create dramatic conflict in order to provide structure to the narrative carries with it the threat of utilizing not just multiple referents, but even too many of them. The requirements of drama enable the possibility of discursive chaos, and the very function of narrative presupposes the creation of counter-readings that mitigate against the memorializing purpose identified by the creators. In short, while both traditional war memorials and their newer counterparts seek consensus through the narrowing of discursive entry points and the minimization of ambiguity, popular culture works awkwardly as a memorializing enterprise insofar as its narrative demands to authorize potentially contradictory, and therefore inflammatory, discursive regimes.

Captain America in a Post-9/11 World

The difficulty of the popular cultural war memorial is particularly highlighted by the efforts of Marvel Comics, America's leading publisher of superhero comic books, to transform Captain America into an ongoing memorial to the victims of the high-jacking of four American commercial jets by Islamic terrorists on 11 September 2001. Captain America is a comic book superhero character originally created by writer Joe Simon and artist Jack Kirby for Timely Comics. He debuted in the first issue of his eponymous magazine in March 1941, nine months prior to the entry of the United States into World War II. In the first issue, which featured an image of the star-spangled hero punching Adolf Hitler in the jaw, Captain America was introduced as a hyper-patriotic artist named Steve Rogers, a 90-pound weakling transformed into a superman through an injection of the experimental Super Soldier serum. With his teenaged sidekick, Bucky, Captain America spent the war fighting German and Japanese special agents, protecting America from fifth columnists, and assisting American soldiers on the battlefront. Following the end of the war, public demand for the adventures of Captain America waned and the title was canceled in 1950. Two failed attempts to revive the character took place in the 1950s, before Captain America was resurrected for good in 1964 as the leader of Marvel Comics' superhero all-star team, The Avengers. Captain America was featured in his own adventures in the magazine *Tales of Suspense*, whose title was changed to *Captain America* in 1968. In 1996, after 454 monthly issues, the *Captain America* comic book was re-launched as *Captain America* volume two, under the creative control of artist-writer Rob Liefeld. In 1998 a third volume was launched, and in 2002, following the events of 11 September 2001, a fourth volume began featuring the work of writer John Ney Rieber and artist John Cassady. It is under their direction that Captain America was re-conceptualized as an ongoing narrative memorial.

The most distinctive feature of the fourth volume of *Captain America* was the fact that it so self-consciously positioned itself as a self-perpetuating popular cultural memorial to the victims of the events of 11 September. Indeed, the first issue featured a cover depicting a flag-bearing Captain America emerging from a smoky background looming over an image of rushing American soldiers and a sky filled with World War II bombers. Captain America, a personage whose insertion into the American military apparatus is implied by the rank that acts as part of his name, is here militarized for a new generation through this alignment of contemporary circumstances with the actions of the so-called "greatest generation." In this way, Rieber and Cassady amplify Captain America's origins as a militaristic hero of World War II to render an explicit connection between otherwise wholly disparate historical and contemporary events. At the same time, the specificity of the memorializing project is made explicit with a dedication at the end of the first issue from writer John Ney Rieber which reads, in part, "may our hearts and hands continue to work together to create an enduring memorial to the victims and the heroes of that day." Given the stated intention, therefore, the pressing issue becomes: what kind of memorial did the hearts and hands of Rieber and Cassady create?

From Realism to Super-Realism

From the very first page of the new *Captain America*, there is no doubt that the comic book series is witnessing a return to topicality unseen since the era of World War II. Entitled "The New Deal," it is a clear reference to President Franklin Roosevelt's "New Deal" that introduced social programs into a Depression-ravaged American economy and emphasized the responsibility of government to oversee the welfare of its citizens. By contrast, Rieber and Cassady's "new deal" seems to only refer to a vague idea that, in terms of geopolitical relations, all bets were off and in the present situation, America had the right to play any cards it had, even ones dealt from the bottom of the deck.[3] The issue opens aboard one of the four hijacked jetliners before shifting to images of a smiling Osama Bin Laden in a cave. The scene then returns to the ruins of the World Trade Center, where Captain America, out of uniform and acting in the role of Steve Rogers, assists in the search for survivors. That Captain America first appears in the story as Steve Rogers, his alter-ego, is telling. While the familiar figure of Captain America would be comforting, or, to use Foss' term, "welcoming" to some readers, the authors opt instead to remind the reader that their hero is, at an important level, merely a man. The de-emphasizing of Captain America's super-heroic capabilities is bolstered by the futility of his search for survivors in the wreckage, and by his acknowledgement that he had been powerless to prevent the attacks; as when he declares "I wasn't here." Clearly, the insertion of the reality of the attacks on the World Trade Center into the fantastical plots of a superhero comic book series carries certain problems. Not the least of these is the fact that, in the long history of Captain America and his fellow superheroes in the Marvel Universe, New York, the United States, the planet, and even the universe had been repeatedly saved from the destruction threatened by marauding super-villains. The question that is immediately posed is how, in the fantasy world of Captain America, could these events have taken place? The poverty of Rogers' answer highlights the first major failing of *Captain America* as a memorializing project: the conventions and generic history implied by the superhero narrative make it an awkward fit for discussions of real world social crises.

Foss identifies the Vietnam Veterans Memorial rupture of the realist tendencies of the war memorial as one of its key strengths.[4] The comic book series *Captain America* similarly breaks with realism, but it does so in order to re-conceptualize it as a form of super-realism that is even more removed from everyday concerns. Significantly, it is only a few pages into the first issue of *Captain America* that he has shed his civilian identity and returned to the streets as a masked vigilante crime fighter. In this scene, he is shown saving an American-born Arab named Samir from a vengeance-driven knife attack. Rieber, using narration by Captain America as a means of speaking directly to the reader, takes this opportunity to preach against retribution: "We can hunt them down. We can scour every blood-stained trace of their terror from the earth. We can turn every stone they've ever touched to dust, and every blade of grass to ash. And it won't matter. We've got to be stronger than we've ever been. As a people. As a nation. We have to be America. Or they've won." With its moralizing tone and celebration of abstract nationalist ideals, the first issue of *Captain America: The New Deal* addresses its readers in a memorializing fashion, moving through tragedy, grief and a return to action. If it stopped there, then its memorializing function may have possibly been complete, but Captain America is not a memorial for those who have perished, but necessarily, as a pop culture narrative, must ultimately focus on that return to action and the kinds of open-ended possibilities and ruptures it engenders.

The particular form of action envisioned by Rieber and Cassady for Captain America, and, by extension, for the United States, is the protection of the innocent against those who would do them unjustified and unjustifiable harm. This "us versus them" logic, which is so centrally embedded in the narrative structure of the superhero story, is built into Captain America's rhetoric of "we have to be America, or they've won," a rhetoric that is deployed over the next several issues of the series in the form of an action adventure. At the conclusion of the first issue, Captain America is dispatched to a small American town on Easter Sunday to battle an Arab terrorist named Al-Tariq, who has taken hostage an entire church full of Christian worshippers. The hero and villain in this drama are broadly drawn caricatures, virtually begging to be read as stand-ins for the American version of a national religion that heals and bonds versus the Middle East's fanatical and destructive Islamicism. Al-Tariq is described as "a monster," and actually describes himself with the phrase "I am hate." This stands in stark contrast to Captain America's statement: "This is America. We don't make war on children." In the ensuing fight scene, a requirement of the genre, Captain America, hero of World War II, fights a group of turban-clad Arab men wielding axes, an image that strongly reinforces anti–Muslim slurs that suggest that Islam is a medieval religion of a backward civilization. Indeed, much of the post–9/11 Captain America could easily be read through the lens of neo-conservative conceptions of America's relationship to those it deems terrorists, from the conception of America as global innocent to the barbaric nature of its Islamic enemies, and through the explicit visual connection that is established between the current "war on terror" and World War II, a connection that tends to reinforce the notion of so-called "Islamofascism" with the Nazis, thereby seeking a moral equivalence of the war fought by the "greatest generation" against a universally reviled enemy with the far more politically contentious invasions of Afghanistan and Iraq.

The Crisis of Dialogue

Based exclusively on the first issue of the fourth volume, it might be easy to dismiss, as some critics do, *Captain America* as simple-minded patriotic propaganda that presents the United States as a place of pure good and its opponents as emblems of pure evil. Nonetheless, the story direction followed by Rieber and Cassady in the ensuing issues problematized that conception of the hero through the introduction of self-doubt and a dialogue with the enemy. In the introduction to the collected edition of the story, writer Max Allan Collins celebrates the work for its "courage and ability to examine the complexities of the issues that accompany terrorism ... specifically, not to duck the things America has done to feed the attacks." The tendency is exemplified by the third issue, in which Captain America begins to have misgivings about his role as a superhero and the role of the United States globally. He asks himself: "Are we only hated because we're free—free and prosperous and good? Or does the light we see cast shadows that we don't— where monsters like this Al-Tariq can plant the seeds of hate?"

Following this logic, the fifth issue takes the deviation from hyper-patriotic rhetoric even further, interestingly using its own rhetorical device against itself. Previous attempts to draw parallels with World War II emphasized its standing as a "good war" with clearly-cut heroes and villains, with America very unambiguously on the side of the former. By the fifth issue, however, the creators draw a connection between the events of

11 September and the firebombing of Dresden by Allied airmen on 13 and 14 February 1945. In so doing, they mobilize a particularly contentious memory of American action against civilian targets during World War II in order to undermine conceptions of American innocence, conceptions that they, themselves, had invoked unproblematically in the first issue. Captain America tells himself: "You didn't understand what we'd done here — until September the 11th. These people weren't soldiers. They huddled in the dark. Trapped.... And when there was nothing left to breathe there in the dark, they died.... History repeats itself like a machine gun." Needless to say, this tendency is at odds with the dominant traditions of the memorializing project, which tends to underplay complexity or any suggestion of mutual culpability.

The introduction of Dresden into the story of Captain America's battle with Muslim terrorists suddenly and dramatically redirects the flow of the narrative. By the sixth issue and the culmination of the "New Deal" story arc, the true villain is revealed not as Al-Tariq, but as an unnamed master-villain who bears a grudge against the United States as a result of an undisclosed incident from one of America's previous colonialist adventures in Africa, Asia or Latin America. During the pivotal battle scene, the mastermind proclaims that American interventionism is what has made him the monster that he is: "You know your history, Captain America....You played that game in too many places.... The sun never set on your political chessboard- your empire of blood." Captain America responds that, presumably since the events of 11 September, the United States has changed: "My people never knew. We know now and those days are over." While such statements offer a conciliatory breath of fresh air that was sorely lacking in public and political debate over 9/11, it also serves to forgive America by proclaiming that the days of economic and military imperialism are over. The dialogue between Captain America and his adversary, and the super-hero's half-hearted acknowledgement of America's role in the tragic circumstances is not only crucial for the creation of a coherent plot within the confines of the superhero adventure comic book story. It also establishes the fatal narrative contradictions that undermine the memorializing project in the eyes of so many readers. Logic necessitates that the villain have a motive for his vengeful plan, and the requirements of realism, even within the conventions of the superhero story, dictate that this motive be psychologically plausible. The requirements of narrative complexity, however delimited by generic constraints, sit uneasily in relation to the therapeutic and propagandistic needs of traditional memorials, which tend to eschew meaningful dialogue of any kind in favor of a monologue of righteousness. Hence, while Captain America's admissions provide necessary psychological support to the narrative, it does so begrudgingly and not necessarily convincingly. Yet, even this small effort was enough to stir controversy.

The presence of self-questioning and dialogue with the enemy posed a significant ideological problem for some critics of the *Captain America* series, who viewed it not as the memorial that Rieber had pledged in the first issue, but as a further attack on the United States itself. Writing in the conservative *National Review*, in an article entitled "Captain America, Traitor?," Michael Medved called the moral equation of the firebombing of Dresden and attacks on the World Trade Center "illogical and obscene."[5] His article accuses Rieber and Cassady of promoting anti-governmental conspiracy theories, and contributing to a "blame-America" logic that is more commonly found among "Hollywood activists, academic apologists, or the angry protesters who regularly fill the streets of European capitals" than in stalwartly patriotic superhero comic books. To reach his conclusion that *Captain America* is a traitorous comic book, Medved necessarily has to presume one of two things. First, that readers will agree with the truth value of statements uttered by the villain in a fantasy piece; or, second, that giving voice to any sentiment critical of the United States, even when the narrative resolves to undermine the validity of that voice, is inherently harmful. In a pluralist democracy the condemnation of polyvocality carries with it significant political and ethical consequences. Simply put, it is an argument against freedom of expression in the name of preserving democratic ideals of freedom. While Medved does not grapple with these implications, it is worth noting how the very introduction of self-doubt and dialogue carry with it the potential of undoing the memorializing project in the eyes of some critics.

Medved's reading of Captain America as distinctly anti–American also needs to contend with the counterargument proposed by Robert Jewett and John Shelton Lawrence who, in their book *Captain America and the Crusade Against Evil*, utilize Captain America as an exemplar of what they term "zealous nationalism."[6] While not specifically addressing the comics by Rieber and Cassady, Jewett and Shelton condemn the legacy of *Captain America* comic books for their doggedly Americanist worldview and their tendency to present the United States as an unproblematized force for truth, justice and democracy. The authors argue that Captain America represents the tension that exists between the type of nationalism that is rooted in the destruction of external enemies and in a "prophetic realism" that seeks to redeem the world for coexistence."[7] Arguing for the superiority of the coexistence model as a response to terrorism, they suggest with regard to Captain America that the "time has come for a dignified retirement."[8] For Jewett and Shelton, the play between entertainment and serious political issues carries the threat of pulling audiences away from "our democratic ideals."[9] Thus, it is possible to see that critics on both ends of the American political spectrum regard the integration of the superhero narrative with real-life events as an inherent danger, one that risks giving aid and comfort to the enemy on the one hand, or which serves through its generic constraints to inoculate readers against the full complexity of real world events on the other. The tension between these readings, a tension that is fundamentally the result of efforts to bring together elements of topicality within the confines of the fantastic melodrama, is a function of the ambiguity that enters the equation when popular cultural texts activate so many signifiers that they can no longer be easily reconciled to a single message.

While Foss praises the apparent ambiguity of the Vietnam Veterans Memorial, it is clear that in the case of Captain America an over-abundance of ambiguity results in the breakdown of the memorializing message. Yet this effect is central to the narrative demands of popular culture. Further, it seems likely that the ideological divide described above is, at least in part, a function of the heightened sensitivity to political issues that occurs when memorializing artifacts are created so closely to the events that they depict. Given the number of controversies that plague memorials to events in wars past, especially World War II which is frequently — and naively — deemed the least problematic and most righteous war of the twentieth century, it is not surprising that any effort to memorialize 9/11 would be met with resistance from all sides. Rieber and Cassady's *Captain America*, launched a mere month after the events of 11 September 2001, seemed destined to draw criticism because the topicality that is demanded by audiences and presented by cultural creators necessarily runs the risk of touching too many raw nerves, generating debate rather than the solace and celebration that is supposed to be the function of traditional war memorials.

The Problem of the Ongoing Memorial

When Captain America tells the super-villain, "My people never knew. We know now and those days are over," a third complication is introduced into the idea of *Captain America* as a memorializing project. Foss observes that one of the strengths of traditional memorials is the way that they place emphasis on those who have perished, rather than focusing on ongoing struggles or conflicts.[10] The case of Captain America is thus problematized in two ways. First, the conflict to which it refers continues to be ongoing in the foreign policy of the Bush White House and has expanded to new fronts including Afghanistan and Iraq. Second, the ongoing nature of *Captain America* as a comic book series, and the demands of topicality established by Rieber and Cassady by their decision to tie the fictional continuity to real-life events, means precisely that "those days" can never be over. The velocity of the superhero comic book series is extremely rapid by the standards of the mass media, with new installments released every month over the course of decades. Yet the velocity of current global geopolitics is even swifter, and by tying the two together, Rieber and Cassady construct a narrative apparatus that runs the risk of being perpetually unsettled by new events.

This tendency is similarly evident in something as simple as presidential approval ratings. For example, George Bush's approval rating in the immediate aftermath of the 9/11 attacks was 86 percent. By May 2006, with the invasion of Iraq losing public support, his approval rating had plummeted to 30 percent and even lower according to some polls. Ongoing historical developments and processes of change are the primary reason that Captain America's status as an ongoing cultural production comes into conflict with the fixed traditions of memorials.

Conclusion

Significantly, Captain America was alone in the comic book field, and perhaps in popular culture generally, in attempting to construct a memorial that might run for all time. A large number of comic books have been released dealing with the events of 11 September 2001, but the vast majority of these were conceived as stand-alone volumes. The most significant and respected comic about the attacks on the World Trade Center is *In the Shadow of No Towers*, by Art Spiegelman, the Pulitzer-prize winning creator of the Holocaust memorial graphic novel, *Maus*. It was initially serialized in a number of European and American newspapers over the course of a year, but was always intended as a single, complete short work (it is only twelve pages long) about the events of that day. Moreover, while Spiegelman's work is highly topical, it is also, in the tradition of *Maus*, extremely personal. The work details this New York-based artist's personal reaction to the events of that day, their impact on his family, and the lasting psychological legacy of what he witnessed. As frequent contributor to *The New Yorker* magazine, and with strong ties to the New York arts and culture community, Spiegelman's voice carried with it deep personal and aesthetic connotations. Furthermore, his cultural capital as the author of *Maus*, regarded by many as the pinnacle of comics art achievement in

America, made him especially fit for the task of comics memorialization. Since it is not conceptualized as a long-running, open-ended memorial in the same fashion as *Captain America, In the Shadow of No Towers* succeeds better as a narrative work with a beginning and an ending because it is able to function in a less ambiguous manner than does the ongoing superhero tale. While both can be seen as important artifacts of popular culture, the generic constraints of the confessional autobiographical essay hold important distinctions from the open-ended adventure series, and the works function in very different ways because of this distinction.

Significantly, the conception of *Captain America* as a perpetually renewing memorial to the victims of the World Trade Center attacks ran into grave difficulties very quickly. As a product of a large publishing industry that ultimately owned all rights to the character, the deeply personal vision that was possible in *No Towers* was both economically and aesthetically impossible here. Taking a more detailed examination of the first six issues of the post–9/11 *Captain America*, it becomes clear that only the first issue could truly be termed memorializing. From the moment that Captain America begins his battle with Al-Tariq, the comic opens itself up to forms of information and dialogue that activate a number of disparate interpretations that undermine the author's stated intentions. Moreover, numerous personnel changes and editorial shifts dramatically altered both the narrative direction and character psychology of the comic series. Shortly after the initial story was completed, writer John Ney Rieber was fired from the title by Marvel editor-in-chief Joe Quesada. Rieber told the comics news site, *Newsarama*, "Probably the simplest way that I can describe what happened is that Joe Quesada has a very clear vision about what he wants Cap to be, and my Cap just wasn't quite what he was looking for."[11] Rieber was replaced by Chuck Austen, who wrapped up the former writer's storylines before he himself was replaced as writer by Dave Gibbons. Gibbons' story was completely removed from topical issues and featured a tale in which the villains were time-traveling Nazis.

With the twenty-first issue, Robert Morales became the writer and sent Captain America as a judge to a trial at Guantanamo Bay, where he learns that Saddam Hussein's weapons of mass destruction have been transferred to Havana by Al-Qaeda agents. This kind of wishful thinking narrative signals clearly that Captain America is no longer questioning American culpability in global conflicts. With the twenty-ninth issue, Morales was replaced by Robert Kirkman, who returned the title squarely to its pre–9/11 roots, with stories featuring Captain America fighting a familiar cast of fantastical super-villains. In 2005 the fourth volume of the title was discontinued and then re-launched under writer Ed Brubaker, who disavowed the topical approach taken by Rieber: "I'm trying to find that balance with him between what Rieber and Morales did in their books, in keeping it connected with the real day, but I don't want to go that political. I don't want to be talking about internment camps. I don't want to be talking about Muslims too much, or much of any of the other things that are happening in the real world, because it's a superhero comic."[12] For Brubaker, the problem with Captain America is that it had gotten away from the fantastic component that is represented by the concept of the Marvel Universe, a fictive space that operates parallel to the world that we inhabit. Popular culture, dealing as it does with fantasy rather than reality, is seen therefore as an inappropriate vehicle for memorializing the real world.

In point of fact, the ongoing memorialization of the events of 11 September lasted only six months on the pages of *Captain America*. By the seventh issue, the hero was fighting native American terrorists; by the twelfth he was "duking" it out with the survivors of Atlantis, as fantasy had clearly overwhelmed reality on the pages of the memorializing comic book. Of course, this has always been the case. In 1972 Captain America made his only visit to the Vietnam War, where rather than fighting the Vietcong he battled the evil super-villain, The Mandarin, a figure intent on prolonging the war to serve his own nefarious ends. In the realm of the superhero, fantasy has always been the order of the day, and in real life no star-spangled crime fighter ever socked it to Hitler in the jaw. This distinction between fantasy and reality is central to the shortcomings of *Captain America: The New Deal* as a memorializing project. In the triumphalist discourse of contemporary American foreign policy, history rolls ever forward, marred only by the occasional crisis. The superhero narrative, on the other hand, is predicated on a narrative context of perpetual and ongoing crises that ill serve the process of remembrance and reflection. Memorials of stone and steel make meaning by enduring unchanged. Yet change is a constant in popular culture and it is a feature that serves to disqualify it from service in a memorializing context. Five years after it was completed, *Captain America: The New Deal* is remembered simply as a well-intentioned and patriotic misstep in the long trajectory of a popular cultural hero. Ultimately, the process of popularizing memories of war through the adventures of a four-color hero was overtaken by structural forces inherent in the cultural industries themselves. Captain America was laid low not by his fictional enemies but by the irreconcilability of real world trauma and popular cultural grief.

NOTES

1. Sonja K. Foss, "Ambiguity as Persuasion. The Vietnam Veterans Memorial," *Communication Quarterly* 34 (Summer 1986), pp. 331–32.

2. *Ibid.*, p. 327

3. John Ney Rieber and John Cassady, *Captain America: The New Deal* (New York, 2002).

4. Foss, "Ambiguity as Persuasion," p. 332.

5. Michael Medved, "Captain America, Traitor?," *The National Review Online*, 4 April 2003. http://www.nationalreview.com/comment-medved040403.asp

6. Robert Jewett and John Shelton Lawrence, *Captain America and the Crusade Against Evil: The Dilemma of Zealous Nationalism* (Grand Rapids, MI, 2003), p. 8.

7. *Ibid.*

8. *Ibid.*, p. 9.

9. *Ibid.*, p. 39.

10. Foss, "Ambiguity as Persuasion," p. 335.

11. Matt Brady, "Rieber Off Cap, Austen On," *Newsarama*, 19 December 2002. http://www.forum.newsrama.com/showthread.php?t=651

12. Matt Brady, "Ed Brubaker on Captain America," *Newsrama*, 24 September 2004. http://www.newsrama.com/pages/Marvel/Bru_Cap.htm

The BBC's "People's War" Website

Lucy Noakes

At the beginning of the twenty-first century, memories of World War II continue to be a very visible aspect of British culture. The late twentieth century has seen a "memory boom" with regard to the means and the extent to which societies remember war.[1] This process shows no apparent signs of slowing down. In recent years Europe has commemorated not only the 60th anniversaries of D-Day and VE-Day, but also the anniversary of the liberation of Auschwitz as Holocaust Memorial Day slowly becomes an established part of the European calendar. Popular television programs, both fictional and documentary, and those which merge the two such as *Band of Brothers* and *Dunkirk* continue to represent the Second World War to eager audiences, as do museum displays such as Portsmouth D-Day Museum's "D-Day Tapestry" and the Imperial War Museum's "Blitz Experience." Significantly, young people and children remain interested in the war years, as evidenced by the popularity of children's novels set during the war years, of University courses examining World War II and the teaching of wartime history to all state educated primary school age children in the country.[2] The British, despite their divergent identities, appear to retain a fascination with the wartime years; a period which is still recalled in popular memory as a time when the nation was united behind a common aim and shared identity.

The presence of the war in contemporary society is achieved and assured by the process of remembrance and acts of commemoration at many levels. While remembrance can be understood as the often complex and shared social memory of an event or period such as wartime, acts of commemoration are the active means by which this process of remembrance is more formally avowed. They can take place on an international stage, as seen in Holocaust Memorial Day, on a national stage, as seen in Australia's commemoration of Anzac Day, and at a more personal level, perhaps by placing flowers at a grave or memorial or by visiting the site of a battle. For many who lived through the war, it remains a significant part of their life story; a period of historical consequence which they experienced and to which they contributed. Many families have wartime stories of both civilian and military life, which are told and retold, passed on through the generations. These individual and family memories are drawn together and become public in the more public, collective acts of commemoration which can be understood as one aspect of the "sites of memory" identified by the French historian Pierre Nora.[3] Nora has argued that the creation of sites of memory necessarily entails a process of sifting or refining, in which particular memories— those which sit most easily with current constructions of national identity — take precedence over other, more difficult memories. These sites of memory are not fixed; rather, their social and cultural meanings and their function, both as sites for collective commemoration and as spaces where remembrance is expressed and shared, can change and evolve over time. As the shared remembrance of wartime continues to evolve and change, so new sites of memory appear. Technological and social change enables the opening up of new spaces where collective remembrance takes place. In recent years the internet has become a key site for the collection and transmission of individual wartime memories, helping to transform separate and sometimes disparate acts of remembering into new, shared, sites of remembrance.

Websites have provided platforms for people to record their experiences of the war and for families to share personal, family memories of wartime, such as stories, letters and photographs with a much wider audience. In contrast to Nora's conception of sites of memory being created "from above," websites provide a more informal space where memories "from below" can be more widely shared and disseminated than in traditional, formally constituted sites such as memorials, museums and textbooks. Students researching World War II for school or college projects regularly post questions about the war on discussion boards such as bbc.co.uk/forums/history, and responses to these come not just from professional and amateur historians, but from those with personal experience and memories of the war. As these technologies become more accessible and more widespread, used and viewed by more extensive numbers of people we can assume that given the ongoing fascination with the war, the number of privately created resources will continue to flourish. Websites which hold large collections of diverse individual memories of an event such as World War II should be understood as a new form of historical remembrance. In some ways analogous to the archives of letters and auto-biographical writing accessed by historians who then go on to produce more widely read syntheses of these materials, websites effectively produce a mass of "primary material" which can be read by anyone with an interest in the subject and with internet access. They thus have the potential to both open up and undercut existing communal remembrance of the war. Unlike museums, novels, television programs, and films—the sites of "prosthetic memory" identified by Alison Landsberg as mediated representations of memory, which enable the modern audience to identify and empathize with others' past experiences—websites such as "The People's War" are less commodified, present a less unified picture of the past, and thus are often contradictory.[4] Indeed, the memories recorded in this way have the potential to be refined and to then feed into publicly produced sites of memory, as evidenced by the BBC's desire to draw on individuals' memories of the war in their programming, "turning the audience into content generators and giving them a platform to tell their stories."[5] Thus, these new technologies have the potential to widen the range of memories accessible on the public stage and to feed into and reshape shared remembrance of the war.

However, despite the promise of new technology opening up the "public stage" to all and enabling the inclusion of memories which were previously marginal to or excluded from collective remembrance of the war, we need to consider whether all memories are equal within these new sites of memory, or whether the actual process of remembering and of deciding to record an aspect of memory means that some experiences and some identities are privileged over others. In recent years a body of work has emerged which interrogates the relationship between gender, war, experience, and identity. Research by scholars such as Janet K. Watson, Sonya O. Rose and Penny Summerfield has examined the relationship between the lived experience of wartime, gendered identity and memory.[6] Both Summerfield and Watson focus on the ways in which wars are remembered and made sense of, while Rose considers the construction and understanding of national identity during wartime. However, they have a shared emphasis on the importance of gender as a factor which plays a central role in shaping both the experience and remembrance of war. Watson demonstrated how the popular memory of World War I has emphasized the experience of the trench soldier on the Western Front above all other experiences of the war, while Summerfield explored the ways in which women's accounts of their lives during World War II were shaped by their experiences of warfare, by their lives since, and, crucially, by the process of remembering and speaking, in this case in interviews with oral historians. In her exploration of the contested nature of national identity in wartime, Rose identified the essential instability of models of femininity in wartime. These recent, important examinations of war, memory, gender, and identity indicate the plurality of identities, experiences and memories of war which continue to co-exist. However, some wartime memories and identities, as Watson suggested in her research on memories of World War I, are prioritized above others. In Britain these tend to fall into two separate but interwoven groups: memories which emphasize the experiences of the combatant man and those which fit within the continuing popular memory of the "people's war." This chapter examines the relationship of gender to the shaping of remembrance of the World War II in contemporary British culture, focusing on the memories recorded on the BBC's "People's War" website.

The BBC "People's War" Website

The website was launched in June 2003 and collected people's memories of the war until January 2006, when the 47,000 written pieces and 15,000 images posted were archived. Many different forms and styles of writing are included on the website. Together with the memories entered onto the website by individuals or spoken to volunteers and then entered, are 367 books, 196 diary entries, 246 letters, and 365 poems. Many of these have photographic illustrations of the author during the war. Thus, alongside the shorter autobiographical stories and family memories entered on the site are lengthier autobiographies and artifacts written and produced both during and following the war years. Within the shorter autobiographical stories, the style of writing varies greatly. While some entries were so lengthy that they were broken down and entered as two or three separate, linked chapters, others were only a few sentences long. Overall, the number and variety of entries on the website indicate a widespread desire among those who experienced the war and their families to share these experiences more widely. The site was originally conceived for the "children and grandchildren of war veterans," where they "would research their family history and tell their family's wartime stories." This idea demonstrated both the ongoing importance of memories of the war to family histories and the belief that older people would be unfamiliar with the technology involved and thus be either unwilling or unable to enter their own memories onto the site.[7] However, it soon became apparent that veterans of the war were interested enough in recording their memories, referred to as stories on the website, to overcome any aversion to, or unfamiliarity with, the new technology involved. Indeed, market research commissioned by the BBC in November 2004 showed that 80 percent of the contributors to the site by that point were aged 60 or over, a remarkable figure considering that in the same year only 12 percent of the British population aged over 65 claimed any familiarity with the internet.[8] To make the site accessible to as many people as possible, the BBC recruited more than 2,000 volunteers who were trained as "story gatherers" working out of approximately 2,500 associate centers such as libraries, museums, schools, and day centers, which war veterans could visit in order to be helped to enter their stories on the site. Stories were also collected at big public events which older people with personal memories of the war were likely to attend, for example 1940s tea parties, air shows and commemorations and celebrations of key wartime dates such as D-Day and VE-Day. Indeed, the large public commemorations of the war years that took place during 2005 appear to have encouraged contributors to enter their wartime memories on the website, with 31,557 separate stories being logged on the site between the 60th anniversary of D-Day in June 2005 and Remembrance Day in November.[9] The very size of the project, with the involvement of the government, the BBC and numerous local councils and voluntary organizations, demonstrates the continued significance of World War II to British culture, history and identity.

The importance of World War II to contemporary culture can also be seen in the original proposal for the "People's War" project by Chris Warren, head of BBC Interactive in May 2002:

> Television series such as 'The Trench' or 'Battlefields' give a vivid picture of different campaigns and some of the underlying human stories, but there is always the unanswered question: what part did members of our family play in the battles of the Western Desert, or in the trenches of the Somme?.... This proposal is for a BBC interactive service which would help set the record straight and let the public piece together for the first time the personal stories of their father's or grandfather's service during the Second World War. Using war-related series such as Deliverance and Battle for the Atlantic to encourage viewers and listeners to take part would then allow them to share their memories and knowledge to build a unique record of the nation at war.[10]

Warren's proposal illuminates both the original ideas underpinning the project and arguably underlying dominant understandings of World War II in Britain at the beginning of the twenty-first century. First, it recognizes the ongoing importance of the memory of the war in both popular and more private memory, demonstrating the role that war stories continue to play in family histories. Second, it highlights the disjuncture which, at times, exists between these two forms of memory, and points towards the ways in which popular memory, by necessity, selects and highlights particular facets of wartime memories, arguably those which best accord with the current sense of national identity. Finally, the proposal points towards the continued primacy of the memories of the male combatant, indicating that while the project's title "The People's War" suggests a popular memory of the war as a time of national unity and togetherness when the Home Front was as much a part of the war effort as the armed forces, it is the memories and experiences of the fighting men that are seen as the most important.

The high percentage of wartime veterans using the site to record their stories and memories demonstrated both the success of the BBC's story gathering program outlined above and the ongoing importance of the war to people's life narratives and sense of themselves. When contributors were asked for their reasons for entering their wartime memories on the site, these included the desire to "leave a legacy," the "pleasure of a willing listener" and the "opportunity to get the autobiography out of the cupboard," this last point suggesting that, as Graham Dawson and Alistair Thomson have both argued, wartime memories are often rehearsed and composed, until they fit with both the individual's sense of self, and with dominant popular memories of the period; the seemingly private process of memory making is actually a public process.[11] This point is supported by stated barriers to writing, which included, alongside "fear of computers," the belief that individual "stories weren't worth telling" and the fact that people were often "unwilling to recall unhappy memories."[12] The combination of popular memories of the war which, while they recognize the death and destruction of wartime, underplay these in favor of an emphasis on the more positive aspects of the war such as national unity, individual heroism and the individual desire not to speak of painful or difficult memories, has led to a preponderance on the site of constructive and affirming stories of the war.[13] This supports Summerfield's findings in her series of oral history interviews with female war veterans: that people are more willing to articulate stories and memories which "fit" with both their sense of self and the life narrative which they are constructing, and with currently dominant popular memories of the period being discussed.[14] Many of the stories recorded on the website demonstrated both the dominance of positive memories of the war in contemporary Britain and the ways in which the expression of these memories is often shaped by gender.

Gender and Remembering on the "People's War" Website

Of the 47,000 stories entered on the Website, by far the largest single category people wrote about was their experiences of wartime childhood and evacuation.[15] This is unsurprising, given that people who were adults during the war would be in their late seventies, at the very youngest, by 2005. Of the other categories, stories about the British Army number the most, although there are slightly more stories catalogued under the general heading "Bombing and the Blitz" under different subcategories. Overall, there are far more stories entered in the categories about "active service" by or about men than women. While 6,364 stories are catalogued under the heading "British Army," the largest of the forces, only 287 are listed under Auxiliary Territorial Service (ATS), the women's branch of the Army and the largest of the women's services. This pattern is continued in the categories for other branches of the Services: while 2,895 stories are catalogued under the heading Royal Air Force, there are only 308 entries for the Women's Auxiliary Air Force; and the 2,570 entries under Royal Navy are followed by only 103 stories relating to the Women's Royal Naval Service. This pattern is reversed in the "Love in Wartime" category where 35 of the 46 "Recommended Stories" were entered by women.[16]

This section will focus upon the stories categorized under the three largest general headings: Bombing and the Blitz, Family and Domestic Life, and Armed Forces: Army and ATS. These categories were chosen as in addition to being the largest and most popular groupings of stories, they could also be expected to be the categories where gender is most visible, with women traditionally seen as being concerned with family and domestic life and more likely than men to have first-hand experience of bombing and the Blitz, while accounts of life and experiences in the armed forces are more closely associated with archetypically masculine narratives, membership of the armed forces sometimes being seen as part of a male rite of passage in which boys become men.

While there are many ways in which the stories recorded here are shaped by gender, a sense of stoicism, a characteristic identified as being intrinsic to discourses of British national identity during the war, is common to many of the stories posted by both women and by men. One man, present at the retreat to Dunkirk, described the "walk to the beach" as "not without incident as the Luftwaffe had taken a violent dislike to our presence and vented their spleen with some gentle bombing and strafing."[17] In its studied understatement and gentle irony, the language used in this entry reiterates the "repressed" language of British war films of the 1950s, perhaps demonstrating the impact of popular representations of the war such as these on the structure of personal memory. Another entry, by a woman recalling the Blitz, recounted how she had miscarried a baby during a raid, her baby nephew being trapped by a falling wardrobe after a direct hit on a neighbor's house and a bombing raid killing 200 women and children, but concluded that "Hitler couldn't get us down" and that despite Britain suffering "a terrible battering, killing hundreds and destroying most of the cities ... the civilians carried on."[18] In its description of the Blitz, this entry combines stories of disaster and death so often either absent from, or marginalized within, popular memory of the war, but it contains them within an ongoing narrative of stoicism and determination so central to this memory. This sense of stoicism, of a British character seen at its best in its shared determination to "carry on" during the war, was mobilized successfully both during the war and in representation of it since and has often been compared unfavorably to reactions to disaster since — as in one woman's comment that "nowadays people would want six months counselling if they had a land mine outside their house."[19] The continuing strength of this particular discourse may well have acted to exclude some memories from the website, or to have contained them within a particular discursive structure that emphasized stoicism over trauma.

Within this emphasis on stoicism and "carrying on," women contributors appeared more likely than their male counterparts to focus on the personal and individual aspects of wartime life, often framing their memories within a romantic narrative. One woman commented, "I was just eight when I saw Alan Tidball. I think I knew I was going to marry him then." Other contributors ended their stories of wartime life with an account of their weddings.[20] Accounts such as these, which emphasize personal events such as love and marriage, often contained accounts of bravery, danger and sacrifice, such as the woman who recounted sleeping most nights of the London Blitz in the Anderson shelter with her baby; and the former WREN who was blown out of her bed by a bomb.[21] In contrast, men were more likely to frame their entries around stories of military service, perhaps reflecting the high status which membership in the military and particularly participation in high profile battles such as the Battle of Britain or D-Day imparted. The higher status accorded to combat during the war has been transferred to the privileged position of memories of this combat today. It appears that a form of hierarchy exists within stories and memories of World War II in Britain, in which memories of active military service by men are of higher status than most other memories, enabling men with such memories to feel a greater sense of entitlement and authority than people with memories of other types of wartime experiences.

However, although some stories, such as the example given above, were shaped by a discourse of stoicism and understatement, others, whilst still recalling events in a factual manner, include memories of fear, injury and death so often marginal to, or entirely absent from, more formalized, public memories of the war. For example, one ex-soldier, recalling his service with the army in Italy, described in great detail the impact of a hand grenade dropped into his tank and the "writhing mass of flesh" left in a German-occupied trench after a shell had landed there.[22] While the memory of Dunkirk cited above perhaps reflects the impact of British war films in reshaping personal narratives of war, it appears to share characteristics with more recent representations of the war, such as Stephen Spielberg's 1998 film *Saving Private Ryan* or the 2001 television series *Band of Brothers*. Both of these representations of World War II focused on the male experience of combat and attempted to represent battle scenes "realistically," using elements drawn from the format of documentary realism to present highly structured and planned images of battle which appear to be unmediated, characterized by the use of hand-held cameras and editing which reflects the confusion of battle. Fear, random death and horrific injury feature heavily in these scenes. While the battle scenes in these representations of war were themselves largely drawn from interviews with veterans, the representations themselves appear to have encouraged a new form of remembering experiences of combat, in which death, fear and injury figure more prominently. For example, one veteran of Juno Beach on D-Day recalled memories of a "shattered" assault craft, described as "a bloody mess" with "two bodies ... hanging over the side where they had been blown by the force of the explosion ... streaks of red ran down the side of the assault craft to the sea where their life blood had drained away."[23] Another veteran recalled seeing the leg of his dead friend lying on the road after they had parachuted into Normandy, while yet another described Juno Beach as a place where "hell had broken out" with "death and destruction all around."[24] It is doubtful whether such graphic images would have been used in public presentations of these memories if *Saving Private Ryan* and *Band of Brothers* had not had such an impact on the ways in which we imagine the experience of battle, specifically the landings of June 1944.

The emphasis given in these stories to vivid, personal accounts of battle was largely unavailable to the women who wrote for the website. While stories of the Blitz and other air raids included images of death and destruction, these were rarely as dramatic as those used to describe experiences of battle, generally written in the past tense, or with a sense of distance from the events being described. Although vivid instances of fear, injury and death are present in remembrance of the Blitz in Britain, these are rarely central to the memory, which largely focuses instead on the experiences of the communal shelters and on attempts to carry on with everyday life despite the bombings.[25] Stories which focused on the Blitz reflect this emphasis, as do stories by women who served with the forces. Women who experienced active service in the ATS often recounted the war years as a period of personal growth and development, reflecting Summerfield's assertion that many women saw the war years as a period of personal liberation. Summerfield argued that servicewomen in particular identified with the modernization thesis of war, retrospectively constructing their experience of military service as bringing about changes in their identity which they perceived as modernizing and liberating.[26] Jean Seeley, who served with the ATS at Bletchley Park, described how she "learned a very great deal, not only in a number of areas of knowledge, but about people, lives, relationships and society."[27] Pat Williams-Burr used a similar narrative of maturation in her account of the ATS as a "finishing school" from which she "emerged a much more mature and understanding person."[28] Despite these narratives of personal change and liberation, the memories of women who had served with the ATS often reflected the position of the Service within the military hierarchy, where it existed to support the higher status of male combat troops.[29] One woman framed her memories within a retelling of the fall of Dunkirk and the work of her ATS company in caring for and feeding the returned troops, describing how "although it was hard and tedious work we all felt we had given valuable service."[30] The entry by Gwendolyne Alice Jones further revealed this hierarchy of service and remembrance in her reflection on her memories of service with the ATS:

> On reading through this it seems very trivial in comparison with the experiences of the men on active service who fought and all too often died for their country. We did the best we could however and hopefully made some contribution towards ultimate victory.[31]

Lacking the certainty and voice of authority which mark so many of the entries by men who had served in the Army during the war, this entry reflects the gendered hierarchy which exists within wartime remembrance.

Conclusion

The impact of new media texts such as the BBC's People's War Website on the complex process of constructing a shared popular memory still has to be fully assessed. Website resources such as this are still a relatively new phenomenon and social and cultural factors such as age, income and gender all undoubtedly contribute to the ease (or otherwise) with which individuals feel able to record their own memories of the past in such a public manner. While computer technology has traditionally been associated with men and largely seen as a male sphere of interest, the increasing domestication of media and technology such as the home-based personal computer and fast access to the internet in many Western homes has meant that computer usage is far less gendered than it perhaps once was.[32] Generational change is also contributing to a widening usage of personal computers and in particular the internet as a new generation grows up to regard the construction and representation of an online identity in networking sites such as Facebook and MySpace as an unremarkable aspect of everyday life. As new media technology becomes further embedded into everyday life, we can expect to see an increasing shift in the ways in which public discourses are created, with more and more people using the internet as a stage on which to share their views, opinions and memories. This technologically-enabled widening of the public stage means that a wider body of beliefs, attitudes and experiences will gain an audience than has been the case in the past. New media such as the internet has the potential to contribute to the democratization of public life and to the reshaping of popular memory. The interactive nature of websites such as the BBC's "People's War" Website may mean that although there are undoubtedly some memories, some stories that are easier to share and to speak of, as discussed below, they fit with a dominant set of memories of the war; the appearance of less often vocalized memories, such as those of conscientious objectors, may encourage others to share their experiences of the war years.

The BBC's "People's War" Website is a fascinating resource to study the popularization of war memory, demonstrating, as it does, the processes by which the personal, private memories of individuals become part of a more widely shared popular memory. The stories entered here can be seen as part of the process of refining and shaping memory until it fits with one's sense of self; the process of composure analyzed by Graham Dawson.[33] As part of this process, existing popular memories and representations of the past are drawn on as a means to create a coherent, recognizable narrative of self which "fits" with public perceptions of the period. The links that exist between private memory and public remembrance, however, are not straightforward and neither are they one-way. Individuals make use of public remembrance in their construction of their own stories, but in a very selective manner, choosing aspects of public representation which "fit" with their sense of self and which enable them to give voice to particular memories in a range of narrative forms. For example, the vivid descriptions on the website of battle, which often use a visual and immediate language, would have been difficult to articulate on such a public stage without the representations of battle found in *Saving Private Ryan* and *Band of Brothers* circulating in contemporary culture. At the same time, other entries use a discourse of understatement and dry humor to describe the same events, drawing on a popular memory of the war which can be traced back to British war films of the 1940s and 1950s. Individual choices of particular narrative registers reflect the subjectivity of memory making; the ways in which we choose memories and express them in such a way as to create stories which fit with our current sense of self. At the same time, the Website demonstrates the "cultural circuit" that exists between personal memory and public remembrance. While the individuals entering stories on the website clearly often draw on the dominant popular memory of the war to frame their stories, this popular memory is itself influenced and shaped by the vocalization of private memories, the range of which is increased by the democratic nature of the Website. One of the BBC's stated aims for the project was that of "turning the audience into content generators," drawing on the stories submitted in their program making.[34] Two commemorative programs broadcast in 2004 focused on two events recognized as central to both the war's outcome and to the popular memory of the war: the withdrawal from Dunkirk and D-Day.[35] Both programs drew widely on the stories entered on the Website, and in their representation of many of the horrors of war reflected the shift towards often very graphic realism seen in the stories which recounted these events. The personal memories entered on the Website thus become part of a wider circuit of production, both being shaped by, and in their turn shaping, public remembrance of the war.

However, within the process of the creation of public remembrance which can be seen on the Website, a hierarchy of memory can also be discerned. Within this hierarchy, some stories are more visible than others. In part, this is a reflection of current views about the war, with the men who fought in Normandy being seen as more worthy of commemoration than, for example, conscientious objectors. The most notable difference, however, can be seen in the ways in which gender shapes both the stories entered on the Website and the language used to describe them. Men, it appears, are still more likely than women to use an authoritative tone in their writing, revealing a sense of entitlement and a belief that their stories are worthy of telling. Women, while they sometimes use this register, were more likely than men to frame their stories within a narrative that focused on the personal and private aspects of life in wartime, recounting weddings, childbirth and friendships in more detail. Descriptions of life under bombardment and of work in the auxiliary forces gave women some access to this authoritative register, but it was more likely to be used by men, especially those who had seen combat during the war. It appears that, although the war is largely remembered within Britain as a "people's war" that touched every aspect of national life, and in which every member of the nation played a part, war itself is still perceived as an essentially masculine affair, sitting comfortably within naturalized discourses of masculinity. The emergence over the past twenty years of the anniversary of D-Day as the key site for acts of wartime remembrance has helped to strengthen these links within public remembrance of the war in Britain.

Even a brief survey such as this of the many thousands of entries to the BBC's People's War Website demonstrates three interwoven themes. The first of these is the ongoing importance of the memory of the war, both to individuals, to families and to Britain's sense of itself as a nation. The second theme is the desire of both individuals and their families to incorporate personal memories and stories within the public memory of the war. The third theme is the hierarchy of memory that exists, with men's memories of combat, especially in battles recognized as particularly significant to the war's eventual outcome, being both prolific and often written with a sense of authority and entitlement. Women and men, it appears, are eager to give voice to their memories of the war and to ensure that their experiences have some place on the public stage, but male combatants were more likely than any other group to write with the confidence that their stories and experiences were important. Collective remembrance of wartime is reliant on the recollection and expression of individual memories of wartime, recorded in sites of memory such as the "People's War" Website. Thus, the process by which collective remembrance of wartime is formed and articulated needs to be understood as gendered.

NOTES

1. J. Winter, *Remembering War: The Great War Between Memory and History in the Twentieth Century* (New Haven, 2006), p.1.

2. See for example Michael Foreman's autobiographical novels, *War Boy* (London, 1996); and *After the War was Over* (London, 1997).

3. P. Nora, *Realms of Memory: The Construction of the French Past. 1. Conflicts and Divisions* (New York, 1996).

4. A. Landsberg, *Prosthetic Memory: The Transformation of American Remembrance in the Age of Mass Culture* (New York, 2004).

5. http://www.bbc.co.uk/ww2peopleswar/about/project_01.shtml. Accessed 2/5/2006.

6. J. K. Watson, *Fighting Different Wars: Experience, Memory and the First World War in Britain* (Cambridge, 2004); S. O. Rose, *Which People's War? National Identity and Citizenship in Wartime Britain 1939–1945* (Oxford, 2003); Penny Summerfield, *Reconstructing Women's Wartime Lives: Discourse and Subjectivity in Oral Histories of the Second World War* (Manchester, 1998). For the relationship between gender, national identity and wartime memories in Britain see L. Noakes, *War and the British: Gender and National Identity in Britain 1939–1991* (London, 1998).

7. Chris Warren, BBC Interactive, May 2002, cited on http://www.bbc.co.uk.ww2 peopleswar/about/project01.shtml Accessed 2/5/2006.

8. http://www.bbc.co.uk/ww2peopleswar/about/project03.shtml. Accessed 2/5/ 2006.

9. http://www.bbc.co.uk/ww2peopleswar/about/project_02.shtml. Accessed 2/5/ 2006.

10. http://www.bbc.co.uk/ww2peopleswar/about/project_01.shtml. Accessed 2/5/ 2006. One aspect of Warren's original proposal that was swiftly revised was the assumption that people would simply use the website to tell "the story of their father's or grandfather's service." When the site went live in June 2003, it soon became apparent that many veterans were keen to record their own stories. http://www.bbc.co.uk/ww2peoples war/about/project03.shtml. Accessed 2/5/2006.

11. G. Dawson, *Soldier Heroes: British Adventure, Empire and the Imagining of Masculinities* (London, 1994), p. 22; A. Thomson, *Anzac Memories: Living with the Legend*, (Melbourne, 1994)

12. http://www.bbc.co.uk/ww2peopleswar/about/project_03.shtml. Accessed 2/5/ 2006.

13. For discussion of the marginalization of painful war memories in public representations of the war, see L. Noakes, "Remembering War," in M. Evans & K. Lunn, eds., *War and Memory in the Twentieth Century* (Oxford, 1997). It should be noted that this stands in contrast to remembrance of the First World War in Britain, to which images of death and suffering are central. For discussion of this see D. Todman, *The Great War: Myth and Memory* (London, 2005); J. Winter, *Sites of Memory, Sites of Mourning: The Great War in European Cultural History* (Cambridge, 1995), and *Remembering War: The Great War Between Memory and History in the Twentieth Century* (New Haven, 2006).

14. Summerfield, *Reconstructing Women's Wartime Lives*, pp. 284–86. Summerfield is drawing on earlier work here by Dawson and Thomson. Dawson, *Soldier Heroes*; Thomson, *Anzac Memories*.

15. 14,336 stories are categorized under the Heading "Childhood and Evacuation," http://bbc.co.uk/ww2peopleswar/categories/.

16. "Recommended Stories" are those chosen by the editorial team for "particularly vivid story telling, an unusual theme not covered in other stories, a dramatic or particularly resonant account of the events." http://www.bbc.co.uk/ww2peopleswar/about/site information.shtml#recommended.

17. http://www.bbc.co.uk/ww2peopleswar/stories/77/a3331577, story i.d. number A3331577, Percy Bowpit.

18. http://www.bbc.co.uk/ww2peopleswar/stories/36/a2886636.shtml, story i.d. number A2886636, Mary Lawrence (entered by Alan Constable).

19. http://bbc.co.uk/ww2peopleswar/stories/53/a3890153.shtml, story i.d. number A3890153, Dr Ivy Oates.

20. http://www.bbc.co.uk/ww2peopleswar/stories/42/a2245042.shtml, story i.d. number A2245042, Hilda Tidball. For stories ending in weddings, see for example, http:// www.bbc.co.uk/ww2peopleswar/stories/34/a2329634.shtml, story i.d. number A2329634, Pam Cuthbert.

21. http://www.bbc.co.uk/ww2peopleswar/stories/36/a2886636.shtml, story i.d. number A2886636, Mary Lawrence, hhtp://www.bbc.co.uk/ww2peopleswar/stories/09/ a3429209.shtml, story i.d. number A3429209, Olive Partridge.

22. http://www.bbc.co.uk/ww2peopleswar/stories/71/a2059571.shtml, story i.d. number A2059571, Gordon Bingham-Hall.

23. http://www.bbc.co.uk/ww2peopleswar/stories/98/a1144298.shtml, story i.d. number A1144298, Reg. A. Carter.

24. http://www.bbc.co.uk/ww2peopleswar/stories/16/a2523016.shtml, story i.d.

A2523016, James Hill, http://www.bbc.co.uk/ww2peopleswar/stories/32/a2082232.shtml, story i.d. number A2082232, Leonard J. Smith.

25. See, for example, "The Blitz Experience," in the Imperial War Museum, London, and the Home Front exhibition at Newhaven Fort. For an example of representation of the Blitz which focuses on human suffering under bombardment, see *Blitz: London's Firestorm*, Darlow-Smithson productions, Channel 4, first broadcast 27 October 2005. Given Britain's ongoing commitment to aerial bombardment as a legitimate method of warfare, it is perhaps unsurprising that few public representations of the Blitz concentrate on the impact of aerial warfare on the humans who experienced it.

26. Summerfield, *Reconstructing Women's Wartime Lives*, p. 261.

27. http://www.bbc.co.uk/ww2peopleswar/stories/37/a2742237.shtml, story i.d. number A2742437, Jean Sealey.

28. http://www.bbc.co.uk/ww2peopleswar/stories/ 34/a4153934.shtml, story i.d. number A4153934, Pat Williams-Burr.

29. See L. Noakes, *Women in the British Army: War and the Gentle Sex 1907–1949* (London, 2006).

30. http://www.bbc.co.uk/ww2peopleswar/stories/31/a2017531/shtml, story i.d. A201753, Kathy Kay.

31. http://www.bbc.co.uk/ww2peopleswar/stories/54/a1361954/shtml, story i.d. A1361954, Gwendolyne Alice Jones.

32. For further discussion of this topic, see T. Berker, M. Hartmann, Y. Punie & K. Ward, eds., *Domestication of Media and Technology* (Open University Press, 2006).

33. Dawson, *Soldier Heroes*, p. 25.

34. http://www.bbc.co.uk/ww2peopleswar/about/projects-01.shtml

35. *Dunkirk*, BBC2, February 2004, *D Day*, BBC 1, June 2004. Both programs combined a mixture of drama and documentary footage.

Inscribing Narratives of Occupation in Israeli Popular Memory

Tamar Katriel

The contact with Palestinian civilians and their plight under the Israeli occupation has given rise to soldierly tales that go beyond both the triumphalism and the lamentation that have been previously associated with Israeli war stories.[1] Soldiers' own accounts of their war experience have significantly contributed to the shift from the glorification of war as a potential site for ennobling heroic acts to a view of combatants as society's ultimate victims.[2] In Israeli discourse this view has been interpreted in inter-generational terms and has been encapsulated in the frequent use of the biblical trope of Abraham's readiness to sacrifice his son, Isaac.[3]

Early expressions of the shift away from war triumphalism in soldiers' own discourses have appeared in the Israeli public sphere through the publication of soldierly group dialogues, which were organized by some kibbutz educators in the wake of the 1967 War. The book in which these group discussions were published became a cult book of sorts, even though the soldiers who had recently participated in that victorious war departed from the triumphalist idiom of the day. They openly expressed their moral unease at the sights of battle they had been exposed to and the combat activities they were implicated in during the war (while at the same time reiterating their commitment to continue fighting the nation's wars when called upon to do so).[4]

Further amplification of these soldiers' troubled accounts and the cultural logic of the Israeli martial ethos could be found in the realm of art. Some Israeli artists poignantly protested not only the Israeli culture of war but also its culture of war commemoration and its pacifying role in public life. Probably the best known example of such artistic protest was found in the iconoclastic 1970 play by Hanoch Levin, *Queen of the Bathtub*, which scandalized the Israeli public by offering its own twist to the Isaac sacrifice trope, explicitly calling the parent generation to account for the sacrifice of their fallen sons. The accusatory lines spoken in the voice of a dead son read: "Dear Dad, when you stand at my grave/ Old, weary, and very much childless/And you see how they put my body into the ground/Ask for my forgiveness, Dad."[5]

Testimonies by contemporary soldiers concerning their military service in the Occupied Territories of the West Bank and Gaza similarly challenge the officially proclaimed ethic of combat and the legitimacy of routine military practices of the Israeli Army. Such troubled accounts have occasionally appeared in the press, in political documentaries, or in the self-justificatory discourse of conscientious objectors. However, it was only in the context of soldier-activists' moral protest that the sustained effort to elicit, collect and disseminate verbal and visual testimonies of the minutae of the military practices upholding the occupation could amount to an open rejection of Israel's military policies in the Occupied Territories.[6]

Arguing that "like artists, activists create new moral possibilities,"[7] James Jasper foregrounds the creative dimensions of what he calls the art of moral protest: "In little ways and big, protestors experiment with novel ways to think, feel, judge, and act. Effective strategizing, especially, relies not only on good timing but artful innovation and choice."[8] Accordingly, this article will address some of the moves made by a particular group of young Israeli men in voicing their protest about the role they were required to play vis-à-vis the Palestinian civilian population during their military service. All the soldiers whose testimonies are included in this chapter were stationed in the Occupied Territories during the Al Aqsa Intifada, the Palestinian uprising that broke out in October 2000, and their experiences there formed a memorable part of their mandatory military service. In contributing photographs and stories to the testimonial project devised by some of their peers, they indicated their support for the moral protest it entailed, even when they chose to remain anonymous.

The group of soldier-activists who solicited, collected and disseminated dozens of such soldiers' testimonies were loosely organized under the name of *Breaking the Silence* [*shovrim shtika*].[9] Their venture became known to the public in May 2004 when they mounted a photographic exhibition made up of pictures shot by soldiers with their hand-held cameras in the town of Hebron in the early 2000s. These photographs captured moments of life under the occupation as noticed and recorded by ordinary soldiers during their routine military service. The exhibition took them from the domestic sphere of personal photo albums and exposed them to public gaze. In addition, the exhibition included material traces of arbitrary military control practices, such as dozens of car keys confiscated from Palestinian drivers at checkpoints. The visual starkness of the photographs and the concrete materiality of the forlorn car keys dangling on the wall in the out-of-context of the exhibition space were powerful metonymic reminders of life under occupation.

Notably, while it focused on a visual medium, the exhibition also became an occasion for verbal narration since the photographs were interpreted and amplified by soldier-activists who guided visitors along the exhibition walls. Stories of occupation were also conveyed in video-taped interviews with soldiers as part of the exhibition. They were also told by visitors as they reminisced about their military service while viewing the exhibition. In publicizing the group's counter-hegemonic message, the photographic display was thus constructed as a powerful exhibitionary site that combined mediated and unmediated messages, visual images and verbal accounts, claims to authentic representation and opportunities for interpersonal exchanges. In many ways, it anticipated the range of protest strategies that came to characterize the group's ongoing activities. Resonating with the expressive idioms typical of moral protest groups worldwide, the soldiers' protest was anchored in a testimonial rhetoric of embodied presence. At the same time, they mobilized the resources made available by the contemporary, digital media, including group-specific websites and online journalism.[10]

Located in the gallery of the Academy for Geographic Photography in Tel Aviv, and curated by the noted photojournalist Miki Kratsman, the exhibition attracted thousands of visitors as well as media attention, garnering support from some and censure from others. After the initial impact of its launching in Tel Aviv, the exhibition had a considerable afterlife as it traveled to other venues across the country, and, particularly, as its young organizers utilized their facility with the resources available to grassroots activists in the digital age. They disseminated photographs and testimonies through the group's website, via popular online newspapers, and with the help of such devices as a DVD recording of a guided tour of the original exhibition. The group's message owed its quick spread to the new possibilities of cyber-activism. Its continued resonance, however, can be credited to the group's effective use of a fusion of digital communication and more traditional, "embodied" protest practices such as the mounting of a play that dramatized a selection of soldiers' testimonies, which was put on in the spring of 2005 by an acting troupe of *Hakibbutzim* Teachers'

College and performed as part of the high-profile *Teatroneto Festival* in Tel Aviv. As well, the compilation and dissemination of booklets containing thematically organized testimonies by soldiers, lectures and discussions involving the public at large, and guided tours to the city of Hebron provided opportunities for their organizers to challenge the Jewish settlers' supremacy by giving voice to their own perspectives on the role of the military in suppressing the Palestinian population under Israeli occupation.

The exploration of the nature and possibilities of contemporary war-related moral protest requires attention to the ways in which the content, forms and media of communication combine to produce a counter-hegemonic statement. In attempting such an exploration as a culturally situated inquiry, I will address the meaning and importance of testimonial narratives as a form of protest by Israeli soldiers as well as the ways in which various forms of communication are utilized in giving voice and flesh to the soldiers' rhetoric of presence and authenticity within today's media-saturated social environment, creating a fusion of the public and the personal. In particular, I will try to show that the multiple ways in which audiences have been exposed to the soldiers' subversive message echo its complex nature. There is an inherent tension in the soldiers' attempt to narrativize their experience, making it meaningful and comprehensible to themselves and others even while invoking a lifeworld that is riddled with puzzlement, contradiction and loss of meaning (as their frequent references to the irrationality, insanity or absurdity of the situations in which they find themselves indicate). In other words, taken together, the set of strategies and media forms mobilized by the soldiers in voicing and disseminating their message of moral protest echo its complex nature and troubled positioning. I will return to the issues of form and medium after presenting central aspects of the message itself.

The Message

The group's launching statement generated considerable public controversy when it first appeared. Although the soldiers regarded their testimonies as essentially apolitical — narrowly defining politics as party-related and partisan — their act of speaking up was widely considered as an intervention in the political controversy over the occupation in which Israeli society has been embroiled for four decades. It is in the context of the political debate over the legitimacy of Israeli policies and military practices in the occupied territories that these soldiers' wakeup call to Israeli society must be read.

In formulating their wakeup call, the *Breaking the Silence* group departed from radical, left-wing criticisms of the situation by focusing not on the heavy toll paid by the Palestinian civilian population but on the moral price each of the soldiers who served in the occupied territories was paying for engaging in oppressive practices. While drawing on their personal authority as eyewitnesses and participants in what they came to consider acts of oppression, they framed the problem at the societal level:

> We feel that service in the occupied territories and the incidents we faced have distorted and harmed the moral values on which we grew up.
> We all agree that as long as Israeli society keeps sending its best people to military combat service in the occupied territories, it is extremely important that all of us, Israeli citizens, know the price which the generation who is fighting in the territories is paying.... **That's why we decided to break the silence, because it's time to tell.**[11]

In choosing testimony as their main strategy, the soldier-activists worked on the assumption that their perspective, anchored in the experiences and insights they had gained through direct contact with the day-to-day realities of the occupation, was unfamiliar to the Israeli public because of an unspoken pact of silence to which they as individual soldiers — along with the official military sources and the mainstream media — had succumbed. At a superficial level, of course, ordinary Israelis are aware of the plight of Palestinian citizens who live under military occupation and are continuously being encroached upon by Jewish settlers. A variety of activist groups and a handful of artists, intellectuals and journalists have consistently tried to keep these stark realities within view. While not usually silenced, they have remained marginal and are frequently discarded as one-sided and disloyal to the Israeli cause. The soldiers' focus on their own plight as victimized-victimizers has positioned them as sensitive to the Israeli cause while at the same time giving them the legitimacy (and opportunity) to recount incidents that bring out the victimization of the Palestinians by way of narrative background to their own soul-searching.[12]

Thus, while much of the soldiers' testimonial activity has a reportorial aura, relentlessly heaping fact on fact and documenting incident after incident, its power lies in its introspective nature. Presenting themselves as reporters of facts, they in fact make a moral claim, attempting to bridge the chasm between the two worlds they straddle in their role as soldiers of the occupation — the tormented, lawless and constricted lifeworld of Palestinian civilians in the occupied territories and the normalcy of life in their own hometowns. The experiential chasm between these two lifeworlds is exacerbated by their geographical proximity. As some of the soldiers testified, their routine movement between these two worlds when on and off military duty became an increasingly unbearable feat. In their preface to the set of testimonies related to service in Hebron they say: "We decided to speak out. We decided to tell. Hebron isn't in outer space. It's one hour from Jerusalem. But Hebron is light years away from Tel Aviv."[13]

Indeed, the soldiers' testimonial mission is double-edged. On the one hand, it uses a documentary idiom, amassing eyewitness reports as an evidentiary base for the claim that the soldiers are portraying a generalized situation, structurally entailed by the power relations associated with the occupation rather than dealing with incidental, disjointed and haphazard injustices that can be corrected through localized disciplinary action or personal good will. On the other hand, even while noting the cumulative effect of the occupation as a structural given, it relies on the power of personal testimony to dramatize concrete moments that encapsulate their experiences as soldier-occupiers. Their testimonies are replete with highly introspective narrative fragments of lived moments that foreground their feelings, self-questioning and moral shock at the part they played in upholding a social order they found both puzzling and distasteful.

The following examples of soldiers' testimonials relating to military service in Hebron bring out the meshing of the structural arrangements underlying the routines of the checkpoint and curfew systems imposed on the Palestinian population and the arbitrary power-games and whimsical conduct of the soldiers upholding them. The first of the following citations brings out the senselessness of the situation:

> Our job was to stop the Palestinians at ... [a particular] checkpoint and tell them they can't pass there anymore... And we knew there was another way they could pass, so on the one hand we were not allowed to let them pass, and on the other hand there were all these old ladies who had to pass to get to their homes, so we'd point in the direction of the opening through which they could pass without us noticing. It was an absurd situation.... Why was it forbidden to pass? It was really a form of collective punishment. Any terrorist could know about and pass through the opening...[14]

The second citation underscores the enormous power put in the hands of each and every soldier, even the ones newly arrived on the scene:

> ...We'd just finished advanced training, got to the assignment and he yells, "Waqif! Stop!" The man didn't quite understand and he advanced one more step. One extra step, and then he yells again, "Waqif!' and the man freezes in fear.... Actually, it's a procedure nobody pays attention to, stopping them exactly on the line. So he decided that ... he'll be detained. I said to him, "Listen, what are you doing?" he said, "No, no, don't argue, at least not in front of them, what are you doing, I'm not going to trust you any-

more, you're not reliable" ... And then I got it, a man who's been in Hebron one week, it has nothing to do with rank, he can do whatever he wants ... it's like there are no rules, everything is permissible.[15]

By recording, collecting, disseminating, and archiving these testimonial narratives, this group of soldier-activists sought to force society to take into consideration aspects of the ongoing war against the Palestinian population that they believed would otherwise remain suppressed and highly compartmentalized in mainstream media coverage.[16] The reality of normative chaos the soldiers witness is customary. Their insistence owed some of its urgency to the continued relevance of the stories and situations the testimonies brought to light, including the fact that their discharge from the army did not relieve them from the scene of occupation as they might be required to return to it as reserve soldiers. As a group, they refused to take a stand with regards to the option of conscientious objection, which was open to them as it was to other soldiers, some of whom had decided to follow this option.[17]

Capitalizing on their unique position as witnesses to both the injustices of the occupation and the reluctance of mainstream Israeli society to properly recognize them, they believed that their first-hand knowledge of the situation carried with it the moral weight of what Linell and Rommetveit have called "epistemic responsibility."[18] For them, this moral weight involved a recognition of their duty to share what they had witnessed in serving the occupation, and in so doing passing on this burden of knowledge to the Israeli pubic — in effect, turning citizens who do not know (and may not wish to know) into bystanders who must make moral choices.[19] In relentlessly throwing their witness accounts into society's lap, they shifted the burden of knowledge unto their elders, at times with an undisguised accusatory tone, trying to shake them out of their "state of denial" and turn them into second-order witnesses.[20] Thus, rather than addressing their polemic directly to their military superiors, or to the political leadership, these young men sought to create a space for a broad-ranging intergenerational dialogue at the familial and societal level. Contradicting the widely accepted picture of familial protectiveness towards young soldiers,[21] they insisted that the same parents who were spending sleepless nights agonizing about their material and emotional wellbeing during military service nevertheless remained willingly ignorant of their moral torments. They accused their parent generation of looking away, of refusing to acknowledge the price their offspring were paying for their failure as adults to see what was happening and to act on this knowledge. As one of them said,

Look what has happened to us. You have corrupted a whole generation, the cream of the crop, the most ideological people, we have all been morally corrupted.... Let every Hebrew mother know,[22] you send your child [to the army] for three years and have no idea what he goes through.[23]

Despite the enormous power they had over the Palestinians, these young soldiers felt utterly helpless to affect their situation. In their social cosmology, as it emerges from many testimonies, violence was primarily structure-oriented and not actor-oriented.[24] The soldiers viewed the violence they took part in as anchored in the occupation context and believed that nothing they would do as individuals in that situation could have any real effect. As one of them said,

At the end of the day, even if the soldiers act as properly as possible without any Palestinians being humiliated and getting beat up and broken, even if you're the best person you can be, you're still carrying out a policy that is a criminal policy."[25]

They tried to overcome their state of paralysis by breaking the intimate intergenerational silence between themselves and their parents—a silence upheld by their unspoken resolve not to tell and the parents' reluctance to ask, as poignantly described by one of the soldiers:

After two days in Hebron I understood that in order to survive there I must lock up all that I am ... all my feelings and thoughts, in a little box. And shut up.... So a high wall of silence grew between and around us. We were silent after guard duty, silent on our leaves at home... I was silent as I watched myself slowly turning into a dumb, cold robot...[26]

Indeed, while they were gratified by the thousands of visitors to their traveling exhibition — including politicians, journalists and public figures— the organizers considered ordinary soldiers and their families as their most immediate and most important target audiences. Above all, they delighted in evidence indicating that family visits to the exhibition provided an occasion for them to share experiences related to military service in the territories in unprecedented ways.

Somewhat ironically, the soldiers employed a soldierly idiom in formulating their civil-familial mission of breaking the silence: "During our combat service we've handled many different missions. We have one mission left: to talk, tell and not keep anything hidden."[27] They thus challenged the polarity between "words" and "deeds," which has been central to Israel's nation-building and militaristic ethos, and embarked on a testimonial project in which *saying is doing.*[28]

With the aid of the visual power and the authentic aura of amateur photography,[29] then, the soldiers sought to bring Hebron to Tel Aviv. They did not, however, challenge their elders' world so much as position themselves as the true custodians of its most cherished values who were willing to court disfavor by breaking the social silence that surrounded the reality of military occupation and the soldiers' impossible role in it.

Moral Shock

In attempting to create a sense of order out their experience of a chaotic situation, the soldiers' narratives were often confessional in nature, seeking to construct a viable moral career out of the disjointed, haphazard episodes that made up their personal memories of military service. This moral career took the form of a double movement of self-brutalization on the one hand, and re-humanization on the other, that makes up the meta-narrative of the soldiers' episodic storytelling. Each of these trajectories was triggered by what Jasper calls a "moral shock." As he points out, moral shocks involve the violation of what are frequently implicit moral principles and they "often begin at the 'gut level,' as moral intuitions trigger emotions."[30] Moral shocks, whether triggered by mundane or unusual events, may give rise to protest in the form of moral testimony. In Jasper's words,

> But most protest involves, not necessarily *doing* the right thing, but *saying* what the right thing is. This kind of moral testimony is itself an important practice. One probes one's own psyche and orders one's beliefs and feelings; one articulates the most important ones... One offers new language for describing the world, and for acting in it.[31]

Many soldiers' testimonials include accounts of their initial shock at encountering face-on the brutality and lawlessness associated with the day-to-day practices of the occupation when they first assumed their post in the territories. They narrate incidents, which became etched in their memories, in which Palestinian civilians were humiliated and brutalized by the veteran soldiers and commanders they joined. They testify to how uneasy these incidents left them during their first days in the territories, repeatedly admitting that they felt dismayed not only by what they saw others doing, but also by their own inability to speak up and intercede. In charting the dark part of their moral career, they openly admit to how quickly they became accustomed to the brutality of the occupation, developing a moral numbness that allowed them to participate in upholding it.

The second moral shock is narrated as due to some other "trigger event" that re-directs the course of their moral career. A "trigger event," as the term is used by Thomas Weber based on research in the area of dispute formation, is an event (or one too many) that brings on a new realization and pushes a person to engage in overt dispute: "The trigger event forces a person to consciously analyze his or her experience of an action, or may cause them to reinterpret previously seemingly insignificant actions in a way that imbues them with added meaning, causing them to see the world differently."[32]

The processes of both dehumanization and re-humanization intimately linked the soldiers' sense of themselves with the treatment of the Palestinian other. Their moral numbness as they got accustomed to their military role, and their relish in the unlimited power they enjoyed, grew out of and contributed to their own self-effacement and to that of the Palestinians.[33] Jolted out of their unthinking enmeshment in the routine maintenance of the occupation by some trigger event, they embarked on a path of re-humanization. Paradoxically, it was precisely the physical proximity mandated by their military presence as soldiers of the occupation that led to the occasional emergence of social proximity. This allowed the Palestinians' plight and humanness to penetrate the soldiers' psychic armor of military indifference and resentment. Trigger events responsible for such shifts in the soldiers' positioning vis-à-vis their Palestinian charges are often reported in their testimonials as moral shocks, as indicated in the following examples.

> [O]ut came a man in his 50s or 60s with a few women and small children... He's the one heading this clan coming at you, and you walk up to him and say in Arabic "Stop, there's a curfew, go home"... In short, weapons are cocked, aimed with a hint, not straight at him, at his legs.... He was all dressed-up, wearing a suit and a *kaffia*, he looked really respectable ... my finger moves to the safety catch, and then I see his eyes are filled with tears, and he says something in Arabic, turns around, and goes. And his clan follows him ... and I felt like the scum of the earth. Like, what am I doing here?[34]

Another repeated instance of moral shock is associated with soldiers' frequent acknowledgement of their sense of intoxication with the unlimited power they held over the Palestinians thanks to their guns and uniforms, as in the following example:

> I was ashamed of myself the day I realized that I simply enjoy the feeling of power.... People do what you tell them. You know it's because you carry a weapon.... And then when someone suddenly says "no" to you — "What do you mean 'no'? Where do you draw the *chutzpa* from, to say no to me? ... I am the Law here..." I remember a very specific situation: I was at a checkpoint ... From one side a line of cars wanting to get out, and from the other side a line of cars wanting to pass ... and suddenly you have a mighty force at the tip of your fingers... When I realized this ... I checked in with myself to see what had happened to me...[35]

Curiously, this sense of omnipotence may go hand-in-hand with a pervasive feeling of helplessness, as is implied by the frequent use of the addiction metaphor. While the first of the above testimonials focused on the shock of empathy aroused by the soldiers' recognition of the respectful-looking Palestinian man's humiliation, and the second focused on the soldier's shock of self-recognition at realizing his addiction to power, other testimonials highlight the narrator's sense of shame at his failure to protest an incident of brutality he had witnessed. Indeed, moments of self-silencing were repeatedly narrated, recollecting how helpless and ineffective they felt on failing to respond to the moral call they sensed but only belatedly came to acknowledge. In recounting feelings of being lost for words, unable to speak up, intimidated into conformity, these soldiers' testimonials were to rectify the moments of self-silencing they had come to regret. This is clearly exemplified by the following underlined narrative codas,[36] which implicitly contrast the recounted incidents of individual failure to protest to the narrator's participation in the group's project of bearing witness.

Thus, telling a story about an officer who abused a family of Palestinian mourners at a funeral, one soldier-witness said,

> I could really see that he didn't consider them equal human beings. *I'm still mad at myself for not saying anything. As in other incidents, I simply lowered my eyes and didn't know what to do with myself....*[37]

Another recounts a situation in which he saw his commander abusing a Palestinian youth who was frequently around and who was known as someone who never made any trouble, saying,

> It's awful. *I can't do anything. I don't have enough air to say anything. I take my helmet and fall on the stone wall, still covering from the front, and I cry. There's nothing I can do...*[38]

And a third tells how a little Jewish settler kid approached him at his post with bravado, telling him of his plans,

> "First, I'm going to buy a popsicle at Gotnik's"—that's their grocery store—"then I'm going to kill some Arabs." *I had nothing to say to him. Nothing. I went completely blank....*[39]

These moments of self-silencing and powerless rage were revisited by the soldiers when they joined the activist group's protest, invoking the power of personal narrative to subvert the authoritativeness of official discourses about the occupation, recognizing that, as Rosen put it, "memory emerging as narrative is one means available to us for asserting our authority against institutionalized power, more precisely the discourses of power."[40]

Conclusion

Through the concrete starkness of their witness accounts and the evidentiary edifice they put together, these young men rejected what to them was the impossible position of "victimized victimizers" that had been thrust upon them. They also rejected the normative chaos of the counter-world they were thrown into, and the effacement and de-humanization of both self and other in which the daily practices of the occupation policy were anchored. Interlacing the political and the personal in ways they hoped would make their elders listen, they utilized a range of persuasion strategies in order to make their protest heard. These included a fusion of performance-based strategies such as lectures, theater and touristic encounters on the one hand and the use of mediated communication, exploiting the new possibilities provided by cyberspace, on the other. Like other activist groups, while they sought the attention of the mainstream media in order to reach a wider audience, the dissenting soldiers were nevertheless well-served by the internet as an alternative medium which allowed them to sidestep press journalism and disseminate information about their activities and positions in their own way.

In addition to their own mailing list, their messages, including segments of testimonies they had collected, were circulated around other lists of activists who sympathized with their cause and at times made their way to online journals. Links to their website were appended to all these messages, inviting interested readers to delve deeper into the group's positions and activities. Although its interactive potential was not much utilized, the group's website presented its mission, and contained materials associated with its activities. In its very structure, it could serve both as an archival resource and a site for relevant news dissemination. Its archival component contained transcribed and video-taped testimonies by soldiers, a picture gallery of photographs of the kind displayed in the group's traveling exhibition, and a collection of mainstream media reports on the group's activities.

Notably, the website's hypertext qualities allowed for the inclusion of both news items that highlight the actor-oriented violence of the occupation and of archived information whose cumulative impact reinforces the group's emphasis on the structure-oriented violence associated with it. This web-facilitated double emphasis on structure-oriented and actor-oriented events points to communicational possibilities that go beyond conventional journalism. But this goes beyond a communicational technology point of interest — indeed, this double-pronged emphasis on structure and actors touches upon the heart of the dilemma that animates the young soldiers' tormented testimonials—the dilemma of self-responsibility as actors operating in a socially coercive context. It is a dilemma that lurks at the edges of glorifying accounts of the soldier role, and one that carries special resonance in Israeli society. As one soldier put it: "This is the most revolting sentence that, for me at least, has the most negative connotations in the world, and you'll hear almost every soldier speak: 'I'm a soldier and I'm just following orders.'"[41]

In the larger context of the political debate in Israel, it was clear that this testimonial campaign was highly controversial. Not surprisingly, people on the right found it objectionable, even treacherous, as for them the Occupied Territories were Promised Land liberated by the Jews in 1967. Less obviously perhaps, this testimonial project was also rejected by some left-wingers who faulted the soldiers for not joining the ranks of the conscientious objectors, but rather engaging in the Israeli version of moral equivocation known as "shooting and crying."[42] Other critics refused to accept the "silence breakers'" central claim that they were victims of "the corrupting situation" or of "society" writ large, calling on them not to downplay their agency and to take responsibility for the abuses they inflicted on Palestinian citizens.

Nevertheless, the effort to circulate soldiers' testimonies that expose the brutal face of the occupation has added its weight to the political campaign against the normalization of Israel's continued occupation policy. Drawing on their credentials as Israeli patriots who are willing to serve their country in uniform, and who deeply care about the moral profile of Israeli society, the "silence breakers" boldly forced an open cultural conversation about morality in war, the abuses of military power, individual agency, national values, and human solidarity. If the political impact of their dissent remains unclear, the cultural import of the alternative paradigm they charted is unmistakable. Propelled by a paradoxical sense of helplessness in a military situation that put so much power in their hands, the soldiers turned to the testimonial act of speaking out to try to reclaim their agency. In a culture that has traditionally privileged deeds over words, they asserted their faith in the power of speech. Countering the Israeli traditional focus on the collective, they privileged personal experience and individual conscience. In doing all this, they brought together the potential impact of human performance and of new media technologies in ways that both reflected and shaped their moral dilemmas.

NOTES

1. As Sivan indicates in his study of the changing contours of war remembrance in Israel, earlier glorifying accounts in the commemoration of the fallen have given way to

more realistic tales of war that acknowledge the soldiers' traumatic experiences and the sense of futility attending the carnage. Emmanuel Sivan, "Private and Public Remembrance in Israel," in Jay Winter and Emmanuel Sivan, eds., *War and Remembrance in the Twentieth Century* (Cambridge, 1999), pp. 177–204.

2. For an account of the cultural roots of the change in 20th century perceptions of war and of soldiers that has resulted in war being perceived as a disillusioning experience and soldiers as victims, see Yuval Noah Harari, "Martial Illusions: War and Disillusionment in Twentieth-Century and Renaissance Military Memoirs," *The Journal of Military History* 69 (2005): 43–72.

3. See Yael Feldman, "Isaac or Oedipus? Jewish Tradition and the Israeli *Akedah*," in Cheryl Exun and Stephen Moore, eds., *Biblical Studies/Cultural Studies: The Third Sheffield Colloquium* (Sheffield, 1998), pp. 159–189; and Avi Sagi, "The Meaning of the *Akedah* in Israeli Culture and Jewish Tradition," *Israel Studies* 3/1 (1998): 45–60.

4. See the collection of soldiers' testimonies gathered, edited and published following the 1967 War in Avraham Shapira, ed., *The Seventh Day: Soldiers Talk about the Six Day War* (London, 1971). For a cultural approach to the study of this text, see Tamar Katriel, *Dialogic Moments: From Soul Talks to Talk Radio in Israeli Culture* (Detroit, 2004), pp. 71–104. A historical treatment of this text in relation to generational shifts within the Kibbutz movement can be found in Alon Gan, "The Discourse that Faded Away? The Attempt to Form a Distinctive Identity to the Second Generation in Kibbutzim," PhD. Dissertation, University of Tel Aviv, 2002; in Hebrew.

5. Hanoch Levin, "Queen of the Tub" in *What Does the Bird Care: Songs, Sketches and Satires* (Tel Aviv, 1987); in Hebrew; English translation cited in Sivan, ibid, p. 203.

6. In the French-Algerian context, a comparably problematic situation of nonconsensual combat was discussed under the label of "the dirty war." See Antoine Prost, "The Algerian War in French Collective Memory," in Winter and Sivan, eds., *War and Remembrance in the Twentieth Century*, pp. 161–76. Clearly, the notion of a "dirty war" stands in sharp contrast to the "myth of war experience" whose development over the past century is discussed in the seminal study of George Mosse, *Fallen Soldiers: Reshaping the Memory of the World Wars* (Oxford, 1990).

7. See James M. Jasper, *The Art of Moral Protest: Culture, Biography, and Creativity in Social Movements* (Chicago, 1997), p. 97.

8. *Ibid.*, p. 66.

9. Information about the *Breaking the Silence* group, including photographs and transcripts and videos of testimonies, can be found in their website, http:/ /www. shovrimshtika.org

10. For several months in 2005 weekly installments selected from "Breaking the Silence" soldiers' testimonies appeared in the online version of the popular daily *Ma'ariv*, called *nrg*, usually thematically organized.

11. "Breaking the Silence" website, http://www.shovrimshtika.org/ downloaded 26.8.08

12. Notably, this earned them some censure from radical left activists who accused them of navel-gazing, claiming that they had no real interest in the Palestinians' plight as a principled issue (as could be occasionally gleaned in talkbacks to their online column in *nrg* and as I encountered in personal conversations).

13. From the Soldier's Letter, February 2004, reproduced on the cover of the booklet compiling testimonies from Hebron, entitled *Breaking the Silence: Soldiers Speak Out About their Service in Hebron* (Jerusalem, March 2004). This and subsequent booklets were distributed for free at events organized by the group and by mail upon request and exist in both Hebrew and English.

14. Hebron booklet (English edition), *Ibid.*, p.8.

15. *Ibid.*, p. 5.

16. For an analysis and critique of mainstream Israeli media coverage of the events

of the Al Aqsa Intifada, see Daniel Dor, *Intifada Hits the Headlines: How the Israeli Press Misrepresented the Outbreak of the Second Palestinian Uprising* (Bloomington, IN, 2003); and *The Suppression of Guilt: The Israeli Media and the Reoccupation of the West Bank* (London, 2005).

17. For the history of conscientious objection in Israel, see Alek Epstein, "In Search of Legitimacy: Development of Conscientious Objection in Israel from the Founding of the State to the Lebanon Campaign," *Israeli Sociology* 1/2 (1999): 385–428, in Hebrew. For information about selective refusal in the early 2000s see, for example, the website of the *Courage to Refuse* group http://www.couragetorefuse.org/English/default.asp.

18. See Per Linell and Ragnar Rommetveit, "The Many Facets of Morality in Dialogue," *Research on Language and Social Interaction* 31 (1998): 466.

19. For a recent treatment of the issue of societal silence in the Israeli context, see Hanna Herzog and Kinneret Lahad, eds., *Knowledge and Silence: On Mechanisms of Denial and Repression in Israeli Society* (Tel Aviv/Jerusalem, 2006); in Hebrew.

20. For analyses of social denial and the position of bystanders, see Stanley Cohen, *States of Denial: Knowing about Atrocities and Suffering* (Cambridge, 2001); Hannah Herzog and Kinneret Lahad, eds., *Knowledge and Silence*, in Hebrew; and Eviatar Zerubavel, *The Elephant in the Room: Silence and Denial in Everyday Life* (Oxford, 2006).

21. On parental involvement in military service, see Tamar Katriel, "Picnics in a Military Zone: Rituals of Parenting and the Politics of Consensus," in *Communal Webs: Communication and Culture in Contemporary Israel* (Albany, NY, 1991), pp. 71–91.

22. The expression "let every Hebrew mother know..." alludes to an oft-quoted statement made by David Ben-Gurion which speaks to the need to assure every Hebrew (Jewish) mother that the army is taking good care of enlisted soldiers.

23. Taken from an installment of testimonies published on *nrg*, the online version of the daily *Ma'ariv* (26.11.04) under the heading of "We Were Monsters," downloaded 18.10.07 from http://www.nrg.co.il/online/1/ART/827/777.html

24. For the distinction between actor-oriented and structure-oriented violence, see Johan Galtung, *Peace by Peaceful Means: Peace and Conflict, Development and Civilization* (London, 1996).

25. "Breaking the Silence," Testimonial booklet #1, English version, p. 22.

26. "Breaking the Silence" website ('Articles' section), Yonatan Boemfeld, "Empty Words," address at the opening of the exhibit, downloaded, 18.10.07.

27. "Breaking the Silence" website ("About Us" statement), *Ibid.*, downloaded 18.10.07

28. For a discussion of this polarity and its implications for Israeli cultural identity, see Tamar Katriel, *Talking Straight: Dugri Speech in Israeli Sabra Culture* (Cambridge, 1986).

29. On the role of photography in relation to the occupation, including some references to the "Breaking the Silence" group, see Ariella Azoulay, *The Civil Contract of Photography* (Tel Aviv, 2006); in Hebrew.

30. Jasper, *Ibid.*, p. 154.

31. Jasper, *Ibid.*, pp. 136–137.

32. Thomas Weber, *Gandhi as Disciple and Mentor* (Cambridge, 2007).

33. For an illuminating discussion of the notion of "effacement," see Zygmunt Bauman, "Effacing the Face: On the Social Management of Moral Proximity," *Theory, Culture & Society* 7 (1990): 5–38.

34. "Breaking the Silence," Hebron booklet, pp. 39–40 (English version).

35. *Ibid.*, p.6.

36. In the Labovian structural analysis of personal experience narratives, the notion of coda refers to that segment of the narrative that links the narrated materials with the storytelling situation. See William Labov and Jushua Waletsky, "Narrative Analysis: Oral Versions of Personal Experience" in J. Helm, ed. *Essays on Verbal and Visual Arts* (Seattle, 1967).

37. "Breaking the Silence," Hebron booklet, p.11 (English version).

38. *Ibid.*, p. 16.

39. *Ibid.*, p. 17.

40. Harold Rosen, "The Autobiographical Impulse," in Deborah Tennen, ed., *Linguistics in Context: Connecting, Observation and Understanding* (Norwood, NJ, 1988), p. 75.

41. "Breaking the Silence," Hebron booklet, p. 15 (English version).

42. See Nachum Barnea, *Shooting and Crying* (Tel Aviv, 1981), in Hebrew.

The *Operation Victory* Video Game

Janis L. Goldie

Over the last thirty years, video games have become one of the most pervasive and popular forms of media entertainment. With the onslaught of game consoles such as PlayStation® and Xbox®, people of all ages are getting involved in gaming and generating impressive profits. Alongside the increased popularity of video games comes a significant expansion of the types of games that are available for consumers. One of the more interesting video games to be released lately, particularly in a Canadian context, is *Operation Victory*[1], a strategy game based on Canada's role in World War II. While video games and war have had a close relationship from the technology's inception, *Operation Victory* is unique in its explicit attempt to present an authentic narrative of the battles and challenges that Canadian soldiers faced in World War II. In this way, the creators of *Operation Victory* have gone to great pains to ensure that players learn about, and directly "experience," the risks, situations and outcomes Canadian soldiers faced in one of the bloodiest conflicts in history.

In its attempt at authenticity and historical accuracy, *Operation Victory* can be seen as a particularly interesting text of commemoration. The digital reenactment of battles and missions that the game provides results in a representation of war as "what really happened" and thus can be understood as a text of commemoration just as films, artwork or celebrations are. Similarly, just as these other texts of commemoration are important in their role in the construction of national identity, the video game *Operation Victory* is important in its construction of a particular version of Canadian national identity via its commemoration of the nation's role in World War II.

The representation of a Canadian experience of war in *Operation Vic-*

tory is the focus of this paper. Thus, I examine how a Canadian experience of war is represented and embedded within the video game and consider what this particular commemoration of warring Canadians suggests about national identity before making claims about what video games may mean for war commemoration more generally.

Video Games—An Overview

Almost forty years since the first video game was released, the industry has proven itself to be a major cultural force across the globe.[2] In 2004 the estimated global market for video game software and hardware exceeded $30 billion. In the United States alone, video game sales amounted to a $7 billion industry in 2006, and it continues to grow, almost tripling in size over the last ten years. Videogames have been noted as the fastest growing entertainment industry in America, even surpassing books, records and movie box office sales. In Canada, video games are an increasingly popular entertainment option as well. As of 2004, the video game market was a billion dollar industry and the country has been noted as one of the world's top producers, as well as consumers, of video games.

Video games are being played by all kinds of people. Recent statistics tell us that 69 percent of video game players are over the age of 18, with 25 percent of gamers over the age of 50, and 44 percent of gamers falling between the 18–49 age category, negating the often-held stereotype that video gamers are socially awkward pre-pubescent male teens.[3] While males continue to dominate in terms of playing video games, females are catching up. In 2006 the Entertainment Software Association reported that male gamers make up 62 percent of the population while females fall in at 38 percent. Overall, in Canada and across the globe, the video game has become "one of the most pervasive, profitable and influential forms of entertainment," making the academic study of it imperative.[4]

Video Games, Commemoration and National Identity

From their inception, video games have had a militaristic bent and thus a significant focus in the game studies literature has been on war and video games— in part, no doubt, because war video games continue to be among the most popular with gamers. The literature on war and video games tends to fall into two main approaches: the traditional "effects" approach ("how do they affect players?"), and the "pedagogical/political economy" approach ("how are they used in training and learning" and "how does the military and the entertainment industry work together to create video games?").[5] In this paper, war and video games are examined from a different perspective — that of war commemoration.

The study of the commemoration of war has increasingly garnered the attention of social science and humanities scholars since the 1980s,[6] in part because of the major political upheavals at the end of the twentieth century, the public visibility of the Holocaust, and the onslaught of major international anniversaries and celebrations, particularly around World War II. This interest in the rituals, celebrations and memorials around war is frequently approached from a theoretical perspective that focuses on the politics of war commemoration.

The politics approach to war commemoration sees the commemoration of war "as a practice bound up with rituals of national identification, and a key element in the symbolic repertoire available to the nation-state for binding its citizens into a collective national identity."[7] In this approach, the issue is often about the power of such commemorations to reestablish social cohesion and the legitimacy of authority. In addition, the politics approach to war commemoration often sees acts of commemoration, especially from state-centered agencies, as an attempt to construct a unitary and coherent version of the past in order to "create comforting collective scripts capable of replacing a lost sense of community."[8] This approach to war commemoration is most often associated with scholars such as Eric Hobsbawm, Terence Ranger and Benedict Anderson.

The politics approach to war commemoration is broadened by Barbara Misztal's dynamics of memory perspective. According to Misztal, the dynamics of memory perspective understands "commemoration as a struggle or negotiation between competing narratives, and stresses that the dynamic of commemorative rituals involves a constant tension between creating, preserving and destroying memories."[9] In this way, commemoration is seen to be a socially constructed and contested process that is shaped by, and shapes, the present as well as the past. The dynamics of memory approach to commemoration also recognizes that commemoration can be constructed by elites and powerful actors or groups such as nation-states; that is, from the top-down, but also that commemoration can be constructed and contested from the bottom-up by ordinary citizens and civil society groups. In this way, a more complex understanding of agency is achieved, allowing dominant constructions of memory to be challenged or rejected by ordinary citizens while at the same time acknowledging that citizens are able to employ personal narratives into various representations. In addition, the dynamics of memory approach leave room for an approach that acknowledges the role of mourning and politics in the construction of commemoration by noting that various elements are often at play at once. Finally, the dynamics of memory approach understand that there are limits in the construction of commemoration as the past is often resistant to efforts to make it over and that permanent and changing visions of the past are always part of one another.

Such an approach to commemoration also necessitates an understanding of commemoration's relation to national identity. Within commemoration studies, an important connection to identity has been noted. First popularized by Eric Erikson in the late 1950s, the term identity was connected to an individual sense of self, or, self-sameness over time. Today, aside from understanding that group identities are also possible, identities are no longer seen as defined and distinguishable entities. Instead, they are considered to be an ongoing process of construction, often in narrative form, which work to stabilize and justify the self-designations that people claim. In other words, identity is now understood to be variable (to a limit) where "the putting on (and also taking off) of identities is a common experience in the contemporary world."[10] We are seen to have many identities at once and are (somewhat) free to change those identities as we see fit. Along the same vein, a country's national identity is seen as a process of construction and no longer a concrete, identifiable entity. Thus, identity, both individual and "imagined communities," are seen as "the product of multiple and competing discourses, and [are] thus unstable, multiple, fluctuating, and fragmentary."[11] In all, both individual and collective identities now tend to be understood as "projects and practices, not properties."[12]

Identity is tied to commemoration at a very fundamental level. The main function of commemoration, from a politics perspective, is to permit cohesion of a social group and to guarantee its identity. As John Gillis explains, "the notion of identity depends on the idea of memory, and vice versa. The core meaning of any individual or group identity, namely, a sense of sameness over time and space, is sustained by remembering; and what is remembered is defined by the assumed identity."[13] In this way, acts of commemoration enable a social group such as a nation-state to create and transmit a consistent narrative of identity to its members. Thus, commemoration often gives a group a sense of its past and defines its aspirations for the future. In all, commemoration helps to form nations via the construction of "common symbols, images, and memories, that, when taken together, constitute the identity of a people and give them an orientation in time and space."[14] In fact, memory is particularly crucial for national identity, so much so, that "the more a community is imagined, as in the case of the nation, the more 'memory' (and forgetting) is necessary to it."[15] Of course, an important part of what creates group identity is what is *not* remembered, or is forgotten. In this way, equally important to what is being remembered by the group is what is being left out.

The study of commemoration and its role in the construction of national identity are important starting places when examining the commemoration of Canada's role in World War II in the videogame *Operation Victory*. While the relationship between video games and war commemoration has been underexplored to date,[16] examining the commemoration of war that is embedded in a videogame is only a natural extension of the research done on war commemoration in films, television shows, museums, artwork, pilgrimages, or reenactments. In other words, when a video game explicitly attempts to historically reenact a battle, a mission or a general encounter that a nation's soldiers have experienced firsthand, a specific representation of war is being presented as "what really happened," and is thus offering a commemoration of war, just as films, novels, history texts, or memorials do. And because *Operation Victory* gives a uniquely Canadian commemoration of World War II, its construction of certain elements of national identity around war is particularly interesting. It is with this perspective in mind that I move on to a brief explanation of the videogame before describing my methodology and findings.

Operation Victory

Operation Victory is centered on the Canadian military experience in World War II. In contrast to first-person shooter games, *Operation Victory* is a turn-based strategy game where tactical thinking matters more than reflexes. Players command teams of soldiers to conduct missions in German-occupied territory that are based on real operations that Canadian soldiers took part in during World War II, such as the raid on Dieppe, the advances into Sicily and Normandy, as well as the Battle of the Atlantic. Players are asked to use their soldiers to accomplish four objectives to successfully complete all of the six missions. Objectives range from overtaking a mountain gun post, to saving a wounded radio operator, to putting out a fire on the HMCS *Alberni*. While these objectives are being carried out, the player's soldiers defend themselves against German troops by strategically placing themselves behind obstacles or keeping hidden in the shadows. In addition, certain soldiers are given special skills, so that one soldier may be a medic and carry a med kit, another may be an explosives expert, and another throws grenades. *Operation Victory* can be played alone or with others in a multiplayer environment and it has a 2-D or a

"God's view" perspective rather than the traditional 3-D format found in most war games (like the popular *Medal of Honor*).

Operation Victory is unique and interesting for a number of reasons. First, it provides a Canadian perspective on World War II. While many war games focus on the American or British experience, this is the first computer game to offer a uniquely Canadian perspective on the war. Second, the game is unique in its historical accuracy, or at least, its explicit attempt at historical accuracy. Produced by Breakthrough New Media in association with Sarbakan, Bell Fund, Telefilm Canada, History Television, and released in 2005 to mark the 60th Anniversary of VE-Day, *Operation Victory* is based on three television productions that are the work of Canadian historian Norm Christie. In this way, the game relies on an historical approach to World War II, is an extension of books and television documentaries, and is marketed as unique in its historical accuracy. That is, the missions that the game provides for the player to accomplish are based on stories and incidents that actually occurred to Canadian soldiers during World War II. The mission briefing that the player receives upon play provides a well-written account and explanation of the setting of the situation, and thus offers important historical context about the war — and the game. Finally, the game is unusual in its focus on tactical action versus being a "shooter" game. As a turn-based game, comparisons can be more easily made between a board game rather than traditional PC-computer war games. Rather than a war game that is focused on killing, the focus in *Operation Victory* is on accomplishing small, manageable missions to help the overall Allied forces make small gains against the Germans. All of these elements of *Operation Victory*— its Canadian perspective, its explicit attempt at historical accuracy and its focus on tactical action — make it particularly appropriate to study in an investigation of how video games and commemoration operate to construct representations of national identity.

Methodology

To investigate how a Canadian perspective of war is represented in *Operation Victory* and to think about what that means for the construction of national identity more generally, I employ rhetorical critical analysis, specifically drawing on narrative criticism.[17] Beyond the connection made by many gaming scholars between narrative and video games, others have also noted the importance of narratives and rhetorical criticism in studying constructions of war commemoration and national identity. M. Lane Bruner for one shows that critical rhetorical theory is useful to investigate the process of national identity construction, in part because "national identity is incessantly negotiated through discourse," and thus is "an ongoing rhetorical process." This study is not an attempt to uncover *the* identity of the Canadian nation, but to analyze a particular moment in time and a particular articulation of national identity in what Bruner calls "in the ongoing discursive negotiation of what it imaginatively means to be a member of a nation."[18] In a similar fashion, T. G. Ashplant, G. Dawson and Michael Roper note the importance of studying narratives as well as the arenas and agencies of war commemoration in order to identify aspects of the struggle over war memories. In all, narrative analysis is particularly useful for the examination of a video game such as *Operation Victory* because it allows the investigation into a particular order and view of the world via a description of a situation involving characters, actions and settings.

Findings

By examining *Operation Victory's* narrative elements—that is, elements of character, event, setting, and narration—the Canadian war experience can be seen to be represented in a number of traditional and surprising ways. Specifically, Canadian soldiers are represented in *Operation Victory* as a fairly homogenous group of people who are morally justified as well as reluctant in their involvement in World War II, but yet who are still resilient and tenacious warriors.

The moral justification of Canadians in *Operation Victory* is evidenced via the representation of characters in the video game as well as throughout the game's narrative. In this way, Canadian soldiers are presented as morally justified in their participation in World War II generally as well as in their specific fight against the Germans. The moral justification of the Canadians' fight against the Germans is evident in the presentation of the different characters in the game. The Canadian soldiers are presented as varied, complex and human agents, while the German soldiers are presented as the non-human "other" enemy. For example, the German soldiers are often referred to as "dogged" or "blasted" by Canadian soldiers. In the mission briefings, the Germans are described as "the Nazi enemy" as well as "fanatical," soldiers who have "cut our men to pieces," are "blocking our advance northward," and turning all of Italy into a battleground. Besides the linguistic moves to position the German soldier characters as the enemy, the game design ensures that this representation is the only option. While this is a turn-based game, the player is unable to select which character set he/she would rather play, and thus operating as a German is not even presented as a viable alternative.

The German soldier characters are also made into the non-human "other" via their uniformity in *Operation Victory*. Generally speaking, they wear the exact same uniform (which consists of a German black helmet, longer green jacket, black belt, grey pants, tall black boots) and they move and act in the same manner. They are faceless and no details about their personalities or their lives off the battlefield are provided — unlike the Canadian hero characters as we will see. Throughout the game, the German characters are the faceless and relentless enemy, and their uniformity and lack of personality enables them to fill the "other" (or the enemy) role nicely so that the moral problem of killing the German characters is removed for the player. The German characters are represented as non-human throughout the game and thus make a natural and unproblematic villain, presenting a simplified version of war, and of humanity.

In contrast, the heroes in the game, the Canadian soldiers, are presented as human in their variety, complexity and agency. There are four different main hero characters on each mission, and each Canadian soldier is named and has a brief biography of his professional and personal life, which the player reads before attempting the mission. In addition, the Canadian hero soldier is posited as an agent, that is, able to make choices about where to go, what to do (shoot, lay down, etc.) via the player. In contrast, no agency is given to the German soldiers. Each Canadian hero is further differentiated by special skills such as being a medic or able to operate a radio, to set off explosives, or throw grenades. In addition, these Canadian hero soldiers are given different faces and uniforms from each other. As well, the Canadian hero characters represent a wide variety of Canadians geographically, linguistically and in terms of their socio-economic class level via descriptions of their professions, educations and backgrounds. For instance, in Mission One we meet Lieutenant Arthur Perry, who we are told is an experienced sailor and a yachtsman who joined the Canadian Navy in 1939 to fight the Nazis. He has been sunk twice by U-boats but, we are told, luckily has survived. We are also told that Perry's fiancée works in London, England, and that when he can, he takes her to the theater or movies—"in spite of German bombs." Besides the interesting stereotypes that these descriptions evoke, the character descriptions also work to "bring alive" the Canadian soldier heroes as complex and varied humans. Sounding much like a short personal ad, these descriptions work to differentiate the characters by giving them unique looks and personalities. In this way, players are more able to identify and relate to the Canadian hero characters as complex humans while at the same time easily to see the German enemy as the morally unproblematic "other" who need to be overcome. By representing the German characters as a non-human "other" entity, the killing and elimination of these characters that takes place in this game is morally permissible, or at least is morally unproblematic. In all, the human hero versus non-human enemy construction of the characters results in the presentation of Canadian soldiers as morally justified in their fight against the Germans.

The moral justification for the Canadian participation in World War II more generally can be found in textual descriptions throughout the game. For instance, the narrator describes World War II as the "bloodiest war in history," explaining that "never have the stakes been so high" because if the Allies are defeated, "whole nations will face slavery — or extermination." The narrator further explains how the Germans have been scoring "victory after victory" in Europe. However, "now, in their darkest hour, Britain, Canada, the United States and their Allies must prepare to strike back." The textual setting described by the narrator, then, evokes a feeling of desperation and implies that the Canadians are fighting in a last-ditch attempt to save the world. Thus, the Canadians are presented as morally justified in their participation in World War II because of the horrible consequences that may result if the Germans were to succeed.

Besides the moral justification of the Canadian involvement in World War II that is represented here, it is clear from the text that the rationale behind getting involved in the war is one of desperation, thereby also working to posit the Canadians as reluctant warriors. Here, because the stakes are so high and the possible consequences so terrifying, Canadian participation is presented as a necessary condition rather than as a choice. In this way, the representation of Canadian involvement in World War II presented in the game seems to suggest that Canadians did not necessarily want to get involved, but were forced to because of the seriousness of the consequences potentially facing the rest of the world if they did not. The Canadian representation of war is one of reactiveness versus aggressiveness, so that Canadians are represented as fighting when necessary, but not as a nation that seeks out conflicts.

Another way that the Canadian soldiers are represented as reluctant warriors is via the overall purpose and goals of the game — which for the Canadian hero character is not to kill the German soldiers, but to achieve objectives to complete a mission. While it may be necessary for self-defense or to complete a mission, killing the villains is not the main focus of the game, unlike the traditional first-person "shooter" war games. Instead, the heroes try to complete small tasks such as putting out fires, climbing a mountain, securing a building, or rescuing a medic. Most of the objectives are fairly benign activities, and when killing is done in the game, it is usually in self-defense or to protect a stronghold. For example, in the off-turn, characters can be placed on over-watch and this enables the Canadian heroes to shoot at any German within firing range. While aiming toward a specific German soldier is possible, actually killing a German soldier with the player's rifle is quite difficult as the player's aim gets worse the closer she is to the soldier. Violence is also permitted when protecting a position or a stronghold. For instance, in the third mission in Sicily, the Norman Castle has to be defended from the Germans. This means positioning the Canadian soldier characters in strategic places to pick off the German soldiers as they come toward the castle. Again, however, the goal was not explicitly to hurt anyone, but rather to protect a stronghold "at all costs." It is not just killing for killing's sake that occurs in *Operation Victory*; instead, it is killing to ensure that the soldiers do not get killed first and to achieve the overall objective. This mechanism in *Operation Victory* represents Canadian soldiers as using violence only when necessary. In addition, it represents violence more generally as being of limited use and appeal — at least on the part of the Canadian soldiers. This is one way that the video game creates a representation of Canadian soldiers as reluctant warriors.

Similarly, the Canadian soldiers are represented as reluctant warriors in the game's embedded preference for cautiousness. One learns via playing *Operation Victory* that it is good to be cautious; that is, it is usually better to be safe than sorry. For instance, when given the choice between gaining 50 meters in distance to get to the ship carrier and being slightly out in the open, it is a much wiser decision to make your Canadian soldier character gain only 35 meters and be completely hidden. In the former situation, time and time again the character will be killed and the mission will end. Thus, protecting the characters and being cautious is rewarded in the game, more so than blind fearlessness. This is interesting in terms of the presentation of Canadian soldiers as smart rather than aggressive, and as defensive rather than offensive in their actions.

A final way that the game portrays Canadians as reluctant warriors is via the distanced perspective of the game. *Operation Victory* employs a "God's view" perspective. This represents a kind of extreme third-person perspective in that the player's actions "are taking place in real time in that other world on the screen, but [his] view is from the outside."[19] While the player is a character in third-person perspective games such as *Operation Victory*, the player does not see the world through the hero character's eyes. Instead, the player sees himself/herself from a "variety of pre-programmed angles, placed in a spatial setting," and thus can see when someone is approaching you behind for instance. In contrast, first-person perspective games put the player into the character's body, so to speak, and allow for the same visual perspective. The third-person perspective in *Operation Victory* is interesting in that it allows the player to be a part of the situation, but as a detached, yet active, master of the situation. In this way, the perspective of *Operation Victory* provides a distanced involvement at the same time that a virtue of direct involvement is portrayed. It is interesting that the feeling of direct involvement is created via the symbolic images in the game, through sound, movement and narrative descriptions, while at the same time is lessened during actual play via the perspective offered. This contradictory perspective of war seems to represent Canadians as reluctant warriors in that they are able to participate in the experience of war, but prefer to keep their distance. Thus, the direct-but-distanced involvement in war that is evident in the game works to further represent Canadian soldiers as reluctant warriors.

Besides being presented as reluctant warriors throughout *Operation Victory,* Canadian soldiers are also seen as tenacious and resilient. This is clear when we examine the difficult odds that the Canadian characters often have to overcome in the game. For instance, while the Canadian soldiers are usually armed with rifles, grenades and the occasional Sherman tank, the German characters have an impressive arsenal including machine guns and Panzers. In this way, the German characters are represented as almost always being in a position of power. This is especially the case in Dieppe and in Sicily, where the German soldiers had a significant advantage in terms of their strategic position. In this way, the German soldiers are extremely difficult to conquer. The difficulty of defeating the Germans via their weapons and position seems to imply that Canadian soldiers managed to overcome difficult odds in their war participation and thus are strong and resilient warriors, despite their reluctance to get involved.

The tenacity of Canadian soldiers is represented via gameplay as well. For instance, it is almost impossible to complete an objective on the first try in the game, let alone complete an entire mission in one attempt. The game is created so that players must keep trying as they learn from trial and error in order to move forward. This virtue of persistence embedded in the game is interesting in terms of what it says about Canadian soldiers and war generally, implying that Canadian soldiers are hard workers and do not give up easily. War is not an easy situation and is not won quickly or easily; it takes time and persistence to achieve goals.

Finally, *Operation Victory* represents Canadian soldiers as strong and resilient because of the chaos that surrounds their missions. The visual setting in the game most often evidences the chaos of the Canadian experience of war. In the Dieppe mission, for instance, there are ground holes and bodies everywhere, tanks are blown up, there are barbed wire and sandbags, guns and bullets flying, and carrier ships stranded. Chaos is also evident in the visual images on the ship in Mission One where fires are raging, steam jets are going off and the boat is sinking. Likewise, in Mission Four in Ortona, tanks are demolished, buildings and walls are blown apart and the opposing sides are so close that death is imminent. The chaos that Canadians are represented to be experiencing again works to portray the Canadians soldiers as strong and resilient, overcoming almost insurmountable odds with persistence and courage.

In addition to positing the Canadian soldiers in World War II as morally justified, reluctant and resilient, *Operation Victory* also presents them as a fairly homogenous group — that is, male and white. Players meet only one female character. Even the civilian characters that are presented are male. While this is an authentic picture of the way things were on the battlefields of World War II, it is interesting nonetheless that the game is mainly focused on the battlefields. In other words, places where women were directly involved in the war effort — say, in a hospital or in the factories— were left out of the narrative of the Canadian experience. Instead, the main way that women exist in the Canadian war experience, according to *Operation Victory*, is through their personal relationships with the Canadian hero characters. Thus, the main representation of women in the game is found in the soldiers' personal biographies— where it is noted that one man's fiancée lives in London, while another is dating a "smashing girl" from Cambridge, and elsewhere. Thus, the Canadian war experience is represented in a very one-gendered and traditional manner, as though women had no objectives in the war. In essence, women are portrayed, by their omission, as people of no real import in the Canadian memory of World War II. This is an interesting aspect of "forgetting" in *Operation Victory*. It seems to imply that the Canadian war experience was no more than what happened on the front lines, and thus was predominantly a male experience. And while women are not completely forgotten in the game, they are present only through their association with men in very traditional support roles, such as wife or girlfriend. In this way, war is represented in *Operation Victory* as a *male* endeavor, as a kind of "militarized masculinity."[20]

In addition to the Canadian war experience being represented as a male endeavor, it is presented as a white one. There is no ethnic or racial diversity portrayed. All of the characters are Caucasian, and thus a Canadian representation of war as a "white" endeavor is embedded in the game. Interestingly, however, regionalism in terms of the provinces the characters come from as well linguistic differences are represented via the Canadian hero soldiers, and thus highlight a Canadian identity that centers around regionalism and linguistic diversity.

Operation Victory and Its Canadian Representation of War

After examining the narrative elements in *Operation Victory*, the Canadian experience of war is shown in four predominant ways. First, Canadians are represented as morally justified in their specific fight against the Germans and in their participation in World War II more generally. Second, Canadians are represented as reluctant warriors. Third, Canadians are represented as resilient and tenacious soldiers. Finally, Canadian soldiers are presented as a fairly homogeneous group.

In terms of what these representations suggest about the construction of Canadian national identity more generally in the game, a number of conventional and unexpected depictions are evident. For example, the presentation of Canadian soldiers as morally justified and reluctant in their participation in World War II follows a familiar feature in the construction of Canadian national identity—that of a Canadian preference for nonviolence.

As a war game, *Operation Victory* flies in the face of this feature of national identity and overcomes it by justifying the Canadian participation in World War II in an ideological manner. The game suggest that it was okay for Canadians to kill and to fight because the Germans were such terrible, inhuman creatures. By portraying the German characters as nonhuman and positing the fight against them as morally unproblematic—as well as by justifying participation in World War II as necessary because of the horrible consequences that could have arisen across the world if Germany was not stopped—the Canadian preference for nonviolence is able to remain intact, even within the context of a war game.

In a similar manner, the Canadian characters are presented as reluctant warriors, which further works to promote or construct the idea of a Canadian preference for nonviolence. Again, the textual descriptions, game play and perspective offered throughout *Operation Victory* presents Canadians as not necessarily wanting to use violence, but doing so—successfully—when necessary.

At the same time that the Canadian preference for nonviolence is embedded in the video game, the construction of Canadians as tough, yet humble, is also evident, mainly through the focus on the resiliency and tenacity of the soldiers. Here, Canadians are constructed as strong and determined when tasked to do difficult things. In this manner, the game seems to suggest that even though Canadians have a preference for nonviolence, when asked to "step up to the plate" they are surprisingly durable and persistent. Thus, in contrast to a traditional construction of Canadian national identity as downplaying our war success, the game seems instead to promote a construction of national identity of pride in national war efforts. In addition, humility is offered alongside this pride, as troubles, failings and challenges along the way have been acknowledged, such as the defeat at Dieppe and the difficulty in overcoming the Germans in Ortona, for instance.

Finally, the representation of Canadians as fairly homogeneous in *Operation Victory* is very surprising in terms of a traditional construction of national identity. In this way, one of the most popular and often-cited aspects of "Canadianess"— multiculturalism — is completely left out of the game. Instead, the focus on difference in Canada in the video game centers on linguistic and regional differences. Thus, Canadians are presented as different in terms of the language they speak, via English and French, and the provinces and areas of the country that they come from, but not in terms of racial backgrounds. This is a very surprising representation of Canadianess in the game.

In all, the construction of Canadian national identity within the game is complex and often contradictory. On the one hand, it presents a Canadian preference for nonviolence. This is a popular feature in the construction of Canadian national identity, especially since peacekeeping has come to the forefront of the Canadian military experience (at least in the popular imagination). It is interesting that even within a war video game, the construction of the preference for nonviolence can be noted. On the other hand, the video game presents Canadian pride and humility in its war efforts. The game suggests that even if Canadians are not naturally aggressive, they can be surprisingly tough, determined and persistent warriors.

Thus, a certain pride in Canadian war accomplishments is constructed, alongside a narrative of nonviolence. Finally, Canadians are represented as humble in their ability to acknowledge their faults and limitations so that the Canadian national identity which is constructed in the game is the ability to confront missteps in history. At the same time that Canadians acknowledge their achievements in war, they remind themselves that they also had failures. The contradictory presentation of national identity within a war context in *Operation Victory* seems to be particularly Canadian. Canada is a nation often noted for its obsession with defining itself, and furthermore, for being consistently confused about who it actually is. This uncertainty is clear in a video game such as *Operation Victory*, where contradictory constructions of national identity lie naturally together.

Video Games and the Popularization of War Memory

As we have seen, the representation of war in *Operation Victory* presents a view of war that is very similar to other popular culture representations, such as those found in films or television shows. It, too, displays
an overall representation of war as a sanitized and simplistic tale that
focuses on the adventure of war, rather than on the human dimension or
cost. Thus, war in this particular video game, despite its realisticness via
narrative and images, tends to retain traditional forms of representation
of war more generally. However, the representation of war in *Operation
Victory* is not the only story. In fact, the use of a video game to commemorate Canada's World War II experience is particularly fascinating in the
kinds of questions that it raises about the future of war commemoration
in an increasingly digital world. For instance, questions arise as to whether
the interactivity and involvement offered in the video game present new
challenges to commemoration more broadly, or whether "playing" at war
memory works to trivialize or enhance it.

Whenever new media forms are made available, concerns about their
effect on the representation of events and acts takes hold. Video games
are no exception. As such, three concerns are commonly voiced around
video games and their potential effect on war commemoration. First, there
are concerns about the representation of war that might be conveyed.
Specifically, these concerns are about the potential for a simplistic and
inauthentic manipulation of war representation. The fact that what were
once only direct, personal experiences of the war are now being replicated
in a digital form, raises concerns about what the replication of an experience means in terms of the transformation of the original experience.
Second, there are concerns about the level of interactivity in video games
and what this may mean for war commemoration. Here, the concern has
to do with the potential for players to alter and affect war commemoration, resulting in questions over who should own or control the commemoration of war and what will become of it in the future. Finally, there are
concerns about the act of "playing" with representations of war in
videogames, and thus its trivialization. In this way, critics worry whether
"playing" with war commemoration may trivialize the seriousness of the
event and the experience for those who have directly experienced it. As I
have already addressed the issue of war representation in *Operation Victory* extensively in this paper, I will now briefly explore the issues of trivialization, interactivity and play that arise within a discussion of video
games and war commemoration.

A close reading of *Operation Victory* shows that its video game format does in fact trivialize war memory. It is a game, after all, and war is far removed from being a game — something that one can choose to stop playing at one's will. But, interestingly, I would argue that *Operation Victory* is trivialized in the same manner that George Mosse proposes. Referring explicitly to kitsch items such as Iron Cross matchboxes, picture postcards, battlefield tourism, theater, toys, and games, he argues that these items and acts worked to trivialize war, thus "cutting war down to size so that it would become commonplace instead of awesome and frightening."[21] Thus, these games and mementos were used to retain pleasant or at least thrilling memories of war, "and, at the same time, exercised control over their memory." In this way, "trivialization was one way of coping with war, not by exalting and glorifying it, but by making it familiar, that which was in one's power to choose and to dominate."[22] Mosse acknowledges that games and play around war tend to trivialize the seriousness of the event, but at the same time are a necessary element to war commemoration as they allowed people to confront the horrors of war, make it mundane and give people the feeling of domination over events.

In *Operation Victory* a mundane process of trivialization also appears to be working to control the memory. In other words, a strict representation of Canada's experience in World War II is presented. By making this representation familiar, domination over it becomes possible. Thus, by weaving this particular version of Canada's World War II experience into the daily life of the video game's players, the confrontation of a war experience that is often plagued by negative representation can be confronted. It is interesting that the first mission that the player experiences, after the initial tutorial mission, is perhaps Canada's greatest military failure — Dieppe. But by reenacting the difficulties that Canadian soldiers experienced, players are able to create a feeling of domination over the events, rather than the sheer mockery and tragedy of the mission that is generally incorporated into public memory. The inane mess that was Dieppe is thus *re*-presented in the video game *Operation Victory* as something that can be controlled and "won" by simply getting out alive. By presenting a different framework around this, and other events for Canadian soldiers in World War II, the difficulties and failures the Canadians experienced can be seen to help take the sting out of the war. The process of trivialization in *Operation Victory*, then, works to transcend the reality of war by making it mundane, and thus operates to exercise control of the memory of Canadians in World War II.

This focus on a controlled memory of Canada in World War II is also evident in the restricted interactivity that the game offers. First, *Operation Victory* presents a very sequential narrative. The game is sequenced so that an objective must be met before one can move on to another, and the same goes for each mission. In this way, Mission One with its four objectives must be completed before Mission Two can be undertaken; a strict narrative sequence is thus kept intact. In other words, there is really only one way to achieve each objective and half of the challenge in this game is to figure out which is the correct way. Thus, *Operation Victory* presents a war narrative in a very limited manner and, as a result, interactivity is very limited here. Just as the game theorists have suggested, *Operation Victory*, instead of offering an interactive experience of war memory, presents a very limited one.[23] Thus, while players are able to move and act in the context of a commemoration act, they are not able to stray from the overall chronological sequence or narrative. Thus, true interactivity, as in free choice and action, is definitely not possible in *Operation Victory*. In this way, concerns about what interactivity means for war memory when history can be altered is a moot point in *Operation Victory*. History cannot be altered in the game as the representation of war that is presented is embedded directly into the game design.

In the same manner, "playing" at war in terms of free-thinking and free-acting is not really a possibility.[24] Instead, Operation Victory becomes a kind of digital reenactment where the player moves the soldiers to the place that they should be, and to do what they should do (or what they did in history). Thus, "playing" with war memory in *Operation Victory* is not really a possibility in terms of free choice or action. However, an attitude of play can be evidenced, which could arguably be detrimental to the commemoration of war (as not being taken seriously).[25] But as to concerns about play as mimesis — that is, as the possibility of transforming war memory into something far removed from what it is not — this is not an option in *Operation Victory*.[26] Because the selection and options within the game are so limited, the player is really taken on a digital storyline, following the predetermined path that the game designers set out for him or her. In this way, there is no real concern in *Operation Victory* in terms of how interactivity or play could affect the memory of war for the worse — as interactivity and play are not possibilities.

These are surprisingly contradictory findings to what one may suppose is happening in a video game commemoration of war. In a strange way, video games such as *Operation Victory* seem to actually offer more control over the memory of war than one would suspect. In this way, just as in films and novels, the representation of war memory that is presented depends to a great extent on the creators or artists of the form. Thus, while video games such as *Operation Victory* may appear to pose concerns about the flexibility and interactivity associated with these forms, the restricted narrative and superficial interactivity found in this game, at least, appear to indicate that video games will represent war in much the same way that "traditional" media have done.

NOTES

1. *Operation Victory* can be downloaded from: ry/index.html.
2. *History of Video Games* 2006, ory-and-genre/.
3. "Essential facts about the computer and video game industry," Entertainment, Software Association, 2006; ial.php.
4. Kurt Squire, "Video Games in Education," *International Journal of Intelligent Simulations and Gaming* 2 (2003): 49–62.
5. For a more detailed overview of the video game literature, see Mark Wolf and Bernard Perron, "Introduction," *The Video Game Theory Reader* (New York and London, 2003).
6. Foundational works in war commemoration include T. G. Ashplant, G. Dawson and Michael Roper, eds., *The Politics of War Memory and Commemoration* (New York, 2000); M. Evans and K. Lunn, eds., *War and Memory in the Twentieth Century* (Oxford, 1997); Paul Fussel, *The Great War and Modern Memory* (London, 1977); E. Hobsbawm and T. Ranger, *The Invention of Tradition* (Cambridge, 1983); George L. Mosse, *Fallen Soldiers: Reshaping the Memory of the World Wars* (New York, 1990); Jay Winter, *Sites of Memory, Sites of Mourning: The Great War in European Cultural History* (Cambridge, 1995); and Jay Winter and Emmanuel Sivan, eds., *War and Remembrance in the Twentieth Century* (Cambridge, 1999).
7. Ashplant, Dawson and Roper, eds., *The Politics of War Memory*, p. 7.
8. Barbara Misztal, "Theories of Social Remembering," in L. Ray, ed., *Theorizing Society* (Maidenhead, 2003), p. 127.
9. Barbara Misztal, "Durkheim on Collective Memory," *Journal of Classical Sociology* 3 (2003): 127.
10. Allen Megill, "History, Memory and Identity," *History of the Human Sciences* 11 (1989): 42.
11. Misztal, "Theories of Social Remembering," p. 34.
12. J. K. Olick and J. Robbins, "Social Memory Studies: From 'Collective Memory' to the Historical Sociology of Mnemonic Practices," *Annual Review of Sociology* 24 (1998): 122.
13. John R. Gillis, "Memory and Identity: The History of a Relationship," *Commemorations: The Politics of National Identity* (Princeton, 1994), p. 3.
14. B. Zelizer, "Reading the Past Against the Grain: The Shape of Memory Studies," *Critical Studies in Mass Communication* 12 (1995): 228.
15. Megill, "History, Memory and Identity," p. 44.
16. Eva Kingsepp, "Immersive Historicity in World War II Digital Games," *HUMAN IT* 8 (2006): 60–89, is one of the few scholars who has begun to think about video games and war memory. In addition, Mosse, *Fallen Soldiers*, pp. 126–27, addresses the role of games in the commemoration of war and its trivialization, noting that games were used to "cut war down to size," to make it familiar, and to "exercise control over its memory" while at the same time "retaining pleasant or at least thrilling memories."
17. Sonja K. Foss, *Rhetorical Criticism: Exploration & Practice* (Prospect Heights, IL, 1996). Following in Arthur A. Berger's footsteps, I take the perspective that video games can be understood as an art form rather than as a new medium, and thus can be read as a kind of text. Berger, *Video Games: A Popular Culture Phenomenon* (New Brunswick, 2002).

18. M. Lane Bruner, *Strategies of Remembrance: The Rhetorical Dimensions of National Identity Construction* (Columbia, SC, 2002), pp. 1, 7.

19. Kingsepp, "Immersive Historicity," p. 5.

20. Stephen Kline, Nick Dyer-Witheford and Gret De Peuter, *Digital Play: The Interaction of Technology, Culture, and Marketing* (Montreal and Kingston, 2003).

21. Mosse, *Fallen Soldiers*, p. 126.

22. *Ibid.*, p. 127.

23. See Berger, *Video Games*; and Kline, et al., *Digital Play*.

24. K. Stagnitti, "Understanding play: The Implications for play assessment," *Australian Occupational Therapy Journal* 51 (2004): 3–12.

25. See Wolf and Perron, "Introduction."

26. Faith Guss, "Reconceptualizing play: Aesthetic self-definitions," *Contemporary Issues in Early Childhood* 6 (2005): 233–43.

The Rwandan Genocide in Film[1]

Kirsten McAllister

Without films such as the academy-award nominated *Hotel Rwanda*, how would the 1994 Rwandan genocide be remembered by North Americans, if at all? As Andrew Hoskins argues, "it becomes difficult to imagine, or to remember, historic events of the modern age, outside of or separate from the media that [produces] them more frequently on a global scale."[2] This chapter critically examines how two dramatic films, *Hotel Rwanda* and *Sometimes in April*, contribute to constructing the public memory of the Rwandan genocide for millions of viewers around the world.

They are part of a wave of dramatic films and television shows produced after the publication of controversial reports[3] in 1998 and 1999 criticizing the United Nations (UN) for failing to stop the genocide. Like *100 Days, Human Cargo*,[4] *Shooting Dogs, A Sunday in Kigali*, and *Shake Hands with the Devil*, both films promise to offer audiences insights into what really happened in Rwanda and disclose why, as the reports claimed, the UN stood aside and watched extremists kill just under 1 million[5] Tutsi and moderate Hutu in less than 100 days.

The reports present many troubling findings. For instance, the 1999 "Report of the Independent Inquiry" states:

> information was available — to UNAMIR [United Nations Assistance Mission in Rwanda]; United Nations Headquarters and to key Governments — about a strategy and threat to exterminate Tutsis, recurrent ethnic and political killings of an organised nature, deathlists, persistent reports of import and distribution of weapons to the population and hate propaganda. *That more was not done to (respond to) this information at an early stage was a costly failure* [emphasis in the original].

This report also identifies the lack of political will to stop the genocide:

> It has been stated repeatedly during the course of the interviews ... that Rwanda was not of strategic interest to third countries and that the international community exercised double standards when faced with the risk of a catastrophe there compared to action taken elsewhere.... The fundamental failure was the lack of resources and political commitment devoted to developments in Rwanda and to the United Nations presence there. There was a persistent lack of political will by Member States to act, or to act with enough assertiveness (emphasis in original).[6]

The findings had a powerful effect on the international community; in this context, *Hotel Rwanda* and *Sometimes in April* can be viewed as expressions of that effect.

Like the other productions about the Rwandan genocide listed above, *Hotel Rwanda* and *Sometimes in April* take up the criticism of the reports launched against UN member states, especially the United States, Belgium and France, and replay the genocide for North American audiences, interweaving historical fact, real events and people into fictional stories. These films make it evident that UN member states were well aware of the atrocities committed by extremists and that France supplied them with arms.[7] But as I will argue below, *Hotel Rwanda* offers Western audiences ways to absolve their guilt and restore the moral authority of the UN and the United States.

This chapter describes not only how *Hotel Rwanda* and *Sometimes in April* offer audiences insight into the (failed) role in the peacekeeping mission, but also how they mediate their burdens of guilt and present them with resolutions. As I will argue, while *Hotel Rwanda* restores faith in Western nation states and attempts to offer closure, *Sometimes in April* shows audiences that there is no closure for those affected by genocide and that only a commitment to the long and complex process of reconciliation offers a possibility for resolution.

Hotel Rwanda and *Sometimes in April* differ from the other dramatic productions about Rwanda in that they present the genocide primarily from the perspective of Rwandans rather than sympathetic Western journalists, foreign missionaries and teachers. As I will describe below, this tends to humanize Rwandans and offers an antidote for the damaging stereotypical images of Africa that made it possible for UN member states to dismiss the genocide as "an African phenomenon."

By watching these films, Western audiences learn about how they, as members of supposedly democratic states, are implicated in the genocide, making it "their" humanitarian crisis. Both films reveal how the West was implicated in the historical roots of Rwanda's genocide. They show that before colonization, the Hutu, Tutsi and Twa shared the same language, history and myths of origin. While Tutsi raised cattle and the Hutu were agrarians, membership was not rigidly determined; for example, membership could be changed through marriage or cattle. Loosely a feudal system, Hutus gained access to the land through service to Tutsis, but by no means were power relations unmediated and the Hutu without autonomy and powerful lineages.[8]

Both films make references to the use of phrenological measurements of skulls and noses by Belgian colonists to divide the Tutsis and Hutus into "scientific" racial categories. Mixing in Christian mythology, Belgians believed the Tutsi were ancestors of Ham because they had physical traits that made them closer to the "white race" and thus more intelligent and attractive than the Hutu.[9] Belgians thus introduced a racial-religious hierarchy that they managed through racial identity cards. The films show audiences the disastrous impact of this colonial system on contemporary Rwanda. Multiple scenes depict how Hutu extremists used the identity cards to target Tutsis at checkpoints in their homes and at work. Without the identity cards, many Tutsi would have been indistinguishable from Hutu members of society. As such, the films attempt to create a public memory of the roots of the genocide, which stretch back to colonization, on Rwandan society, intertwining Rwanda's history with that of the Western world.

Both films also show Western, and especially United States, audiences that they are implicated in the current humanitarian crisis. For example, in *Sometimes in April*, a parallel storyline follows real-life Prudence Bushnell (Debra Winger),[10] an official in Washington. She warns her government about the impending outbreak of violence in Rwanda. Once the genocide begins, she pressures her government and Rwandan commanders to intervene. The plotline following Bushnell shows audiences that without a doubt, the United States government knew about the carnage and refused to do anything.

Sometimes in April also reveals the failure of the American media. More obsessed with the Tanya Harding skating scandal and the suicide of musician Kurt Cobain, the Rwandan crisis is given little in-depth coverage. In a press conference reporters only want to know "who are the good guys?" and "are American citizens safe?" In this context, it could be argued that the Bushnell character serves to alleviate our burden of guilt, reassuring film viewers there were a few good Americans. Yet, unlike the "good" Westerners in *Hotel Rwanda*, whether individual Red Cross workers or UN colonels, she is ineffectual, unable to use her position to save Rwandans.

As I have suggested above, *Hotel Rwanda* and *Sometimes in April* educate audiences about the role of UN member states in the genocide. The viewers' willingness to be educated suggests that they are also willing to accept the fact that their governments had some degree of responsibility for what happened. Accepting responsibility is a way to make amends for wrong actions. In this way, both films offer a means to ameliorate the audience's guilt over the abandonment of thousands of Rwandan civilians desperately attempting to escape the genocide.

The films address viewers not just as citizens belonging to guilty UN member states, but also as members of societies where the news media and popular forms of entertainment are filled with dehumanizing images of Africans.[11] Each film has a number of scenes that confront viewers with these dehumanizing images. In *Hotel Rwanda*, for example, when the UN decides to reduce troops from 2,539 to 270, the UN Colonel (Nick Nolte) bluntly lays out the assumptions behind the UN's decision. The colonel turns to the main character, Paul Rusesabagina (Don Cheadle), who has just offered him a drink, and disgusted by his superiors, he blurts out, "You should spit in my face [Paul]. You're dirt; we think you're dirt." Shocked, Paul asks "who is 'we'?" The colonel replies, "the West, all the superpowers ... you're worthless, you're black, you're not even a nigger. You're African."

Here the UN colonel forces viewers to reflect on their own images of Africa. Mainstream media heavily relies on images of Africa as bewitching yet barbaric,[12] ignoring the region's complex politics, histories and cultural movements.[13] For example, recent films such as *Black Hawk Down* (Somalia), *Tears of the Sun* (Nigeria) and even *The Constant Gardener* (Kenya) and *Lord of War* (West African countries), which expose the corruption of Western transnational corporations and governments, distinguish Africans from Westerners using black-white, evil-good, irrational-rational, and child-adult dichotomies, drawing on powerful colonial discourses.[14] By confronting audiences with the dehumanizing images that inform Westerners about Africa, the films make us feel that we are working to correct our problematic views. But the films offer more than education and correction. They give us a chance to identify with individual Rwandans. Our identification with the characters in the films promises to redeem us, reinforcing our humanity.

Both films follow the plight of Rwandans struggling to protect their families and escape Hutu extremists. Working against media constructions of Africans as anonymous masses of helpless victims savagely slaughtered by barbaric members of their own society,[15] the characters are principled individuals with strong social consciousnesses. Both films focus on loving father figures trying to save their families from extremists. The sympathetic multi-dimensional portraits of the Rwandan characters encourage audiences to identify with them. Like conventional patriotic war films, the characters are given heroic qualities; for example, their willingness to sacrifice themselves to save their families and strangers. They are given emotional depth through humor and scenes of warm intimacy with their loved ones. As viewers, we become invested in their survival, experiencing fear when extremists threaten them and emotional pain when loved ones are killed. Moreover, through our vicarious identification with victims, we place ourselves in their roles, giving us access to (dramatizations of) their terrifying experiences. Access to these (dramatizations of) experiences allows audiences access to memories of the genocide. Audiences thus create their own "prosthetic memories": "memories [that] ... originate outside [their] lived experience and yet are taken and worn by [them] through mass cultural technologies of memory."[16]

In this regard, both films use various techniques to offer viewers the victims' experiences of fear and anxiety that feed in the production of prosthetic memory. While the films resist exploiting graphic images of extremists killing innocent civilians—which could reproduce images of primitive violence found in films like *Black Hawk Down* and *Lord of War*—they rely heavily on what the viewers already know from media reports, such as the widespread use of machetes and clubs. Each film has only one scene showing this form of killing. The scenes are long shots so that details cannot be seen. Yet many refer to machete killing. In *Sometimes in April* a militant checks the identity card of a young woman and then pulls her aside. We are not shown what happens next, although given the previous shots of the Interahamwe (civilian Hutu death squads) waving their machetes, her fate is easily imagined.

Shots of unruly Interahamwe operate as an ever-present threat, suddenly appearing from nowhere as if spilling out of the cracks of society and then dispersing and disappearing into alleys, crowds and forests. As viewers we are never certain when or where they will appear. Immersed in this landscape of fear where no one can be trusted and nowhere is safe, viewers can appropriate dramatizations of the victims' experiences as their own, creating prosthetic memories of the genocide.

As many Western audiences have little knowledge of Rwandan politics and history, prosthetic memories of the genocide can rely just as much on dangerous fantasy as on fact. For instance, the films turn the Interahamwe into the terrifying other — unpredictable, violent figures found in horror films and nightmares. It is true that the films show the Interahamwe were simply not spontaneous bloodthirsty mobs but rather trained by the Rwandan Armed Forces (RAF) and given machetes, which as mentioned above, were supplied by France. Yet neither film delves into the complex political history between the Tutsi and Hutu. Nor do the films refer to the power colonial Belgians gave to the Tutsis while subordinating the Hutus.[17] Perhaps the directors, George Terry (*Hotel Rwanda*) and Raoul Peck (*Sometimes*), felt these details would make the plots too complex for Western viewers to follow and jeopardize the ability to identify with the genocide victims. Also at stake is the impact of these films on Rwandans still suffering the aftermath of the recent genocide. Would reference to the colonial treatment of Hutu feed into the extremists' propaganda about "Tutsi oppressors"? Responsible directors must have considered how internationally distributed films could exasperate divisions rather than encourage reconciliation.[18] The proper timing and priorities for working through painful events must be considered. In addition, certain media and forums might be better for exploring such events, like the gacaca (grass) courts where common people traditionally gather to resolve conflicts. It might also be only future generations that can publicly explore the 1994 genocide in detailed relation to the colonial history.

In this respect, both films are careful to instill a sense of hope despite their depiction of horrific scenes of death. Focusing on families where Hutu and Tutsi have intermarried, the films show the social fabric of Rwandan society has remained intercultural despite divisive colonial rule. This functions to draw out memories of an earlier Rwanda that offer a vision for the future. The intermarried families represent what could be larger Rwandan society, where Hutu and Tutsi are members of the same family and the same society.

The films also avoid vilifying Hutus. They show that extremists killed Tutsis as well as moderate Hutus. Significantly, the main characters, Paul and Augustin, are Hutu. The films also show Hutus helping Rwandans escaping extremists. In *Sometimes in April* a Hutu farmer, a peasant woman, gives Martine, Augustin's future fiancé, and her two students shelter in her simple dwelling as they escape the extremists. She took a risk since the men in her household belong to the Interahamwe. Thus, the films attempt to engender memories of the solidarity between Hutu and Tutsi during the genocide, refusing to resort to the simplistic divide between Hutu "bad guys" and Tutsi "victims."

For both films, resolution relies on the reunification of the family. It involves escaping extremists with the hope of finding safety under the protection of community (restoration of community life). But while there are similarities between the films, each presents Westerners with radically different resolutions. *Hotel Rwanda* uses a conventional linear narrative that follows the transformation of Paul Rusesabagina, the manager of the

Hotel des Mille Collines, a four-star Belgian hotel in Kigali. In the beginning of the film he is simply concerned with the delivery of outstanding service, upholding the reputation of the hotel. When the ethnic cleansing begins, he is forced to make decisions about the Tutsis seeking shelter in the hotel. Initially, the UN Security Forces protect the hotel because of its North American and European guests. But after the UN evacuates the guests and reduces security forces to 270, there are not enough soldiers to protect the hotel. Yet even with the security forces gone, the hotel retains the aura of its colonial authority and the status as an international zone. It thus remains, at least symbolically, outside the jurisdiction of the Rwandan Armed Forces—in contrast to churches where they do not hesitate to kill thousands.

Paul works to maintain the hotel's authority, using his contacts with high-ranking Hutu generals and his status as the manager of a foreign hotel. He keeps a direct line of communication with the Belgian owner who uses his relations with his government to apply pressure on the RAF to leave the Tutsi "hotel guests" alone. Paul also maintains formal relations with influential extremists through the exchange of favors and luxury goods such as imported liquor. These exchanges place him in a relation of negotiation rather than dependence, made possible through the authority granted him by the colonial power of the Belgium-owned hotel. The film presents the Belgium-run hotel as the only remaining space where Rwandans on different sides of the political fence can engage in negotiation. As a space that is still used and run by a former colonial power, it comes to represent the last remaining space of civilization as Kigali is overtaken by Hutu extremists. Thus, the film inadvertently reproduces images of the West bringing civilization to Africa, drawing on romanticized colonial memories that threaten to bury the oppressive rule of countries such as Belgium in Rwanda.

As the tensions increase, the UN colonel eventually saves Paul and his "guests" by negotiating a deal with the RAF and Tutsi RPF to exchange them for extremist RAF prisoners. The colonel is fashioned after Canadian UN Force Commander Romeo Dallaire, who was left in Rwanda to oversee UN peacekeeping after the Belgians withdrew their troops and the UN drastically reduced its operations. But in *Hotel Rwanda*'s version, there is no reference to his name or nationality, making him just as easily American as Canadian. The film makes the "colonel" a hero in public memory, giving audiences assurance that there are Western individuals (likely United States individuals) with moral integrity that we can rely on to save victims in humanitarian crises, even if they are abandoned by our governments and the UN.

In the final scene Paul's wife, Tatiana (Sophie Okonedo), miraculously finds her two nieces in a refugee camp among hundreds of orphaned children. The family is reunited in a dramatic crescendo of jubilant emotion and tears. While this is the film's climax, it is difficult to be completely carried away in their emotional reunification. In the camp we see hundreds of children with no families and uncertain futures. The narrative has difficulty containing their terrible scale of loss. Yet the film pushes for closure, ending with an epilogue: Paul saved over 1,200 Rwandans and he and his family settled in Belgium. *Hotel Rwanda* is thus a story about an exemplary individual, who through bravery and a commitment to higher principles becomes a hero. It is primarily a personal story with the resolution hinging on Paul's ability to save his family, as the emotional climax of finding his nieces shows. On another level, the film absolves the West: it grants protection to Rwandans seeking shelter in the Hotel des Mille Collines; the UN colonel saves Paul and his "hotel guests" by negotiating a deal with the RAF; and Belgium ironically becomes Paul's new home. Resolutions for the other conflicts are summed up in the rest of the epilogue: the Tutsi RPF stop the genocide and gain control over Kigali in July 2006; Hutu General Bizimunga is captured by UN security forces; and George Rutagunda, the Interahamwe's leader, is sentenced by the War Crimes Tribunal.

Hotel Rwanda thus constructs a public memory of the genocide that offers neat resolutions that assure Western audiences that brave UN commanders saved hundreds of individuals, war criminals have been brought to justice, fathers have saved their families, and countries like Belgium have given new homes to deserving refugees. But there is much not resolved by the heroic deeds of Paul. If audiences rely on prosthetic memory, they would not necessarily know that after the genocide, masses of Hutu civilians flee Rwanda fearing retribution from Tutsi rebels; assassinations and massacres continue; thousands of Hutus are locked up in prisons with no trial in sight; and it is unclear how killers and victims living side by side will come to terms with the genocide.[19]

In contrast, *Sometimes in April* shows audiences that reconciliation for Rwandans is going to take years. It is a film, in fact, that is about the memory of the genocide and how it continues to traumatize the survivors. The film begins ten years after the genocide. It follows the main character, Augustin Muganza (Idris Elba), on his painful emotional journey to learn about the fate of his family. Like Paul in *Hotel Rwanda*, he is a principled loving father and husband, but not a hero. As an officer with the Hutu Rwandan Armed Forces, he failed fully to realize his superiors were planning genocide. When he and his friend Xavier (Fraser James) are blacklisted as Tutsi sympathizers, Augustin turns to his brother Honoré (Orus Erhuero) to help Jeanne (Carole Karemera), his Tutsi wife, their children and Xavier's wife. Even though Honoré works at a radio station broadcasting hate propaganda, Augustin trusts him and asks him to drive his family past the extremists' checkpoints to safety. The last time Augustin sees his family alive is with Honoré. The resolution of this film does not depend on reunifying his family since they are killed. The resolution depends on Augustin's ability to confront his brother and come to terms with the killing of his family, a metaphor for Rwandan society.

When the film begins, Augustin has started a new life as a teacher. He is in a warm loving relation with Martine (Pamela Novete), another survivor. Although a decade has passed, Augustin is unable to live fully in the present. This is symbolized by his inability to remove the wedding ring that binds him to his first wife, Jeanne. He is plagued by the past, especially in April when the rains bring back memories of the genocide.

The film replicates the skewed temporality experienced by traumatized subjects. They are overwhelmed by unpredictable floods of terrifying images from the past and disconnected from whatever is happening in the present. Likewise, in *Sometimes in April* Augustin is overwhelmed by his memories about the fate of his family and friends. As Augustin begins to confront what happened during the genocide, he retrospectively weaves the past into three narratives that follow his escape with his friend Xavier (he is killed), the escape of Martine with his daughter (she dies from gun wounds), and the death of Jeanne and their two sons (he doesn't know how they died). These scenes are intense, violent and action-filled, immersing viewers in the traumatic recall of the genocide. By contrast, the present is an ethereal space where time is suspended. For example, in the beginning of the film we hear Augustin's voice, strangely disconnected from himself, reflecting on what has come to pass: "When did paradise become hell"; "When we finally grasped the horror, it was too late."

In the second scene, Augustin reads a letter from his brother, Honoré, who is now on trial at the War Crimes Tribunal in Arusha. Honoré beseeches Augustin to visit him: "When I [came to accept] I was part of this [genocide] ... I thought my death would bring me peace, would bring me relief—but only the truth can ease my guilt." Augustin crumples up the letter. Yet the camera pans to photographs of his brother with Augustin's wife Jeanne and their children during happier times. He has kept the photos of his brother, indicating a longing for unity. But Augustin refuses to see his brother. His emotional pain is registered in close-ups of his face. As in other ethereal scenes from the present, the faces of characters are rendered into slow-moving subtle landscapes of reflection and feeling. It is as if Augustin is suspended in time, in a slow moving dream, unable to connect with the living world around him.

Martine gently insists that Augustin must visit his brother Honoré, aware that he is haunted by the thought that his brother might have killed his family. This is another example of how *Sometimes in April* emphasizes the necessity of facing rather than avoiding painful truths in remembering the genocide for both victims and perpetrators. When Augustin finally goes to Arusha, Honoré is able to unburden his guilt to his brother. He recounts his failure to save Jeanne and their boys when militants attacked them. After the attack Honoré realized Jeanne was not dead and pulled her into a ditch, returning later that night to take her to a church. But his attempt to save her fails. He later hears that the priest cooperated with extremists when they executed people and abused women, including Jeanne, who sought sanctuary in the church. The film gives Jeanne, as one of the thousands of Tutsi women violated and killed by extremists, a dignified death as a martyr. When Jeanne discovers the extremists plan to kill her and the other women, in an act of bravery she finds a hand grenade, blows up her captors and dies in the explosion. As I will discuss below, *Sometimes in April* in many ways acts like a "celluloid memorial"[20] to remember and honor those killed during the genocide.

Like *Hotel Rwanda*, the family has a central role in *Sometimes in April*. But in *Sometimes in April*, the family is a powerful symbol for larger Rwandan society. The initial inability of two brothers to reconcile means neither can live in the present. Instead, they are trapped in the anger and guilt of the past. Now their past is on trial. Augustin is skeptical about the War Crime Tribunals. As the epilogue underlines, few war criminals have been sentenced. Yet the film suggests that the tribunals are still essential in determining accountability and restoring an equitable moral order. Could they be the basis for a new collective Rwandan story? As the hate propaganda demonstrated, collective stories about the past are a powerful means of mobilization. This new story must reach across fear, pain and ideological differences if Rwandans are to live together in the present.

The film also shows that resolution requires coming to terms with what happened in the past by accepting the painful loss of loved ones. Final resolution comes for Augustin only when he encounters Valentine (Cléophas Kabasiita), another survivor, at the tribunals. When he meets her, he begins to work through the guilt and pain regarding the loss of his wife Jeanne. In many ways, for Augustin she symbolizes Jeanne. In his hotel room, alone and depressed, he hears a woman weeping in the next room. Her anguish pulls him out of his own desolation. He begins singing, trying to comfort her, tenderly, as he would have comforted Jeanne. He cannot see her, just as he can no longer see Jeanne. Through the wall they begin talking and Augustin learns she is a protected witness giving testimony at the tribunal. She asks him to come hear her testimonial. He points out that with the protective screen in the trial room, she will be unable to see him. She replies that she will know he is there, even if she cannot see him.

While it seems as if Augustin is comforting Valentine, in many ways it is she who comforts him, helping him overcome his guilt for failing to save Jeanne. When the witness insists that she will know he is there *even if she cannot see him*, it is as if she reassures Augustin that Jeanne knew he was with her during her last terrible days, even if he was not present. While he failed to save Jeanne, his (unseen) presence comforted her. This is a crucial moment also because in comforting the witness, Augustin reaches out beyond his personal pain and connects with a stranger, another member of society.

The way Valentine symbolizes Jeanne is made even more evident on Augustin's last day at the hotel. When he finally meets Valentine in person, there is clearly a strong attraction between them, again suggesting that she stands in for Jeanne. When she tells her sons to say good-bye, Augustin salutes them as he would his two dead sons. Thus, Augustin is given the chance to say good-bye to his family and finish mourning them. A torrent of sexy jazz follows the departure of his airplane, marking his entry into the living present with his fiancé Martine and their soon-to-be-born son.

Valentine is just one example of the role of women in *Sometimes in April*. Valentine, Jeanne, Martine, and Bushnell are significant figures in the film. It suggests women will transform society where men have failed. Augustin and Honoré failed to realize the gravity of the extremist propaganda. They failed to save their families and country from genocide. While it could be argued that the women, whether Valentine or Martine, are given the traditional female role of social reproduction, rebuilding the bonds of society, they are also heroines. Jeanne dies as a martyr, killing extremists. Valentine gives testimony against accused war criminals, despite dangers to herself and her family. Martine tries to save her students. And the female farmer risks offering them shelter while her husband and son-in-law are away killing Tutsis.

The film is a celluloid memorial, recovering the honor of women denigrated by extremists, especially Tutsi women who were constructed as treacherous seductresses.[21] Tutsi Prime Minister Agathe Uwilingiyimana was among the first politicians killed by extremists.[22] As mentioned above, *Sometimes in April* avoids scenes of gruesome violence and humiliating violations. The film gives her a dignified death, despite accounts of her denigration.[23] She calmly meets the RAF approaching her home and asks them to take her to their commanding officer. A soldier panics and shoots her. The moment of her death is engulfed in a choral requiem, turning the scene into a visual commemoration. The film also honors unknown female figures, including Martine's students. As the extremists approach her school, they state, "we are sisters, we are staying together." As the extremists attempt to separate Hutu and Tutsi girls, they tell the soldiers in quavering voices they are staying together. As soldiers shoot them, again a choral requiem transforms their deaths into a scene of martyrdom.

By avoiding graphic violence and turning victims into martyrs, do *Sometimes in April* and *Hotel Rwanda* make viewing the genocide safe for the viewers? Do they simply show us what we want to believe, keeping our moral universe intact by presenting individuals who follow their principles and remain kind and loving despite the horrors they witness and, in some cases, commit?[24] This raises a question about the purpose of realistically representing *acts* of violence. Is the purpose to convey the experience of violence to viewers? What is the purpose and, importantly, what would be lost if the films focused on these acts? For example, can scenes of killing convey the enormity of violence — what happened at a social and political level that made the killing possible in the first place or its impact over time across generations? At another level, trauma scholars such as Judith Herman and Cathy Caruth explain that meaningfully representing violent acts is impossible.[25] Violent acts defy the basic terms of humanity — relations of trust to others— and the basis of meaning itself. Despite the impossibility of meaningfully representing violent acts, trauma scholars still argue that the attempt to give meaning to events such as genocide is necessary for seeking justice and transforming the damaging effects on subsequent generations.[26] The question is thus not how to represent genocide in graphic detail, conveying its unspeakable horror, but rather what forms of representation as well as communication make it possible to rebuild relations of trust. As Augustin shows, until he confronts his brother, who puts the fate of his wife into words, he remains trapped in the terrifying past, unable to live fully in the present with his new family.

Hotel Rwanda and *Sometimes in April* have contributed to constructing the public memory of the 1994 Rwandan genocide for North American audiences. As I have argued, it is a prosthetic memory/cinema. And as Guy Westwell and others argue, it has had a fundamental role in shaping the memories of war in a New World Order where most of us know little about the humanitarian crises and regional conflicts where our governments send peacekeeping forces.

As part of a wave of dramatic productions following the publicizing of controversial reports documenting the decision of the UN and its Western member states to refuse to take measures to stop the genocide, *Hotel Rwanda* and *Sometimes in April* gave North Americans insights into the failure of their governments to stop the genocide. Audiences learned about their responsibility for what unfolded in Rwanda by watching the films, making it their humanitarian crisis, their "war." On the other hand, the films gave them a quick way to ameliorate their guilt. By offering audiences a chance to identify with Rwandan characters and become emotionally invested in their escape from extremists, the films also gave Westerners an easy way to redeem themselves, to show they cared and thus reaffirm their humanity. At another level, by vicariously giving audiences access to facsimiles of the victims' experiences, the films produced prosthetic memories of the genocide that could be easily consumed. The danger here is that with little knowledge of Rwandan politics and history, the film can generate memories for audiences that draw as much on fantasy as fact. As I argued in the case of *Hotel Rwanda*, it offers problematic closure—for the Rwandan family when the main character's wife, Tatianna, finds her nieces in a refugee camp and their family is reunited. Closure for Western audiences comes when the UN colonel ends up saving the Rwandans, Belgium offers Paul's family a new home, and the War Tribunals put extremists on trial. Thus, the film reaffirms the moral integrity of Western individuals, states and bodies such as the United Nations. Like President William J. Clinton during a CNN address, the film assures North American audiences that the West is committed to international justice.[27]

In contrast, *Sometimes in April* does not offer closure. The film follows the main character ten years after the genocide as he goes through the painful and complex process of reconciliation at the intimate level of family and the broader level of society. As I argued, *Sometimes in April* is a film about memory itself. In particular, the film's scenes of dead bodies act as a metaphor for the memory of genocide. Like memory of the genocide, the sites of death cannot be contained in particular areas, cordoned off from public view. Middle-class neighborhoods in Kigali and the countryside are strewn with rotting corpses and remnants of clothing. The main characters witness piles of recently killed people in trucks and along roads. In contrast to the idyllic life of the main characters at the beginning of each film, these scenes immerse the film's audiences in a world of death. The images of recently killed women, men and children, the remains of bodies decomposing in classrooms, churches, ditches, and fields create a landscape that is literally saturated with the slowly disintegrating physical remains, the smell, and the terror of fleeing victims. Like the scenes of dead bodies, then, which pervade the senses and landscape with death, the film suggests that the terror of the genocide cannot be easily washed away from the body or from memory.

While *Sometimes in April* shows audiences that memories of genocide cannot be neatly contained and final closure is impossible, it nevertheless stresses the necessity of reconciliation, both personal and public. Whether in the intimate space of the family or the public space of international tribunals, reconciliation requires rebuilding relations with others in the search for painful details about what happened. For Western audiences, what type of reconciliation is possible? Rather than seeking redemption and reaffirming our own humanity and the moral integrity of our governments as audience members if we do indeed identify with Augustin, the main character in *Sometimes in April*, then he provides insights into what is involved in the slow painful process of reconciliation. As discussed above, it necessarily involves rebuilding relations with others. In this respect both films identify North Americans and Europeans as political actors, soldiers, colonizers, journalists, and aid workers in Rwanda. While at an ideological level, acknowledging our involvement makes the Rwandan genocide part of our story, part of our war memory, at another level, humanitarian crises like Rwanda increasingly become part of our war memories because they include the memories of refugees who have fled to Canada for shelter, traumatized soldiers and families grieving their loved ones, as well as the dark side of military culture which can erupt in scandals such as the Somalia Affair and the Abu Ghraib prison incidents.

By refusing to offer closure, *Sometimes in April* shows Westerners that in many senses, the genocide continues through the damaging impact it will have on generations to come. Thus, rather than weeping in grief and joy when Paul's family reunites, *Sometimes in April* leaves us with a continuing crisis where there is hope only through commitment to the ongoing work of reconciliation locally, nationally and internationally. *Sometimes in April* thus reminds us that security in the New World Order requires more than military power.

NOTES

1. Many thanks to Michael Keren and Holger Herwig as well as Glen Lowry for their insightful and incisive feedback.

2. Andrew Hoskins, "'New Memory': The Media and the Past," Conference Paper, BISA, St. Andrews, Scotland, 2005

3. See the 1999 report by the UN special investigative committee on the Rwanda genocide, "Report of the Independent Inquiry into the Actions of the United Nations during the 1994 Genocide in Rwanda," htm — Introduction; also, "Lessons from the Rwandan Experience," March 8, 1999, IMG/ N9939547.pdf (OpenElement), which was sponsored by 20 donor nations and Human Rights Watch's 1999 "Leave None to Tell the Story: Genocide in Rwanda," TopOfPage.

4. See Kirsten McAllister, "Human Trafficking: Global Connections in the Living Rooms of the Canadian Nation," in Zoë Druick and Patricia Kotsopoulos, eds., *Border Fiction* (Waterloo, 2008).

5. Reports vary from 500,000 to 1,000,000.

6. *Border Fiction*, "Report of the Independent."

7. The UN was well aware of the atrocities in Rwanda in 1993 when it implemented the Arusha Peace Agreements to stop the three-year civil war between the Rwandan Patriotic Front (RPF) and the Rwandan government. But when the genocide began in April 1994, against the advice of the RPF and its Force Commander in Rwanda, the UN and most of its Western member states left Rwanda. Only once the RPF halted extremists did the UN resume operations. See United Nations, *Mandate for the United Nations Assistance Mission for Rwanda (UNAMIR)*, irM.htm; and Paul J. Magnarella, *Justice in Africa: Rwanda's Genocide, Its Courts, and the UN Criminal Tribunal*, 30–33 (Aldershot, 2000).

8. Josias Semujanga, *Origins of Rwandan Genocide* (Amherst, NY, 2003), pp. 104–05.

9. *Ibid.*, pp. 111–20.

10. At the time, Bushnell was the deputy assistant secretary of state for African affairs.

11. See Jo Ellen Fair and Lisa Parks, "Africa On Camera: Television News Coverage and Aerial Imaging of Rwandan Refugees," *Africa Today* 48 (2001): 35–36.

12. *Lord of War* and the *Constant Gardener* criticize the West's role in the Third World, but Western corruption is always of another order than African "evil." In the *Constant Gardener*, the corruption of British politicians and transnationals can only be fully unleashed in a lawless violent region like Africa.

13. For example, Patrice Lumumba (Congo) and Stephen Biko (South Africa) inspired generations of anti-colonial, pan-African and black consciousness movements.

14. Karen Ross, *Black and White Media: Black Images in Popular Film and Television*, (Cambridge, 1996); Chinua Achebe, "An Image of Africa: Racism in Conrad's *Heart of Darkness*," in *Hopes and Impediments: Selected Essays 1965–1987* (Oxford, 1988), pp. 1–19; Sander L. Gilman, "Black Bodies, White Bodies: Toward an Iconography of Female Sexuality in Late Nineteenth Century Art, Medicine and Literature," *Critical Inquiry*, 12 (1985): 223–61; Jordan Winthrop, *White Over Black: American Attitudes Towards the Negro 1550–1812*, (Baltimore, 1968).

15. Alain Sigg, "Historical and Political Perspectives on the Genocide: Introduction," in John A. Berry and Carol Pott Berry, eds., *Genocide in Rwanda: A Collective Memory* (Washington, DC, 1999), p. 26.

16. Alison Lansberg, *Prosthetic Memory: the Transformation of American Remembrance in the Age of Mass Culture*, (New York, 2004).

17. See Magnarella, *Justice*, pp. 11–14; also, Alison Liebhafsky Des Forges, "History," in *Leave None to Tell the Story: Genocide in Rwanda*, (London Human Rights Watch, March 1999), TopOfPage.

18. See Xan Rice, "Rwandans See Genocide on the Big Screen," the *Guardian*, 3 April 2006 http://www.guardian.co.uk/world/2006/mar/27/film.rwanda; and Alice O'Keefe, "Anger at BBC Genocide Film," the *Guardian* 19 March 2006 http://film.guardian.co.uk/news/story/0,,1735139,00.html.

19. Mahmood Mamdani, *When Victims Become Killers: Colonialism, Nativism and the Genocide in Rwanda* (Princeton, 2001); Wole Soyinka, *The Burden of Memory: the Muse of Forgiveness* (New York, 1999).

20. Guy Westwell, *War Cinema: Hollywood on the Front Line* (London, 2006), p. 114.

21. Christopher C. Taylor, *Sacrifice as Terror: the Rwandan Genocide of 1994* (Oxford and New York, 1999), pp. 171, 176.

22. As Education Minister she removed the quota system restricting the number of Tutsi students, angering Hutu extremists. Taylor, *Sacrifice as Terror*, p. 164.

23. Loc. cit; Berry and Berry, *Genocide in Rwanda*, p. 14.

24. Lawrence L. Langer, *Holocaust Testimonies: the Ruins of Memory* (New Haven, CT, and London, 1991), pp. 26–27.

25. Cathy Caruth, *Trauma: Explorations in Memory* (Baltimore, 1995); Judith Lewis Herman, *Trauma and Recovery: the Aftermath of Violence — From Domestic Abuse to Political Terror* (New York, 1992).

26. Herman, *Trauma and Recovery*.

27. CNN "Clinton meets Rwanda Genocide survivors, " 25 March 25 1998, n/.

About the Contributors

Bart Beaty is the author of *Fredric Wertham and the Critique of Mass Culture* (University of Mississippi Press, 2005); and U*npopular Culture: Transforming the European Comic Book in the 1990s* (University of Toronto Press, 2007). His monograph *David Cronenberg's A History of Violence* will be published next year in the *Canadian Cinema* series from University of Toronto Press. He is an associate professor in the faculty of Communication and Culture at the University of Calgary.

Sam Edwards undertook his doctoral research in the Department of History and the Institute for Cultural Research at Lancaster University (UK). He was awarded his PhD — entitled "War and Collective Memory: American Military Commemoration in Britain and France, 1943 to the Present" — in March 2008 and he currently teaches American studies, and American and European history at Lancaster University.

Janis Goldie is a PhD candidate and instructor in the faculty of Communication and Culture at the University of Calgary. She is currently completing her dissertation in political communication on the role of Royal Commissions in Canada and their connection to political scandal. She has also published on privacy and the Internet as well as on research ethics.

Rebecca Lynn Graff-McRae, originally from Alberta, Canada, completed her PhD in the School of Politics, International Studies and Philosophy at Queen's University, Belfast. Working under the auspices of the "Commemorating 1916 in 1966" project, in co-operation with the Humanities Institute of Ireland, her doctoral thesis presents a post-structuralist, deconstructive approach to the politics of commemoration, and seeks to explicate the discursive links between commemoration and conflict in the Irish context.

Holger H. Herwig is professor of history and Canada Research Chair in Military and Strategic Studies at the University of Calgary. He is the author of numerous books on German military-diplomatic history in the twentieth century, including *One Christmas in Washington: Churchill and Roosevelt Forge the Grand Alliance* (McArthur, 2005).

Tamar Katriel is a professor in the Department of Communication and in the Department of Education at the University of Haifa, where she conducts research in the Ethnography of Communication. Her most recent books include a Hebrew collection of essays entitled *Key Words: Patterns of Culture and Communication in Israel* (Haifa University Press, 1999); and *Dialogic Moments: From Soul Talks to Talk Radio in Israeli Culture* (Wayne State University Press, 2004).

Michael Keren is a professor and Canada Research Chair in Communication, Culture and Civil Society at the University of Calgary. He is the author of many books and articles on political theory and political communication.

Kirsten McAllister teaches in the School of Communication at Simon Fraser University. She has conducted research and published in the area of cultural memory and the incarceration of Japanese Canadians during the 1940s. Her current research focuses on refugees and contemporary discourses of exclusion and inclusion in Canada and the UK.

Arthur G. Neal is an Emeritus Distinguished University Professor at Bowling Green State University. His recent books include *Sociological Perspectives on Modernity: Multiple Models and Competing Realities* (Peter Lang, 2007); *National Trauma and Collective Memory: Extraordinary Events in the American Experience* (M.E. Sharpe, 2005); and, with Dena Eber, *Memory and Representation: Constructed Truths and Competing Realities* (Bowling Green University Popular Press, 2001).

Lucy Noakes is a senior lecturer in history at the University of Brighton, UK. She researches the relationship between war, memory, gender, and nationhood. Publications include *War and the British: Gender and National Identity 1939–1991* (I.B. Tauris, 1998); and *Women and the British Army 1908–1948: The Gentle Sex at War* (Routledge, 2006).

Bruce C. Scates is the director of the National Center for Australian Studies at Monash University. His research into pilgrimage and commemoration has been funded by national and international agencies including the Australian Research Council and the Australian War Memorial. He is the author of *Return to Gallipoli: Walking the Battlefields of the Great War* (Cambridge, 2006); and co-author of *Women and the Great War* (Cambridge 1997). His history of Victoria's Shrine of Remembrance will be published by Cambridge University Press in 2009.

Dan Todman is senior lecturer in modern history at Queen Mary, University of London, UK. He works on the cultural, social and military history of modern war, with a particular focus on remembrance.

Index

Aberbach, David 14
Albert of Aachen 10–11
Allingham, Henry 30, 34
American Historical Review 38
Anderson, Benedict 61, 64, 168
An Anzac Muster 57–58; *see also* Baylebridge, William
Arc de Triomphe 122
Ashplant, T.G. 3, 172
Australian New Zealand Army Corps (ANZAC), Anzacs 57–72, 136

Band of Brothers 135, 143, 145–146
Barthel, Diane 87
Bartov, Omer 2
Baruch of Magenza 5, 9, 13–21; *see also* Tchernichowsky, Shaul
Barzel, Hilel 19
Baylebridge, William 57–58, 63, 67, 71
The Belfast Telegraph 51
Best, George 45
Bialik, Haim Nachman 144
Blackadder Goes Forth 32
Bloch, Marc 25
Bracher, Nathan 77
Breaking the Silence 151–162
The Bridgehead Sentinel 79–80, 86
Brinker, Menachem 18, 20
British Broadcasting Corporation (BBC) 6–7, 30, 31–32, 33, 34, 35, 43–44, 135–147
Broido, Ephraim 14
Bruner, M. Lane 171–172
Bulge, Battle of the 93
Burdick, Eugene 100
Bush, George W. 102, 130–131
Bushnell, Prudence 187
Butler, Paul 52

Calder, Simon 42, 52
Canada, Canadians 2–3, 4, 7, 166–183; *see also* Dallaire, Romeo
Canadian War Museum 2–3
Canetti, Elias 115
Captain America, Captain America 6, 124–133
Captain America and the Crusade Against Evil 129–130
Carr, Graham 67
Carson, Ciaran 43
Caruth, Cathy 196
Cassady, John 124, 125, 126, 127, 129–130, 131
Christie, Norm 171
Clark, Alan 32
Clarke, Lee 102
Clinton, William J. 197
Clowes, Edith 18
Cohen, Jeremy 12
Cold War 94, 95–96, 97–101; and films 99–101; and music 98–99, 101; and novels 100, 101; *see also* nuclear war
Collins, Max Allan 127
comic books 120–133
Confino, Alon 38
Coombes, Anne 71

Dallaire, Romeo 191; *see also* Shake Hands with the Devil
Dawson, Graham 3, 140, 145, 172
The Day After 99–101
De Gaulle, Charles 81, 83
Derrida, Jacques 42, 46–47, 50, 53
Dr. Strangelove 99
Dodds, Nigel 48–49
The Donkeys 32
Doomsday Clock 95
Dresden, firebombing of 93, 127–128, 129

Dunkirk 135
Dunning, Richard 34

Edkins, Jenny 42, 47
Eher, Franz 111
Einbinder, Susan 12
Ekkehard of Aura 10–11
Enola Gay 2; *see also* Hiroshima
Erikson, Eric 169
Everything Is Illuminated 41

Facey, Bert 66
Fail Safe 99–100
Family Frames 27
Le Figaro 76, 86
First Crusade 5, 9–13
1st Infantry Division (U.S.) 79–80, 85
Foer, Jonathan Safran 41
Foss, Sonja K. 120, 121, 123, 126, 130
Foucault, Michel 51–52
Franco, Francisco 116

Gallipoli 5–6, 57–72, 86; and *Gallipoli* 66
The Genocidal Mentality 94–95
Gettysburg 77, 80
Gillis, John 169–170
Goebbels, Joseph 116
Gorbachev, Mikhail 101
Greenlaw, Duncan 53–54
The Guardian 45

Hamlet 50
Herman, Judith 196
Himmler, Heinrich 110
Hiroshima 2, 6, 93–103
Hiroshima in America 106
Hirsch, Marianne 27, 31
Hitler, Adolf 6, 105–117, 124, 133, 142;
  see also Nazi Germany
Hobsbawm, Eric 61, 168
Holocaust 2–3, 92, 94–95, 168
Hoskins, Andrew 185
Hotel Rwanda 7, 185–198
Hurban 15; *see also* Mintz, Alan
Hynes, Samuel 33

Imperial War Graves Commission 59, 60
Imperial War Museum 38, 135
In the City of Slaughter 14
In the Shadow of No Towers 131–132
The Independent 42
internet websites 6–7, 136–147
Iron Curtain 95–96

Irwin family 60–63, 64, 68–69, 72; *see
  also* Gallipoli
Israeli-Palestinian Conflict 7, 150–162

Jalland, Pat 59–60
Jarman, Neil 46
Jasper, James 151, 158
Jewett, Robert 129–130

Kammen, Michael 78
Kirby, Jack 124
Klausner, Joseph 13
Klein, Kerwin Lee 24, 29
Kratsman, Miki 152
Kreis, Wilhelm 6, 105, 108–117; *see also*
  Nazi Germany

Landsberg, Alison 4, 27–28, 33, 137; *see
  also* prosthetic memory
Lawrence, John Shelton 129–130
Lehrer, Tom 98–99
LeMay, Curtis 93
Leoussi, Athena 14
Levin, Hanoch 151
Lewis, C.S. 45
Lifton, Robert Jay 94, 102
Lin, Maya 120, 121, 123; *see also* Vietnam
  Veterans Memorial
Linell, Per 156
Lloyd, D.W. 80–81
Lochnagar crater 34, 35
Lowenthal, David 64, 87
Lucisferrato 117

Mainz Pogrom 10–21
Manhattan Project 95
Markusen, Eric 94
Marvel Comics 124–133
Maus 131; *see also* Spiegelman, Art
McFayden, Melanie 47
McGuiness, Martin 49
McGurk, Neil 30, 37
McKeown, Laurence 50, 51
Medved, Michael 129
Megill, Allan 29, 36
Mein Kampf 107
Memorial to the Murdered Jews of Eu-
  rope 121
memory boom 23–24, 26–29, 36, 37–38,
  82, 83, 135
Mintz, Alan 12–13, 15
Miron, Dan 14
Misztal, Barbara 168–169

Mitchell, Greg 102
Mitterand, François 83
Moorhead, Cyril 45
moral shock 158–160
Moses, Isaac Ben 11, 12
Mosse, George 1–2, 77, 115, 181
MTV 2
Müller, Jan-Werner 65
mutually assured destruction (MAD)
    96–97, 99

Nagasaki 93, 94, 95, 98
National Army Museum (U.K.) 38
National Review 129
Nazi Germany 92, 93, 127; and architec-
    ture 105–117; and in *Operation Victory*
    video game 172–173, 176; *see also*
    Hitler, Adolf; Holocaust
Neisser, Ulric 82
The New York Times 77
The New Yorker 131
Newsarama 132
Nietzsche, Friedrich 18–19, 20
Nora, Pierre 28, 58, 64, 136
Normandy 6, 76–89; and the D-Day
    landings 135, 139, 142, 143
Northern Ireland 5, 41–54; and the
    Good Friday Agreement 43, 47; and
    the Maze Prison (Long Kesh) 47–54
nuclear war 37, 92–103
Nugent, Jan 44

On the Beach 99–100
Operation Barbarossa 6, 109
Operation Victory 7, 166–183
Oppenheimer, J. Robert 95

Paisley, Ian, Sr. 48
Passerini, Louisa 71
Patch, Harry 30
Pearl Harbor 93–94, 95–96, 101–102
Peck, Raoul 190; *see also Sometimes in
    April*
People's War 136–147; *see also* British
    Broadcasting Corporation
Peukert, Detlev 115
Poots, Edwin 49
postmemory 27, 31
Prince Charles 30–31
prosthetic memory 4, 27–28, 33, 137,
    189

Queen of the Bathtub 151

Ranger, Terence 168
Ranger Veterans (U.S.) 83, 88
Reagan presidency 82, 83, 84
Rieber, John Nay 124, 125, 126, 127, 129–
    130, 131, 132, 133
Robinson, Peter 49
Rommetveit, Ragnar 156
Roper, Michael 3, 172
Rose, Sonya O. 137–138
Rosen, Harold 160
Rosenberg, Emily S. 82
Rousso, Henry 82–83
Royal Naval Air Service 30
Rwandan genocide 185–198

Samson, Solomon Bar 10–11, 13
Saving Private Ryan 143, 145–146
Scates, Bruce 86
September 11, 2001 101–102, 121, 123, 124–
    133; similarities to Pearl Harbor 101–102
Shake Hands with the Devil 185
Simon, Joe 124
Sivan, Emmanuel 3
Snyder, Timothy 66
social memory 1–2
Sometimes in April 7, 185–198
Somme, Battle of the 5, 23–39
Specters of Marx 46–47; *see also* Derrida,
    Jacques
Speer, Albert 106–107, 109, 113, 114, 116
Spiegelman, Art 131–132
Splasher Six 83
Struken, Marita 87
Summerfield, Penny 137–138, 140

Tamms, Friedrich 108
Tchernichowsky, Shaul 5, 9, 13–21
Terry, George 190
Teutonic Knights 6, 106, 108, 109
Thiepval 30–31
Thomson, Alistair 25, 140
The Times of London 81
Tischler, Robert 116
Titanic, RMS 45
Tomb of the Unknown Soldier 122
total war 92–93
Totenburgen 105, 109, 110–112, 114, 115–
    116; and difference from *soldatenhalle*
    108–109; *see also* Nazi Germany
The Trench 35
trigger event 158–159
Troost, Gerdy 106, 114
Truman, Harry S 95

United Nations 185–193
Urry, John 80, 95

The Valour and the Horror 2
Vasselais, Guy de la 78, 81
Veterans' Week Workshop (2006) 4
Vietnam Veterans Memorial 120–121, 123, 126, 130
Vietnam War 65–66, 70, 82, 133

Wagner, Richard 19, 113
Walsh, Seanna 50, 51
Walter, Tony 85
War veterans 1–5, 34, 77, 79–89
Warren, Chris 139–140
Watson, Janet K. 137–138
Weber, Thomas 158–159
Weeks, Jim 80
Westwell, Guy 196–197
Wheeler, Harvey 100
Wier, Peter 66

Wilson, Sammy 49
Winter, Jay 3, 24, 26, 27, 37, 82; *see also* memory boom
Woodward, Shaun 49
World Cup 37
World Trade Center Memorial 121; *see also* September 11, 2001
World War I, Great War: the Battle of the Somme 4, 23–39; death toll 92; and Gallipoli 6, 57–72; and monuments 109; and nationalism 1–2
World War II, Second World War: and BBC's *People's War* 6–7, 135–147; *Captain America* 124, 127–128, 130; death toll 92; and the Irish airfield Long Kesh 47; Nazi architecture 6, 105–117; Normandy commemoration 6, 76–89; nuclear bombs 93–95, 98; and *Operation Victory* video game 7, 166–183; and veterans 2–3, 34, 79–89
Wright, Billy 45